THE KRAYS
UNFINISHED BUSINESS

THIS IS A CARLTON BOOK

Design copyright © 1999 Carlton Books Limited
Text copyright © 1999 Martin Fido

This edition published by Carlton Books Limited 2000
20 Mortimer Street
London
W1N 7RD

A CIP catalogue for this book is available from the British Library

The Krays: Unfinished Business accompanies the Carlton Television
documentaries "The Krays: Unfinished Business" and "The Krays:
Inside the Firm". Copyright © Carlton Television Limited 1999.

ISBN 1 85868 925 2

Printed and bound in Great Britain

THE KRAYS
UNFINISHED BUSINESS

A SENSATIONAL STORY OF EAST END
MURDER AND BETRAYAL

MARTIN FIDO

CONTENTS

INTRODUCTION

There have been fifteen books specifically dealing with the Kray brothers and their crimes. Reg, Ron and Charlie have written or contributed to seven of them. Most have been revised at least once. Additional memoirs and studies of London crime in the 1960s inevitably mention them. Each new book or edition purports to "set the record straight", especially if one of the brothers had a hand in it. Yet nothing can be less "straight" than the self-serving and blatantly lying memoirs of old villains with some unindicted felonies to conceal or a wrongful acquittal to claim as justified. Even Freddie Foreman's confession to the murders of Ginger Marks and Frank Mitchell does not make his autobiography, *Respect*, a comprehensively reliable account of his and others' doings.

Villains are not scholars, so we should not be surprised that they print errors as well as lies. Ronnie Kray, in particular, seems to have been utterly incapable of accuracy. He confuses Home Office pathologist Professor Keith Simpson with Metropolitan Police Commissioner Sir Joseph Simpson. He misremembers details of Lord Boothby's overt connections with himself. He even misremembers the location of his own pub, the Carpenter's Arms.

Nor is it easy for honest commentators to sort out the truth from the dross in what they have been told. Kate Kray, the second woman to marry Ronnie while he was in Broadmoor, wrote a couple of books and evidently believed everything he told her. Which led her to publish a certain amount of manifest error and absurdity. John Pearson, writer of the original and initially "authorized" life of the Kray twins, has had to add, amend and withdraw details as his book ran from edition to edition and increasing numbers of lies and cover stories collapsed. Yet somehow, with all this correction, his editions from 1972 to 1977 retained a birth date for the Kray twins a week earlier than that given by Ronnie and Reggie themselves and recorded on their birth certificates. Books disagree about the intervals between the twins' elder brother Charlie's birth and theirs; about their grandfather's christian name; about the spelling of the street where they were born. The need for some assessment of what all these differing accounts really amount to is apparent.

I mistrust my own ability to detect lies being told me. My expertise lies in examining documentary evidence and assessing its worth after careful reading, rather than interviewing protagonists and hoping I can perceive the truth or falsehood in what say. I don't mix with people who habitually tell lies, and so, unlike a policeman, a judge or a spymaster, I don't anticipate being lied to. Though I value unsolicited information that has come to me from time to time in conversations with police officers, journalists and occasional criminals, it has been a shock, since I entered the field of crime history, to come across people who tell enormous whoppers, simply for self-aggrandizement. So I have added no interviewing of my own to the work done by Frank Simmonds and Andy Weir for Carlton Television.

From 1988 to 1993 I conducted regular guided walks in the East End. As I sat in pubs and chatted with the walkers after the tours, I was occasionally accosted by strangers who had gathered from our conversation that I write about true crime.

"You write about crime? Why don't you write about me?" was the usual question. And as often as not the speaker added, "I used to work for the Krays."

Sometimes the story was simple. "I used to do their accounts. They were very good guv'nors as far as I was concerned."

Sometimes my tour-guide spiel was challenged. "You was quite wrong to say they got life. They got 30 years. They'll be out soon." (I was quite right. They got life, with a recommended minimum of 30 years. Ronnie died before the minimum was completed. Reggie was not given the speedy parole for which he hoped and at the time of writing seems to have little more certainty of a release date than had his protégé and victim Frank Mitchell.)

Unknown and self-acclaimed villains are not the helpful sources a crime historian likes to cultivate. Really successful criminals prefer to remain anonymous, at least as long as they are relatively sober. And the Krays' ramifying interests meant that a lot of people were employed by them in essentially law-abiding jobs, with no real knowledge of the workings of "the firm". Indeed, my closest colleague in the walking-tour business, an East Londoner with a wealth of political experience and a first-rate local historian's knowledge of the city, once almost accepted a job that turned out to be Kray controlled. But he lacked criminal tendencies and knew no more about their activities than other newspaper-readers.

It was a safe assumption that every English visitor I took on a tour to The Blind Beggar on Whitechapel Road knew that this was where Ronnie Kray openly murdered George Cornell. The Lion in Tapp Street, the pub the Kray firm called "The Widow's", was further off the beaten track, less well known, and more atmospheric. The Grave Maurice beside Whitechapel underground station still had the layout and decor of the twins' day and I often used Ronnie Kray's favourite banquette, where he could keep an eye on the street door, the bar and the entry to the gents'.

The Kray twins, the best-known gang bosses England has ever experienced, were really very incompetent criminals. They never scored a coup like the Great Train Robbery, the British crime committed during their heyday that still attracts transatlantic admiration. Indeed, Americans ask how on earth we could ever have been impressed by "little pissant hoodlums" like the Krays.

Maybe all criminals are incompetent. If a criminal's aim is wealth, he could probably achieve it more certainly and securely by going straight. If his goal is prestige, he is buying a shoddy version. If his retirement dream is Macbeth's noble vision of "Honour, love, obedience, troops of friends," then he is going Macbeth's way about ensuring the alternative, "Curses, mouth-honour, breath, Which the poor heart would fain deny, and dare not".

But then, the other leading subject of East End walking tours, Jack the Ripper, is proof positive that celebrity may be acquired without distinction.

What, one wonders, would have been the verdict of history if the Kray firm had not been rounded up and convicted before John Pearson's *Profession of Violence* was completed? Would the standard life merely have described two rough diamonds, businessmen club-owners who had worked up from the bottom to become the celebrity friends of stars and politicians and well-known philanthropists in and around Bethnal Green? Pearson's book became a best-seller because it gave the background to what was then the longest murder trial in British history, and the second sensational trial giving an account of the savagery going on in 1960s gangland. The first was the Richardson "torture trial"; the Krays' downfall was linked to their rivalry with the infamous Richardsons. And with the termination of these two major gangs, the traditional London gangland of racketeering extortionists was on the way out, even if it was not apparent at the time. Gangland has moved on. The twins' brother Charlie has gone down for drug trafficking, once the exclusive preserve of the Chinese of Limehouse and the Ratcliffe Highway.

The Kray twins have become uncomfortable icons of the swinging sixties. David Bailey's portrait of them is now, of all unlikely things, a popular design for large and expensive tattoos. As happens with notorious rogues, the Krays' cold cruelty and selfishness tend to be overlooked. So does the extent to which they were culturally conservative-minded and hardly representative of the era of flower power and acid rock. They were a bit behind the times, cultivating Lita Roza, Sophie Tucker and Judy Garland, Billy Daniels and Johnny Ray, and Joe Louis and Sonny Liston, in a London whose night-life was famous for the patronage of The Beatles, the Rolling Stones, George Best and Marianne Faithfull. Ronnie Kray preferred Italian opera to rock n' roll. Reggie listened faithfully to "Friday Night Is Music Night" on the radio when he found himself in prison. The Krays' recreational drugs of choice were alcohol and tobacco. Their natty suits came from Frank Wood, the tailor in the Kingspond Road, Dalston, who traditionally supplied East End gangsters, not from Oz Clarke, and they scorned the fancy dress of "Sergeant Pepper". Nary a floral tie or ruffled shirt clashed with their formal Prince of Wales checks or dark blue gents' suitings. Their gold was worn in bracelets and rings, not draped around turtleneck shirts. Their tastes were far from swinging.

As a matter of fact, the Krays became considerably better known once convicted and incarcerated than they had been while they made themselves highly visible in Stepney, Mile End and Bethnal Green. Their local reputation was only local. Their brief appearances in the national press did not make them household names. That all came after the trial, and with their brother Charlie's ventures to keep their reputations alive and earn them more than a few bob. So as they endured their life sentences, they appeared on T-shirts and ashtrays. And writers on true crime began to speculate about their other possible murders. What had become of their driver Billy "Jack" Frost? Where was their one-time friend "Mad Teddy" Smith? Were they in fact behind the continuing rumours that the ex-boxing champion Freddie Mills had not, as the police and the inquest declared, committed suicide, but had been murdered? The humorist Peter Cook told a cheerful story of having snubbed the Kray firm's attempt to shake him down when he opened the Establishment Club. After his own untimely death, other writers suggested that following this temerity he had quickly and discreet-ly taken a holiday abroad.

In the 1980s, I asked a friend in Parkhurst who knew Reggie whether the Krays had had anything to do with Freddie Mills' death. He was quite certain they hadn't. He was somewhat con-temptuous of the twins' claims to have been a sort of force for social good, given that Reggie had befriended a granny-basher in prison. He was not unduly impressed by the regimen of physical fitness Reggie famously maintained. Other fit inmates could always take a poke at him on equal terms if they felt like it. And he was gently scornful of the idea of the Krays as important criminals. "Some people call them thieves' ponces", he said. It was the first time I had heard the term.

In 1986, more detailed truths began to emerge. John Dickson who had testified against them, wrote a full account of how he had driven Ronnie to murder George Cornell, and how he had been one of the minders looking after Frank "the Mad Axeman" Mitchell in the Barking Road flat where he was held until he was murdered. The twins reacted within a couple of years. With the help of a ghostwriter they produced "their story", a blatantly self-serving account that accused other people of lying. It provoked yet more associates to venture into print. The Lambrianou brothers wrote separate and in some ways disparate accounts. Albert Donoghue collaborated with the experienced writer and documentary-maker Martin Short, which may explain why his book evinces an unusual awareness of the Kray firm's puerility. And most importantly, after Ronnie Kray's death, Freddie Foreman confessed.

For once, a criminal did not follow that exasperating habit of both villains and policemen of insisting, when it suits them, that a dubious "result" in the courts must be accepted as historical truth. Foreman now put up his hand to certain murders for which he had been tried and acquitted. And in so doing he blew apart the Krays' longstanding pretence that they didn't know what had happened to Frank Mitchell after he left Lenny Dunn's flat.

It was clear that the files on the notorious Cornell and McVitie murders were closed and would remain closed. Three of the most murderously vengeful men ever to come before the courts had gone to prison, but they had known backup from conscienceless killing organizations and the witnesses have to be protected from irresponsible publicity. But with Freddie Foreman's admission that he had killed Frank Mitchell, Carlton Television producer Frank Simmonds realized the possibility of further revelations when, assuming the 30-year rule were followed, the papers relating to the trial became available in the public domain in January 2000. A television programme cannot be put together overnight like a newspaper article. And so Frank Simmonds and Andy Weir asked the Lord Chancellor's Office for permission to see the papers in advance of their release, to ascertain whether there was new and important information.

There was. The papers included the various convicted gang members' appeals, and the statements in these gave a new picture of events. Those who had "staunchly" denied everything Scotch Jack Dickson and Ronnie Hart said at the trials couldn't wait to retract once they saw a decade in prison looming up. Not only was there new detail on the 12 days Frank Mitchell spent locked up, there was more detail on the Cornell and McVitie murders. And there was clear indication about the short-lived nature of honour among thieves – the alleged non-viability of the strict code against grassing. Ronnie Kray's paranoid belief that one of his "staunchest" supporters had secretly cracked as soon as he was arrested proved untrue. But the statement Ronnie claimed to have seen exists and is reproduced in this book, along with other revealing statements and extracts from the long interviews Carlton Television conducted with surviving protagonists.

There are however, differences between this book and the major Carlton Television documentary "The Krays – Unfinished Business". A book is a more leisurely enterprise than a television feature, and this gives more historical background. And in all my time in true-crime writing and broadcasting, I have editorialized freely and passed moral judgements. The many opinions expressed are mine, and not the responsibility of the TV producers or the publishers. But there is new inside information on the Frank Mitchell and Jack McVitie murders: now it can be told.

1

TRADITIONAL GANGLAND

Theft, the acquisition of other people's property without their permission by means including pocket picking, burglary, robbery, extortion, blackmail and fraud, is the traditional lifeblood of professional crime. The major criminal, respected by his peers, has almost invariably started as a thief.

Robber gangs stretch back into the mists of history. Robin Hood's merry men were nothing more than a gang of muggers, infesting a wooded piece of highway near Barnsley in the 13th or 14th century. "Friar Tuck" was the nom-de-guerre of the heavily armed Sussex and Surrey livestock rustler Richard Stafford. Shakespeare's Falstaff and Hal, Bardolph, Nym, Peto and Poins were an amateur gang whose rumbustious camaraderie camouflaged the violence with which they terrorized peaceful carters. Dick Turpin was not a lone romantic figure on a black mare, but the leader of a gang of brutal housebreakers on the outskirts of London. The Great Train Robbers comprised two gangs of thieves: Bruce Reynolds' and Gordon Goody's, who were experienced plotters of skilful capers that relied on advance planning, terrifying threats and professional getaway drivers; and Tommy Wisbey's and Jimmy White's south London mob, who knew how to stop trains without pulling the communication cord. Loosely, all such criminals are "organized", unlike the loners, from Charley Peace to "Black Panther" Donald Nilsen, who may compensate for their lack of supporting muscle and lookouts by carrying and using firearms recklessly.

Most murder, however, is committed by people who are not professional criminals at all.

Really sophisticated criminal organization started in England with Jonathan Wild, "the thieftaker-general" (c.1682–1725), who came to control all the thieving gangs of London by the simple expedient of impeaching and giving evidence against any who refused to work for him, thereby establishing a near monopoly of the receiving trade. Fencing stolen goods is a vital aspect of the theft industry. Receivers are unlikely to be loved by the clients who can rarely squeeze more than a tithe of the value of "hot goods" from them. But, like Wild, receivers may find themselves in a strong position to organize and manage other criminals' activity. James "Jim the

Penman" Saward, the Inner Temple barrister and master criminal of the 1850s, financed the theft of a safe full of bullion from the train carrying it to a Channel ferry and then brokered the sale of the gold. Adam Worth, the great cat burglar of the end of Victoria's reign, perpetrated most of his thefts as an individual. But his apartment in Piccadilly became a Mecca for international thieves where, as he fenced their goods, he helped plot their crimes, earning the title "Napoleon of Crime" from the Assistant Commissioner at Scotland Yard.

These were exceptional figures. The majority of criminal gangs were ordinary working-class lads who started with petty theft and then ganged together to fight with rivals and steal as co-operative groups. The Swell Mob were Victorian East Enders who specialized in picking pockets at race meetings where crowds gave them cover. Election meetings in the days of open-air hustings were similarly lucrative for the gang who once famously got away with a victorious candidate's watch from the steps of the Carlton Club. The Blind Beggar mob in the 1890s congregated in the famous Whitechapel Road pub, but carried out their mugging and pocket-picking in the richer West End, scornfully dismissing their native neighbourhood as "Tom Tiddler's Ground". Although they got themselves into serious trouble when one of them killed an innocent passer-by in Gower Street, this was the accidental result of some odious anti-Semitic horseplay, not their professional activities. All these people were straightforward thieves.

The Nichol gang from Old Nichol Street off Brick Lane practised a nasty form of extortion. They preyed on the street prostitutes of the East End, threatening to beat them up if they didn't turn over their takings. This "blackmail" was developed by Jewish gangs (formed after the great immigration of the 1880s) into extortion from legitimate shopkeepers. Much as Jewish gangsters liked to portray themselves as honourable knights defending their co-religionists against anti-Semitic thugs, they were just as likely to live as predators upon their fellow Jews. A gang of extortionists known as the "Bessarabians" were headed by a professional boxer who called himself Max Moses in private life and "Kid McCoy" in the ring.

Prizefighting was a way of escape from a marginalized ghetto existence. Pugilistic skill could be turned to criminal use, too, when territorial gang wars started. A brave Jewish cafe owner named Kikas drove the Bessarabians out of his Odessa Cafe. Admiring local thugs started calling themselves the Odessians and made a concerted attempt to run off the Bessarabians and take over their business. After a number of clashes, knives were drawn in an inter-gang affray in Philpot Street, beside the London Hospital. An Odessian called Henry Brodovitz was killed. McCoy and two of his henchmen stood trial and went to penal servitude for manslaughter in 1902. From then on the East End gangs appeared to feel that manslaughter rather than capital murder was the reasonable judicial assessment of violent death caused by their infighting.

Another, less violent, kind of criminal gang came into being in the last quarter of the 19th century, once again composed largely of immigrants, who provided contraband foodstuffs, wines and fabrics from the continent. Smuggling had always been a good second to thieving as long as privately owned cross-Channel vessels had a reasonable hope of outrunning coastguard cutters. After the Industrial Revolution and ever better-equipped excisemen, running ordinary consumer goods was never a continuously commercial proposition – though if puritanical politicians started banning people's pleasures, the criminal world was only too happy to supply them at inflated prices.

The Josephine Butler Society and the National Vigilance Association had high hopes of eliminating vice by legislating against it. Though they never succeeded in having prostitution declared illegal as such, they welcomed laws that prohibited disorderly houses and harassed street soliciting, and they joined with continental reformers in agitating about supposed "White Slavery". It was widely believed that Belgian brothel-owners held foreign women against their will after they had been kidnapped and forced or tricked into prostitution. International protocols were signed by most European nations prohibiting the transportation of women across national boundaries for immoral purposes and police forces (including Scotland Yard) set up bureaux and task forces to suppress the trade. Year after year, at international conferences, police chiefs reported that, in their own countries at least, White Slavery did not exist. And the bureaux supposed to be stamping it out instead helped charitable organizations with rescue work among juveniles who could be persuaded to give up prostitution. But in truth and in fact, once the vile traffic in virgin children had been stamped out by raising the age of consent, there was no international trade removing unwilling women to stock the brothels of the continent. The moral reformers were deaf to this information. They kept the annual international conference on White Slavery in being until World War I, at which point most police forces closed their bureaux down, though the contacts established were revived after the war in the more fruitful form of Interpol.

But if sexual enslavement of women was imaginary, prostitution was not. And the international protocol with its attendant police activity was a serious nuisance and hindrance to women who wanted to practise their trade in a different country. There were German and English women who welcomed the chance of a spell under contract to a French or Belgian brothel, with the security and companionship such institutions offered. There were French and Belgian women who wanted the independent lifestyle and rich pickings enjoyed by London prostitutes in the capital of the greatest empire in the world. In 1905, three Australian prostitutes, seeking the bright lights of Europe, took a leisurely passage to Paris and London, with a couple of weeks' voluntary "busman's holiday" en route, working in a Buenos Aires brothel. They did not come alone. Like all would-be international transient prostitutes, their freedom of movement was hindered by White Slavery policing. And so their Latvian ponces accompanied them to help them cross borders and find accommodation and working premises. These men were despised by the police and by some of the criminal fraternity for "living off immoral earnings". But they were not pimps, bullying stables of frightened women into submission nor, usually, brothel-owners (who in England provided a valuable service for prostitutes by bearing the risk of prosecution for keeping disorderly houses). They were effectively travel agents, couriers and managers in strange and officially unfriendly places. Their arrival in London ensured that a major strand of prostitution would be controlled by organized crime. One of these Latvians, Max Kassell, was still running a small stable of hookers in the 1930s, when he was murdered in Soho – one of a sequence of victims in the poncing gangs' clashes. (By that time the ponces' major service was the arrangement of marriages of convenience to give foreign women British passports. This had been unnecessary in the happy days before 1915, when passports were recognized as the exclusive imposition of over-policed nations like the Czarist Empire or post-Revolutionary France).

The National Vigilance Association enjoyed more success with its opposition to gambling and drinking. The Jockey Club and the turf, with strong royal support, were unassailable. Nobody could prevent gentlemen from wagering with each other. Nobody could stop the Prince of Wales from playing the mind-numbing game of baccarat with his friends, though he took up the more intellectually strenuous pastime of whist after the alleged cheating of Sir William Gordon-Cumming at Tranby Croft in 1890 created a national scandal. But the law could and did prohibit gaming in public premises, especially those that served alcohol. And it could restrict cash bookmaking to the racetracks. The 1872 Licensing Act forced the notorious night-houses of Panton Street and Leicester Square to close at midnight, thereby ruining their not very exciting trade in cheap champagne, flirtatious conversation with "soiled doves" and a very little, very occasional sex. The 1906 Street Betting Act theoretically prevented the working classes from wasting their substance in regular little flutters when they could not afford a day at the races. And the reduced pub licensing hours introduced in World War I encouraged a revival of night-clubs, serving drinks to subscribing members for a few hours after closing time.

All this legal restriction opened the way for new illegal ventures by gangs. The street bookmaker, (or his runner), collecting bets and disappearing as the police arrived, became a part of the urban scene until the 1960s. For drinkers who could not afford membership of reputable private establishments, illicit drinking clubs opened. For lower-class punters who wanted to play cards with the same freedom as members of White's or Boodle's, illegal gambling clubs arrived. Jewish dominance of the East End and its crime was reflected in their Yiddish name, "spielers" (places for games). In the Brick Lane neighbourhood, Isaac Bogard, a Jewish villain whose swarthy complexion and tightly curled black hair earned him the nickname "Darky the Coon", extended his interests. He began in the early years of the 20th century by supplying muscle for street traders who wanted to prevent newcomers from moving in, but he moved on to managing prostitutes and drinking clubs. And he became one of the protagonists in the worst gang war London had hitherto seen.

His rival was Arthur Harding, a brash young thief from the Old Nichol, whose own gang had grown increasingly bold, intimidating shopkeepers and street traders and openly helping themselves to goods or money. Harding stole and brawled within clear view of police officers whenever a sufficient number of passers-by impeded their catching him. He had no hesitation in attacking a police patrol that arrested one of his friends and when two of his gang waylaid and beat up a solitary policeman one night, he made an official complaint, falsely accusing the officer of unprovoked assault.

"Darky the Coon" undertook to put Harding in his place. There were fights with knives and by 1910 Harding was openly carrying a pistol on the streets. When both men were summoned before Old Street magistrates to be bound over to keep the peace, Harding planned to surround the courthouse with armed thugs, with the intention of gunning down Bogard and his chief lieutenant. To everyone's shock, Bogard appealed for police protection and Inspector Wensley, the leading CID officer in the East End, concealed a large body of men in tarpaulin-covered wagons who arrested Harding and his gang when they surged toward the court steps. Harding went to prison for that escapade, his gang thereafter nicknamed "the Vendetta mob". But he and Wensley were both mistaken in believing Bogard was finished from that moment. Bogard continued to flourish in Brick Lane until the 1920s and his heirs played their part in the East End underworld for another couple of generations.

All these gangsters of the days before World War I were generally unknown to the public at large. If an ordinary law-abiding citizen tried to imagine a professional criminal, it was probably as a broken-nosed, unshaven man in a cap and mask carrying a bag labelled "Swag"; he might have envisaged foggy Dickensian streets populated by the likes of Fagin, Bill Sikes and Flash Toby Crackitt saying things like, "Stow the glim!". Such characters really had existed once. Sikes' residential neighbourhood in Bethnal Green Road and the districts of Fagin's two dens off Saffron Hill and in Whitechapel all remained genuine nests of criminality. Boy pickpockets had actually been organized by a Jewish fence off Gray's Inn Road when Dickens wrote *Oliver Twist* and were still more shockingly managed by two West End policemen, Henry King and Jesse Jeapes, in the 1850s. But early 20th-century "gangsters", to the general public, were likely to mean "hooligans", teenaged urban ruffians who adopted a uniform of flat cap and broad heavy-buckled belt in supposed emulation of the legendary hell-raising "Hoolihan" family who fought with their belts. Hooligans, of course, existed. But like most adolescent trouble-makers, the overwhelming majority were not the slightest bit interested in professional crime and settled into righteous and sober lives once their hormones had stabilized.

All this altered after World War I. By a remarkable coincidence, Italian gangsters with Sicilian Mafia connections changed the whole public image of gangland in both England and America during the same decade. Prior to the war, New York and London were both infested with ethnically divided gangs of young tearaways who combined a certain amount of haphazard theft with a good deal of scrapping with each other and a limited amount of hired-out violence to those who wanted it. Adult American gangs had certain advantages over their British counterparts, however. Prostitution and off-track gambling were both rigidly illegal in the USA (except for Nevada). American criminal gangs willingly organized the provision of these recreational "vices" for punters. But in England prostitution was merely harassed and off-course betting was open to the middle classes through "turf accountants". There was no room for the mobs to move in and monopolize vice.

Meanwhile, American employers and unions had embarked upon labour disputes that encouraged one side to employ gangsters as violent strike-breakers and the other to inflict reprisals on owners and blacklegs. Fairly sophisticated gang-controlled marketing, supply and distribution systems were therefore in place when, in an act of unparalleled legislative folly, the USA prohibited the sale of alcoholic beverages for a decade, and thereby established really powerful organized crime as an apparently permanent feature of society, with its attendant corruption of local legislatures and jurisdictions. Adult English gangs could not advance much beyond theft, receiving, arranging street-betting or organizing transport and accommodation for transient prostitutes. They were certainly not household names.

The Sabini brothers improved on that. Darby Sabini – his real christian name was Charles, his closest associates called him Darbo – was the first British gangster since Jonathan Wild to become nationally notorious. He was born in Saffron Hill's "Little Italy" in 1889, one of the youngest in a large Irish-Italian family. At 13 he went to work for an Irish bookmaker who promoted boxing matches. The young Darby was a fancied middleweight, but he didn't care for the hard work of training and became a bouncer at the Hoxton Baths promotions instead. And around 1910 he started looking for alliances with the Jewish mobs from Aldgate to make his way into racecourse extortion.

Greedy English bookmakers in the 1870s had laid up a lot of grief for their successors. Bookmakers found that days when they lost heavily to the punters could be ameliorated by having a few ruffians on hand to discourage the timorous from collecting their winnings. It served them right when the ruffians turned the extortion back on them. Racing crowds, which had long provided cover for mobs of pickpockets, now sheltered the mobs of protection racketeers preying on bookmakers. The trade was a natural for the Sabinis, who were said to have Sicilian Mafia connections. The Italian secret societies that had once genuinely protected and avenged Italian peasants against foreign tyrants were the great masters of turning protection into extortion. America's first major gang war was between Sicilian Mafiosi and Neapolitan Camorristi, competing for the rich pickings to be extorted from Italian immigrants in New Orleans.

English racetrack extortion in 1910 was dominated by a Birmingham man called Billy Kimber, most of whose mob originated from the Elephant and Castle district of London. Kimber seems to have had some corrupt relationship with Tom Divall, the Divisional Detective Inspector of H Division (Whitechapel). Divall first tried very hard to prevent the outstanding young police officer Frederick Porter Wensley from being accepted into the CID, then tried to block his promotion. And on his own retirement he took a position with the Jockey Club, which he assured that Kimber was an excellent man to have around the racetracks. He also sang Darby Sabini's praises, despite the fact that race-going was rendered miserable in the early 1920s by the vicious gang wars between Sabini's mob and Kimber's "Brummagen Boys".

The Sabinis – brothers Harry-Boy, Joseph, Fred and George loosely acknowledging Darby's leadership - began to make an impression around 1920. By one account, Darby won the undisputed leadership of Little Italy's tough youngsters when he fought and humiliated an Elephant and Castle bully called Bennyworth who deliberately insulted an Italian girl in a Saffron Hill pub and tore her dress. Another view is that Darby benefited from the creation of the Flying Squad in 1919, as he quickly established good relations with its members (who policed the Epsom racecourse); sympathetic squadmen arrested Brummagen Boys rather than Clerkenwell Italians when fights broke out. In any event, the Sabini gang came to dominate the racetracks in the south, partly because they invariably went to the races in force, whereas the Brummagen Boys spread themselves around a larger number of meetings. By 1921, Kimber had effectively retreated to the Midlands.

Not that gang war ceased. Kimber paid a visit to Darby's home in Clerkenwell where somebody put a bullet in his side, though he didn't know who. Two drivers who worked for Darby were attacked and one was shot at the old Alexandra Palace racetrack. They didn't know who their assailants were, either. The Mafia code of *omerta*, silence, which worked so well in New York and Chicago, was also working in England.

Ethnic division was stirred up from a peculiar source. Horatio Bottomley, the crooked politician, pseudo-patriot and journalist who would ultimately go to prison for printing fraudulent competitions and bogus bargain offers once too often in his vulgar newssheets, protested that Darby Sabini and his men were taking work away from good honest English race-goers who had fought for king and country in the Great War. This was because Salisbury bookmakers, to defend themselves from having their pitches seized at gunpoint, had created the Racecourse Bookmakers and Backers Protection Association, with eight stewards to look after their interests – the five Sabini brothers, with three friends of Darby's.

Inspired by Bottomley's gutter-press jingoism, a Birmingham businessman financed the Brummagen Boys to go to Epsom for the Derby and settle the Sabinis' hash once and for all. Kimber signed up allies and Arthur Harding's Vendetta mob came up from London to lend a hand, supported by a rival Italian gang led by the Mancini family. The Brummagen Boys brought a charabanc south and used it to set up a road block to trap the Sabinis returning to London. The best-laid plans, however, may be defeated by mistiming. The Sabinis went home earlier than expected. The Brummagen Boys waylaid and fought furiously with their own London allies.

The Sabini-Kimber gang war raged on through 1921 and 1922. Darby Sabini shot his way out of a possible serious beating at Greenford trotting track. A Brummagen member was beaten up and shots fired when he went for a walk with his wife in Camden Town. The gangsters fought with each other in public and private places, in clubs, in pubs, on the underground, on the streets. They didn't use bombs or machine-guns. Indeed, although the Sabini gang were once famous for their Italian stilettos, they soon turned to the safer weaponry developed in the North and Midlands. A razor blade stitched into the edge of a cap peak made a vicious weapon when the cap was swung. A razor blade embedded in a potato could inflict horrible cuts without ever risking killing the victim and attracting a possible capital charge. Cutthroat razors could be wrapped in

Elastoplast, leaving only the tips to inflict surface wounds. "Striping" and "cutting" to scar an enemy's face became preferred assaults in London gangland, and would be favoured for 40 years. Throwing vitriol was also favoured in the inter-war period. Both kinds of disfiguring brutalities were employed horribly against women who stepped out of line. The London gangster's traditional sentimental love of his old mum and gallant assault on anyone who uses foul language in front of a lady should never be mistaken for the mark of a chivalrous nature. Darby himself disliked blood and rarely stayed around when the cutting started. But he took to carrying a pistol in his back pocket. And his were the orders that ensured rivals were viciously injured. The lawlessness Al Capone and his rivals would bring to Chicago within a few years was antcipated by the London gangs.

Blood flowing in the underground trains and on the streets alarmed the public, even though they were spared the pistol-firing car chases and the tommy-guns of the Capone and O'Banion mobs. It was not the police who halted Kimber and Sabini. It was the Jockey Club. Faced with a serious threat that all racetracks where trouble persisted would be closed down, the Jockey Club revised the system of allocating bookmakers' pitches with a strict "first come first served" rule, which prevented the mobsters from buying them up and sub-leasing them at extortionate rates. Darby and Kimber quickly came to an agreement and divided up the tracks between them. Roughly, Darby retained the South of England, Kimber the Midlands and North. There was still plenty of money to be made from the unfortunate bookies. They had to buy their printed lists of runners from Darby Sabini. They had to accept the services of Darby's sponge-boys who came round with a bucket and wiped out the chalked odds after each race, accepting half-a-crown in the bucket for this pennyworth of unwanted assistance.

But no sooner had inter-gang peace fallen than Darby was faced with mutiny inside his own mob. Some of the Jewish members wanted a higher percentage of the profits. The five Cortesi brothers, sent to negotiate with them, changed sides and joined the mutineers. Violent fighting followed the breakaway faction's appropriation of the take from Kempton Park bookmakers, and Harry-boy Sabini was convicted of assaulting George Cortesi, while five Sabini mobsters went to prison for attempted murder. When Darby and Harry-boy were caught in a Clerkenwell Club, however, where Harry-boy took a bullet and Darby had his false teeth broken, the temporary loss of face presaged long-term victory. Assault convictions took the Cortesis to prison for three years and their faction fell apart. The Sabinis ruled, ok?

Over the decade they built up their interests and developed the style that would be followed by successive 20th-century gangsters. Like Capone and his ilk, they posed as public benefactors. (The ego-massaging pretence of redistributing wealth by crime is as old as Robin Hood.) The Sabinis' private charity made them friends among their neighbours. Darby Sabini was the man to turn to if you couldn't pay your rent in Clerkenwell. He would produce a white fiver and ask for no repayment...until the time came that you could do him a favour. The pattern of "the godfather" derived, of course, from Sicily, where the Mafia's "men of respect" picked up prestige by their cheap and showy kindness to needy individuals, while the general inflation caused by their extortions ripped off the poor as a class. A Clerkenwell girl who threw herself in front of Darby to shield him from a threatened shooting emotionally described him as "her godfather" 50 years before Marlon Brando made the honorific title famous.

Like Mafiosi everywhere, Darby Sabini spread his interests. In addition to racecourse protection, he moved into spielers and drinking clubs. He devised, too, one new form of extortion. If club owners on the margins of illegality could not turn to the police for serious protection, burglars certainly could not. The Sabinis started to prey on thieves, demanding a cut of their takings and threatening to beat them up if they appeared in the West End without having paid tribute. The Sabinis were the first gangsters to earn the contemptuous description "thieves' ponces".

Yet Darby Sabini continued to win golden opinions from his neighbours as a "godfatherly" crime czar with the best interests of the weak at heart. He did stay out of sexual poncing. He protected girls, he didn't exploit them, they said on Saffron Hill. Not that he objected to others exploiting them. The Messina brothers came to London during the 1930s while Darby was the supreme criminal power in the West End. Their Italian father had been a brothel keeper in Egypt and Malta, had married a Maltese and thus acquired for himself and his children the right to live in England. Darby Sabini could have blocked them if he wanted to protect the women in the West End, after the last of the old Latvian, French and Algerian poncing gangs had eliminated and driven each other out of London in the series of lethal quarrels over money that ended in the murder of Max Kassell. Instead, he let the Messinas build up a lucrative business. They brought girls in from the continent with passports acquired through arranged marriages to destitute Englishmen. They established them in tiny West End flats with maids to check the takings and ensure that no punter was allowed more than ten minutes. They set up pavement patrols to check that the Messina girls were reliably on their beats and any competition was warned off. "The Maltese", who would become such a power in the English commercial sex industry, established their foothold in London with Darby Sabini's blessing. And they allowed him to appear clean-handed when sleaze was in the news. (Not that the newspapers paid much attention to the real sex industry in the 1930s. Crime reporters were more interested in trying to revive fears of the mythical White Slave trade).

Neither the Sabinis nor any other major gangsters had anything to do with drugs in those days. The Chinese restaurateur and dealer "Brilliant Chang" (Chan Nan) was excoriated when a girl died from an overdose of cocaine after the Victory Ball in the Albert Hall. Chang withdrew from Regent Street to Limehouse. There he lived like Dr Fu Man Chu in a building with a slummy exterior and palatial interior apartments. There he continued to deal in drugs. And when a second girl died and the police found cocaine in his flat, he was imprisoned and then deported. His place in Soho was taken by Jamaican Eddie Manning who ran a few whores, dealt a little dope and spun a bent roulette wheel at his Lisle Street flat and Berwick Street cafe. Manning also handled stolen goods and acted as an occasional police informer. This last activity led colleagues to set him up for a bust and he went to prison in 1929, dying there of syphilis three years later. Drugs were not important to English organized crime in the inter-war years, (though a Japanese operating from Marseilles made some tidy profits trading internationally among the intellectuals and sophisticates who liked playing with fire). Little was known about drugs, which would not be a serious menace until the well-meant Dangerous Drugs Act of 1967 naively let traffickers gain a secure footing in London. Even the pharmaceutically trained Agatha Christie nursed the delusion that one quick shot of marijuana could turn a woman into a sex slave.

The interrelated worlds of London boxing and London gangs had curiously different holds on ethnic loyalties. Traditional old London extortionists with British names like Dodger Mullins (and, later, Tommy Smithson) didn't do especially well at holding their own against the various immigrant groups in the East and West Ends. So the brutal young thug Cecil Louis England, whose alleged underworld exploits were said to include chopping one enemy's arm off with a meat axe and stuffing the hand of another into a mincing machine, changed his name to Tony Mancini before hiring out his muscle. And under that Italian guise he got away with the second Brighton trunk murder, much to his own surprise. His counsel, Norman Birkett, argued that Mancini's string of convictions (all for non-violent offences) had put him in the dock – a case of give a dog a bad name – and he was really entitled to be believed when he claimed that he had found his prostitute girlfriend battered to death after leaving her with an unknown punter.

Conversely, boxer Pasqualino Papa changed his name to Bert Marsh to attract true blue British ringside supporters. Charged with his sidekick Bert Wilkins as participants in a greyhound-track brawl in which a man was stabbed to death, Marsh devised a ploy that would be copied by others for a sympathetic hearing in court. While on remand, he and Wilkins bribed another inmate to attack a warder, to whose defence they then leaped. This won them grateful thanks at the Old Bailey and secured Marsh a very short sentence for manslaughter rather than a topping for murder. After the war, he passed the wheeze on to his protégé "Italian Albert" Dimes, who also used it to cop a reduced sentence.

The greyhound tracks had brought the Sabinis an unexpected challenge from the White brothers of Islington for control of this new and potentially corrupt sport. In the underworld, the "battle of Lewes" does not refer to Simon de Montfort's victory over Henry I in the Barons' War. It describes a savage riot at Lewes racecourse in 1936 when the Whites' allies, the Hoxton mob, turned up in force to try and wipe out the Sabinis. Since the Italians weren't there, the Hoxtonians set upon the Sabini-protected bookmakers instead and ultimately 16 men drew an aggregate of over 50 years' imprisonment for the affray. Compromise was the sensible answer. The Sabinis retained the West End and ceded the King's Cross area to the Whites. Darby Sabini went to live in Brighton and sent his daughter to an expensive girls' school in Sussex. Graham Greene modelled Colleoni, the master gangster in *Brighton Rock*, on Sabini who certainly had all that sinister crime lord's power over criminal small fry. But in one respect Greene glamorized his character. Colleoni (like most '30s gangsters) is a sharp dresser. Darby Sabini favoured brown suits and black waistcoats, with a perpetual flat cap. Some thought he wore the whole outfit to bed. He disliked the fiddle of a collar and tie, sported a collarless shirt in private and favoured a black muffler for smart occasions. He usually looked more like Andy Capp than "Snorky" Capone.

Sabini was a very bad man and a very rich one. When he sued a newspaper for describing him as a criminal, he denied that his income was a staggering £32,000 a year (say, over £1-million today). He probably didn't know, but that it could be estimated so high gives an indication of his success.

The downfall of the Sabini gang was not down to good policing. It was down to Mussolini. When the Duce meekly followed the Führer into making war on Britain and France, all but one of the Sabini brothers were rounded up as enemy aliens and interned on the Isle of Wight. The one who escaped the round-up was arrested and put into a civil prison for evading the summons. Unlike their American confrere Lucky Luciano, gaoled for poncing, the Sabinis were unable to continue running their business from behind bars. And they had not the Sicilian connections to give them pull with the government when the island was invaded. They emerged into a peacetime world where they were remembered, but no longer counted. However, they hung onto their wealth. Darby took a little pitch as a bookmaker at the end of his life, more for something to do than to make money. When he died in 1950, he didn't seem to be rich, but his faithful clerk was stopped leaving the country with £36,000 which, no doubt, would have joined other large sums in continental bank accounts.

The Sabini name still meant something in the 1970s. Johnny Sabini, an old man then, visited Ronnie Kray in prison. And the flamboyant Ronnie evidently felt that he was enjoying very serious recognition if the last of the Sabinis came to see how he was.

As the Whites moved in to take control of the West End, the Sabini empire fell completely apart in 1941, with violent fighting between the surviving Italians and Jewish factions. An Italian genuinely named Tony Mancini (and nicknamed "Babe" or "Baby Face") joined a fight in a Wardour Street club where there had been numerous brawls between the two sides. On this occasion Mancini picked up a knife and stabbed Harry "Little Hubby" Distleman, a Jewish club manager, gambler and possibly part-sharer (with his brother) in a chain of brothels. Gasping, "Baby's stabbed me in the heart. I'm dying", Distleman expired, and Mancini found himself on trial for murder. Had he been willing to plead guilty to malicious wounding, the heavier charge might have been reduced to manslaughter. But Mancini relied on the traditional omerta and despite there being 40 or so witnesses, no coherent account emerged of what had happened. However, despite the judge drawing attention to the weak evidence, the jury found Mancini guilty and he was sentenced to hang. His appeal failed, and he became one of the very few gangsters to suffer death for killing a rival in a professional gang fight. The incident was otherwise important for the involvement of RAF deserter "Italian Albert" Dimes (originally Alberto Dimeo), who was bound over to keep the peace before being returned to uniform. He would become an important figure in post-war gangland.

The future major gang leaders other than the Whites had started to emerge in the Sabini days. Jacob Comacho, aka John Colmore, better known as Jack Comer, but best known as Jack Spot, was born in Whitechapel in 1912. In 1927 he started work as a bookie's runner. The following year he joined forces with another East End villain in "Darky the Coon's" old business of "protecting" the street-market stallholders in Petticoat Lane. Spot was starting to establish the reputation for the violence that would cause his rise, and the hubristic love of fame that would be his downfall. After beating up his partner and taking over the business solo, he began to call himself "the King of Aldgate". He set up as a welching bookmaker in his own right. He also worked with a local housebreaker, acting as lookout on about 40 occasions, which he asked to be taken into account when arrested and convicted.

When Oswald Mosley's Fascists started to infest the East End chanting, "We gotta get rid of the Yids", Spot became a local hero, taking a lead-weighted chair leg to inflict a savage beating on one of Mosley's roughnecks at the battle of Cable Street. Spot's exultant recollection of the incident from his placid law-abiding retirement in the '80s was still capable of startling a young journalist by the revelation of relished brutality.

After 1935, Spot nominated himself the official protector of Jewish shopkeepers, who were likely to find their premises seriously damaged (by Fascists, no doubt!) should they fail to pay his high premiums. Around this time, according to his story, he acquired the nickname "Spot" because of his opportune appearance "on the spot" whenever he was needed. A much later claim is that the nickname derived from his finally preferred surname Comer, pronounced "Comma", and so a spot of punctuation. But it is far more likely that he was nicknamed for the large black mole on his left cheek.

In 1937 Spot suffered the only prison sentence of his career, going down for six months for inflicting GBH on a Fascist.

Apart from a brief spell in the Royal Artillery, from which he was discharged on medical grounds, the great Anti-Fascist didn't contribute much to putting down Hitler. Instead he used the war years to consolidate his prominent position in the underworld, especially by travelling to the North and helping club-owners, greyhound racing operators and bookmakers in Manchester and Leeds. He liked to think of himself as the strong man who could be sent for by any Jewish businessman in trouble anywhere, from Glasgow to London. He would then bash the businessman's enemies, and in return help himself to clothing, food and drink, and spare cash as he needed it. Rabbis recommended him to their congregations, as Spot tells it.

Crucially, however, Spot realized that the Whites' hold on the racetracks was shaky. They were getting older, and Spot had little difficulty in kicking in the face of the 65-year-old man who looked after their interests in Newcastle. Spot wanted the lucrative point-to-point business that had not come under Jockey Club control, allowing the Whites to take £2 a head from every bookmaker who wanted to do business at a meeting. In 1947, Spot went mob-handed to a drinking club in Sackville Street where he accused Harry White of being anti-Semitic and beat him up. Then he teamed up with another up-and-coming gangster, Billy Hill, to put together a huge army that searched for the Whites all over King's Cross. By Spot's account, the Whites just melted away. By Hill's, one was first captured and tortured by being held over an open fire. In either case, Jack Spot took over the White's racing business. He upped the bookmakers' premium for the right to work at point-to-points from £2 to £7. And he took 25% of anything Harry White made at the races. From then on, Jack Spot started to regard himself as "King of the Underworld".

Billy Hill was a tearaway from the old Dickensian criminal slum of Seven Dials behind Charing Cross Road. He was one of 21 children and his sister Maggie became well-known as a member of Alice Diamond's shop-lifting gang, "the Forty Thieves". Single eyes played a large part in Maggie's legend. She was said to be one-eyed; said to have received four years penal servitude for stabbing a policeman in the eye; said to have put out the eye of another thief's mother with a hatpin. Billy claimed to have started using malicious violence when he was 14, at which age he found he could push a pair of scissors into a fellow human being without feeling anything but satisfaction. He started his larcenous career as a housebreaker and proceeded to clumsy smash-and-grab robbery as that became the fashionable crime of the motorized inter-war years. He was not especially good at it. He came out of prison from a four-year sentence just as the war broke out in 1939 and returned to prison twice, spending most of the time that he might have been fighting Hitler as His Majesty's guest. Nothing suggested that this hopeless recidivist would become a prominent and successful criminal in peacetime. It is probable that his association with Jack Spot in overthrowing the Whites gave him the start he needed. He was helped, too, by his Scottish wife Aggie, who knew how to manage money.

It may have been Spot who gave Hill the idea of setting up serious robberies instead of hit-or-miss snatches and break-ins.

Spot is alleged to have been behind the 1948 London Airport robbery which went wrong though it was an ambitious, professional job, planned along the lines developed in America by "Baron" Lamm, a former Prussian army officer drummed out of his regiment for cheating at cards. Calling on his military training, Lamm carefully recced his targets and prepared floor plans. He coached his gang thoroughly and put them through timed rehearsals, and he had getaway vehicles and fallback positions. He imposed strict discipline and insisted on meticulous timing, forcing his hoodlums to leave behind surplus loot rather than delay their exit from the scene. His death in a shoot-out with the police in 1930 was a serious loss to the criminal world, but his methods were followed by others, including John Dillinger and, 30 years later, Bruce Reynolds.

The London Airport caper, like nearly all really important robberies, depended on inside information. Teddy Machin and Franny Daniels, two villains who sometimes supplied muscle for Spot, were part of the gang that learned when £250,000 in bullion was to be held at Heathrow in the warehouses of BOAC (British Overseas Air Corporation, the intercontinental forerunner of British Air). A bent warehouseman was engaged to put knockout drops in his colleagues' tea so they would be unconscious on the night the robbers broke in. Unfortunately for the team, the warehouseman bent in two directions at once, and told the police. When the gangsters arrived, the sleeping "watchmen" were actually three Flying Squad men simulating unconsciousness, with two more hidden in cupboards and another nine waiting in a bus parked outside in the darkness. The nine thieves were outnumbered, but armed with iron bars, they gave a good account of themselves. Men on both sides were concussed. The Flying Squad chalked up a number of convictions with 12-year sentences handed out. Machin and Daniels escaped, the latter suffering severe burns from the lorry chassis to which he clung.

Four years later the Eastcastle Street mail-van robbery announced that serious and effective heists à la Lamm had really started in London. £287,000 was taken after the van had been boxed in by other vehicles; the driver and guard pulled out of it; the van driven away to be dumped in Camden Town. Thirteen sacks remained from the original 31. The fact that any had been left behind showed that professionalism and the quick getaway took priority over greed. Nobody was charged with the theft, none of the money was recovered and although two men were charged with handling, they were not convicted. Billy Hill supposedly had managed to nobble the jury. Billy himself was summoned to Scotland Yard where a senior officer anticipated charging him but, again supposedly, Billy made known his friendship with a villain who enjoyed a corrupt relationship with the officer and no charge was brought. By Billy's account he handed over £14,000 to Jack Spot as feudal tribute, suggesting that Spot really did rule gangland in 1952.

Spot and Hill were enjoying a spell of exceptionally fine weather for organized crime. Post-war rationing encouraged large numbers of normally honest citizens to view black marketeering as crime that "didn't count". The female cartoonist Anton's drawings of spivs in Punch created a new and friendly image for the criminal wide-boy, offering the nylon stockings that were so cruelly export-only on the legitimate market. Fedora hats, extravagantly padded shoulders, jazz-patterned ties and moustaches like ladies' eyebrows, the insignia of the downmarket carnival barker or three-card trickster in America, became the uniform of the lovable London street-smart dealer. The spiv was so popular as the provider of forbidden and rationed goods that his appearance was imitated by other criminals. Spot's fedora became familiar at racecourses. Billy Hill's slicked-down Brylcreemed hair seemed to up-and-coming CID officer "Nipper" Read to be the image of the contemporary spivs' style.

The unpopular villains of the time were the violent and ill-organized young tearaways. The Jenkins family from the Elephant and Castle supplied two figures for post-war demonology. Signally failing to profit from Billy Hill's example, they went on crudely smashing and grabbing. In 1944, accompanied by Ronald Hedley, Thomas Jenkins attacked a jewellers' shop in narrow Birchin Lane in the City of London. As the getaway car swung out into Lombard Street, 56-year-old naval commander Ralph Binney stepped in its way to try and bring it to a halt. The thugs drove straight over him, dragging him under the wheels right the way across London Bridge. Commander Binney was killed, and a commemorative medal named for him is annually awarded to someone performing a similarly brave act to oppose violent crime. Ronald Hedley died on the gallows and Thomas Jenkins was lucky to get away with a long prison sentence.

Which taught his little brother Charles nothing. In 1947 he joined Christopher Geraghty and Terence Rolt in another smash-and-grab raid, this time off Tottenham Court Road. Motor cyclist Alex de Antiquis tried to stop them and they shot him dead. The younger Jenkins was hanged with Geraghty. Rolt, only 17 at the time, was lucky to be detained at His Majesty's pleasure.

In 1948, the young army deserter George Thomas shot PC Nat Edgar who was questioning him about his housebreaking activities. He escaped hanging because a bill for the abolition of capital punishment was before Parliament at the time. In 1953 16-year-old Christopher Craig was too young to be hanged for shooting PC Sidney Miles, but his co-defendant Derek Bentley went to the gallows – though the bias with which Lord Chief Justice Goddard conducted the case led the Lords of Appeal, 40 years later, to overturn Bentley's conviction, despite what they recognized as strong (if not overwhelming) evidence that he was, as charged, guilty of the technical murder for which he was hanged. The authorities constantly worried that having a conscript army engendered the spread of guns in criminal hands.

All this concentration on juvenile violence was excellent camouflage for Spot and Hill. Warned by Detective Chief Superintendent Peter Beveridge that the police would not tolerate the sort of gang warfare on the streets which the Sabinis had practised, Spot and Hill celebrated their defeat of the Whites by tossing their guns and hand grenades away, some into the Thames and others down a manhole. They could maintain a sufficient reign of terror with knives and shoes and knuckle-dusters. And the newspapers paid them no attention. Neither man was interested in prostitution or vice racketeering, so neither was implicated when the *People* ran its famous campaign against the Messinas. Spot and Hill preferred a territorial agreement that the Maltese could sell sex while they sold gambling and arranged heists and protection racketeering. They left it to individualist Tommy Smithson to take on the Malts. He came out of the navy and back to his native Spitalfields, found them opening clubs and running prostitutes, and tried to impose protection on them. He earned two savage stripings before he was contemptuously murdered outside George Caruana's west London house. Jack Spot was content to be a "King of Soho" who left Soho's most famous industry in the hands of others. Like "Darky the Coon's" mob after Darky's death, Spot and Hill at first kept a low profile, and nobody interfered with them.

How much this was a matter agreed between the mobs and the police may never be known. For the police, too, were enjoying a golden era, the "Dixon of Dock Green" era when the public image of a copper was fatherly Jack Warner and nobody doubted that our police were wonderful. In consequence, nobody ever asked whether the CID had a cosy relationship with certain criminals and nobody believed that a British bobby would ever plant evidence, invent a statement or use intimidation and violence to secure a confession. The Metropolitan Police commissioners of the 1940s and 1950s had other things on their mind than the close supervision of the CID. Sir Philip Game would have retired in 1940 had not the war kept him loyally in office, overseeing the largely civil defence policing duties of wartime London. His successor was not a police officer but, uniquely, a senior civil servant with no experience of either law enforcement or armed service. Sir Harold Scott's major preoccupation was maintaining a severely undermanned service in the climate of economic austerity and his claim to fame was giving Ealing Studios every assistance in making *The Blue Lamp*, a decision that paid handsome dividends in public admiration for "PC George Dixon". Scott had no intention of interfering with the glamorized careers and popular retirement memoirs of Robert Fabian and other assorted Knackers of the Yard. The Flying Squad could use whom it liked as informants; cultivate them in ways that seemed most profitable; enjoy the nickname "the Heavy Mob" when it came to fierce hand-fighting like the battle of Heathrow. Scott's successor, Sir John Nott-Bower was a serving officer, but he was nearing retirement and content to interest himself mildly in the Mounted Branch and the Dog Section.

The serpent in this idyllic paradise for major organized crime was the peculiar and rather unsavoury journalist "Tommy" Duncan Webb, legendary – in the sense of being essentially mythical as well as hugely successful – for his moralizing exposé of the Messina brothers' vice empire in 1950. In fact, Webb's real knowledge of prostitution was as a tiresome client. Four years earlier he had been convicted of common assault when he refused to leave a prostitute, Jean Crews (whose services he had just used and paid for), and attacked a passer-by who came to her aid when she ran out of her flat with her sister to call for help. Webb was lucky to escape the serious charges of malicious wounding and impersonating a policeman, since he used his Metropolitan Police-issued press ID card to try and hoodwink the victim of his assault into believing he was arresting him. As it was, his conviction led to his dismissal from the *Daily Express*. (He had already cost them a reprimand and himself a conviction by incautiously phoning in wartime shipping movements from Plymouth in such a way as to give away classified information.) In 1948, after eight days as news editor of the *Daily Graphic*, Webb was sacked for his "unorthodox" methods of obtaining information.

In 1950, when Donald Hume was on trial for the murder of his fellow spiv Stanley Setty, Webb opportunistically cultivated a past casual introduction to Mrs Hume (a former Torbay carnival queen). He telegraphed her the avuncular advice to have nothing to do with reporters who were pleading for an exclusive interview. As a result, he himself got it – and was nearly prosecuted for interfering with a witness when the Director of Public Prosecutions heard about it. But he won the affections of Mrs Hume, who later married him while Donald served his sentence for the admitted disposal of Setty's body. Webb was uneasy about a gangland revenge for the sin of pinching a convicted villain's woman, and definitely scared that Hume might seek personal revenge when he came out of prison.

Webb's exclusive interview with Mrs Hume had appeared in the *People*, whose editor, Sam Campbell, was a notably creative journalist. He had turned the virtually unknown reporter Arthur Halliwell into an "expert" on the underworld of spivs and crooks (or at least on the largely fictitious version of it that Campbell knew would appeal to his readers). He now gave Webb even greater elevation as a spectacular crime reporter. His was the by-line on a front-page series that opened with photographs of the Messinas and the headline, ARREST THESE FOUR MEN. Sam Campbell pretended that Duncan Webb had been investigating the Messinas' vice empire for over a year, heading a team comprising two private detectives and two ex-police officers. Careful reading of Webb's articles shows that in fact he had visited two or three prostitutes' flats as a client and asked them a few casual questions before they found out his true occupation. Sam Campbell pretended that Webb's "dossier" was of interest to the Home Office and Inspector Mahon of the "Vice Squad". The Home Office's weary acknowledgement that they would have to consider an investigation if Webb made a formal complaint was blithely interpreted by Campbell as an invitation to Webb to help the authorities set up an inquiry. Readers were never told that there was no formal Vice Squad in 1950, or that Inspector Mahon was, in fact, investigating two Messina girls' allegations that Webb had bribed them to give phoney information against their ponces. Sam Campbell concocted a story that Webb's life was in danger as the series had so damaged the furious pimps that they were likely to engage contract killers to rub him out. Webb's desk in the *People* newsroom was surrounded with bullet-proof glass, much to the admiration of visiting members of the public and the amusement of his fellow hacks. Working journalists were well aware that the soft-living Messinas might beat up girls who flouted their rules (fixed beats, exclusive short times to maximize earnings and compulsory condoms to minimize absenteeism from sickness or maternity leave). But the brothers were not going to take on men, let alone men who were sufficiently legit to appeal for police protection. It was Sam Campbell who invented the catch-phrase with which Webb alleged he ended his investigative interviews with prostitutes: "I made an excuse and left". Few in the know doubted that like most such "covert investigators", Webb was more likely to have paid an extortionate fee for a pathetic sexual return and put it down to expenses.

This father of sleaze journalism might become his editor's nominal spearhead in driving out the small family of foreign-born ponces who controlled most of the lucrative Shepherd Market trade. But he should never have been able to affect home-grown successes like Jack Spot and Billy Hill. That he did so was a matter of their own folly, vanity and competing egos, all characteristic features of professional criminals.

In 1954, when he was widely thought of as an established and respected crime columnist, Webb started a series on the criminal underworld. His guide through this swampy territory was Billy Hill. That the series assigned underworld primacy to Hill got up Jack Spot's nose. In fact, the old "King of the Underworld's" gangland prestige was slipping. With a young and beautiful wife, Rita, he was, some people thought, too happily married to be a gang boss any longer. He led a peaceful and unostentatious domestic life in his Hyde Park Mansions flat. He and Billy Hill had always been most interested in the commercial success of their crime empires. They had never gone to war for prestige. Yet now Spot apparently felt that Webb's series belittled him in ways that could not be tolerated and threatened to sell his own series to Kemsley newspapers, the *Daily*

Telegraph group. He took Webb to lunch in Old Compton Street and threatened to break his jaw if he interfered with his Kemsley contract. Webb claimed to have responded brashly, "Here is my jaw, break it. I am not going to be intimidated by a cheap little gangster like you". Which was rash of him (if he ever said it, which seems highly unlikely). Spot set up a false meeting for Webb with another contact in the Dominion Cinema, turned up himself with a couple of minders, led Webb round the back and nutted him, with the words, "Take that you fucking bastard. I'll show you who runs the underworld and this fucking town".

"For heaven's sake, Jack, what is this all about?" cried Webb. Spot only repeated his claim, adding, "I'll show you who's the governor round here", with which he donned brass knuckles and pummelled Webb about the face and body, finally knocking him down and kicking him. Next day the Charing Cross Hospital confirmed that Webb had a broken wrist. Spot was convicted of causing grievous bodily harm and was lucky to escape with a £50 fine. Webb then brought a civil suit and received over £700 damages, leaving Spot with a further heavy bill for legal costs. It was the beginning of the end for Jack Spot.

Billy Hill, using Webb as ghostwriter for his memoirs, rather contemptuously took the journalist under his wing. He delighted in taunting him with the forthcoming release of Donald Hume, suggesting that the killer never forgave a grievance and would surely come after the man who stole his wife. For his part, Hill was hoping to leave England for Australia and possibly retire. His empire of Soho spielers and drinking clubs (which left prostitution and dirty bookshops to the Maltese) was largely controlled by his lieutenant Albert Dimes, who still had ties to the Italian gangland survivors, headed by Bert Marsh, the ex-boxer who began his life as Pasqualino Papa. A good-natured gentle giant in the eyes of the underworld, Dimes had actually killed a man in a street fight before the war. This, together with his participation in the brawl that led to Babe Mancini's execution for the murder of Hubby Distleman, gave the "gentle, good-natured" Italian Albert considerable prestige in gangland.

To challenge Spot's continuing dominance at the racetracks, Hill and Dimes started picking up new and younger gang members. They recruited hard men like "Billy Boy" Blythe and Richard "Dicky Dido" Frett and their friend "Mad Frankie" Fraser, a promising young thief who had met Hill in gaol and respected him. Having been certified a couple of times did "Mad Frankie" no harm in gangland. A reputation for having the potential to go berserk and create uncontrolled mayhem is useful to an enforcer. Spot followed suit on the recruitment front. He hired the rising East End protection racketeers Ronnie and Reggie Kray to turn up, carrying firearms, as his minders at the Epsom spring race meeting. It was the twins' first professional outing among the West End "faces" and despite their later claim that they despised their employer and only turned out to establish that they were the up-and-coming firm who intended to take over from him, it was actually a big step up. Spot also hired 19-year-old Joe Cannon as a permanent minder and bodyguard.

Spot's public humiliation and downfall came that summer. Billy Hill attempted to emigrate to Australia. Albert Dimes started trying to give orders to Jack Spot and declared that he was to be driven off the racetracks. Infuriated, Spot attacked Dimes with a knife in Frith Street, Soho. The fight was vicious and moved from the street into a shop, where a lady fruiterer whacked Spot with a brass weighing-pan in an attempt to stop it. Spot dropped his knife after cutting Dimes severely. Dimes picked it up and inflict reciprocal injuries. Both men went to hospital where they were arrested after treatment. The battle of Frith Street made the front pages and Jack Spot became a household name.

The trials that followed suggested that gangland could run rings round the courts even when affrays were openly witnessed by the public. Dimes' counsel submitted that a man fighting for his life could not be said to be causing an affray. Mr Justice Glyn-Jones accepted the argument and the affray charges were dropped against both men (a precedent which appears to suggest in logic that it is perfectly legal for two men to try to kill each other on the streets, but criminal if they only try to hurt each other). They were then tried separately to decide which had first assaulted the other. Bert Marsh had testified before the magistrate that Spot attacked Dimes. And despite the obvious likelihood that Marsh was around expecting trouble and willing to lend his Italian compatriot a hand, this seemed to be supported by passers-by. The prosecution decided not to proceed against Dimes. At Spot's trial a witness called Christopher Glinski who had underworld connections testified that Dimes had attacked Spot. And this was supported by the apparently unimpeachable testimony of an 88-year-old parson who happened to have been in Frith Street at the time. Spot was acquitted and the fight the whole world knew about had become, in the eyes of the law, a fight that never was.

It was small compensation for the police that the Reverend Basil Andrews was back in the witness box a year later, admitting that, as a geriatric clergyman with huge gambling debts, he had been an easy target for Spot's friends "Sonny the Yank" Schack and "Moisha Blue Boy" Goldman to bribe with a measly £25. He had perjured himself on Spot's behalf, but now his testimony sent Schack and Goldman to prison.

Jack Spot's empire collapsed just as he achieved national fame. Billy Hill returned from Australia, having been barred entry because the woman accompanying him was not his lawful wedded wife Aggie. But the Hill vs Spot war anticipated by some crime correspondents never materialized. Spot's men changed sides and word went out that Spot was a police informer, which was not impossible - it has been the last recourse of many gangsters past the age of fighting for dominance. Fearing that he was going to be carved again, Spot went to Superintendent Peter Beveridge and asked for police protection. This could not be supplied and Spot lost face when word went round. With Mad Frankie Fraser acting for Hill and Dimes, the carving duly took place. Spot dithered about naming names. Rita did not. Frankie Fraser, "Battles" Rossi, "Billy Boy" Blythe, Bobby Warren and William Dennis went to prison for the assault. With the twisted self-interest that passes for morality in gangland, they criticized Spot for not saving them with a perjured declaration. He stayed just within the code of not grassing by saying he could not recognize who had done it.

But Spot was washed up. His repeated court cases landed him in bankruptcy and he was evicted from the Hyde Park Mansions flat. He took work as a meatpacker and remained perky, menacing and full of boastful memories, but he was never again a real power in gangland. When he came to have his memoirs written, he achieved a surprising new low, finding an author even sleazier than Duncan Webb to commemorate his achievements. *Jack Spot, Man of a Thousand Cuts* is accredited to Hank Janson, the pseudonym under which Stephen D. Frances wrote mildly salacious thrillers that passed for dirty books, until Mickey Spillane legitimized the genre by writing mildly dirty books that passed for salacious thrillers.

Billy Hill's autobiography, *Boss of Britain's Underworld*, was ghosted by Webb and launched with a publisher's party attended by Sir Bernard Docker, chairman of the Birmingham Small Arms company, whose extravagant and flamboyant wife was constantly in the news, to the dismay of shareholders who feared that the company profits were being poured into a yacht floating on champagne. Frankie Fraser, not yet back in the prisons where he spent most of his adult life, was photographed at the party and has claimed that he and Albert Dimes wandered into a room where they found Lady Docker happily bonking with Billy Hill. So Albert gave her a friendly slap on the bottom for being a naughty girl. Whether the story is true one can't say, but it does have a certain charm.

That was the final flourish of Hill's career, however. The Flying Squad had always been directed against robbers rather than racketeers and Hill's fame was as a robber. Tommy Butler and Peter Vibart, the legendary detectives of the late '50s and early '60s, might not have been able to bring down Hill. But they did the next best thing. They brought down his brief. Barrister Patrick Marrinan, who lived in the same block of Barnes flats as Hill and was always available as the gangster's legal adviser, was disbarred for improperly associating with men of known bad character and acting on their behalf without instructions from a solicitor.

Hill had never been a man like Spot who delighted in violence. And now, by the accounts of all but his greatest admirers, his bottle really had gone. He feared the savagery his quarrel with Spot had unleashed and he retired to Spain, starting the fashion for taking ill-gotten gains to sunny "Costa del Crook" and thence on to Tangiers. Suddenly the rich pickings of the West End's vice and gambling were open territory. Albert Dimes was the senior figure connected with the old protection racketeers. But Albert was no longer seen as a man of effective violence. "He couldn't fight for fuck" was one contemptuous dismissal. In fact, Albert concentrated his attention on the racetracks and a few crafty fraudster's scams. He was still "Italian Albert" and "King of the Points". So when the rather naively managed legitimizing of gambling clubs attracted Mafia attention to London in the early '60s, Dimes cemented his contacts with Angelo Bruno of the Philadelphia family. And he used his standing alongside Bert Marsh to preserve peace in gangland, as far as could be done in that world of uncontrolled greed and overweening egos. Soho's burgeoning porn and strip industry was left largely in the hands of Bernie Silver and Frank Mifsud, who settled down to the sensible work of thoroughly corrupting the Metropolitan Police Obscene Publications Squad. Once that was done, they could rely on the law to push out competitors without calling up their own muscle. Nobody claimed the silly title "King of the Underworld".

In the inner suburbs new crime families were springing up who would cast greedy eyes on the money and prestige available in the West End. The Nashes from northwest London. The Richardsons from south of the river. And in the East End, Ronnie and Reggie Kray. The Kray twins came to criminal maturity in the heyday of Spot and Hill without the sense to see that Spot and Hill's celebrity status was exactly what lost them their power.

2

THE GANGLAND ETHOS

It would be satisfying to deny villains all virtue and insist that their thuggery has no redeeming feature. But it would be unfair. The first essential prerequisite of a traditional robber or extortionist is physical courage. For a certain length of time, a brawny coward with a knuckle-duster, a knife, a razor or a gun may get away with bullying the timorous or prudent. But in the end, everyone comes across a stronger or better-armed opponent or mob-handed opposition. You can't win 'em all. And the East End, birthplace of London thugs from Dick Turpin to Ronnie Kray, has always demanded that a man stand up and take his lumps when the fight goes against him.

The 1908 Royal Commission investigating street policing found one horrific case of brutality in Spitalfields, in which a beat constable tried to take over a prostitute's open-air services from her client and, knocking the young man to the ground, kicked him so savagely that his urethra was permanently damaged. His Majesty's Commissioners, apparently influenced by the ethical standards of the witnesses appearing before them, seemed to feel that the victim had been somewhat pusillanimous in falling at the first blow, and thereby almost invited grave injury. The police themselves took a more serious view and saw to the conviction and imprisonment of both the assaulting constable and his sergeant who had condoned the attack. Half a century later Tommy "Scarface" Smithson made the audacious error of trying to force protection on the Maltese running the commercial sex industries. He earned two savage stripings, at least one of which might have been lethal, but continued his endeavours. In another clash he was mortally wounded but still dragged his dying body across the road in a hopeless attempt to counter-attack, finally bleeding to death outside the front door of his adversary. He was widely admired for being game. Mad Frankie Fraser, his thighbone smashed by a bullet, hopped 300 yards down the road supported by friends; then told them to scarper while he dived through a privet hedge as the police arrived. Practically all his criminal contemporaries hail him as one of the gamest men alive. Commentators from the worlds of politics and law enforcement are fond of calling men of violence "cowards" in view of their natural human preference for fighting opponents weaker than themselves.

But until age weakens them or too many beatings cause them to lose their bottle, most "hard men" accept pain that the rest of us would dread. They don't last long if they can't take it.

There are two corollaries to this. The first is that being a hard man is to a great extent being perceived as a hard man and those villains who don't have the requisite ability to bear a beating have to pretend they are unafraid. Gangland, in consequence, is a world of rather absurd swaggering. Nobody admits to being frightened of anybody else. Nobody admits having lost a fair fight at equal odds to anybody else. In a gangland brawl, no team is reported as coming off second best, unless disgracefully ambushed or hopelessly outnumbered, in which case there is no shame in being overwhelmed. Mad Frankie Fraser and Frank Mitchell the Mad Axeman made themselves reputations by inviting repeated savage and well-earned beatings from prison officers for briefly hurting or humiliating the odd screw, and foolishly gloried in winning plaudits from their confreres. The second corollary is that you must take your beatings without complaint. Never whinge to the Law that you have been beaten. And never, never, never let it be known who inflicted the beating.

This has a superficially attractive appeal. We were nearly all socially conditioned from our earliest schooldays to hate sneaking, snitching or telling tales. We can nearly all sympathize with E. M. Forster's express wish that if he had to choose between betraying his friend or his country, he hoped he would have the courage to betray his country. Indeed, many may wonder why Forster thought such an obvious ethical preference took any moral courage at all: living, breathing people we know and have come to love obviously have higher priority than the abstraction of a nation state we happened to be born into. We don't like the acquaintance who feels inclined to call the police because someone lights up a joint. We don't look for a traffic warden to report someone with an overrun parking meter. We can understand Willie Donald's taunt that policemen may be defined as people who don't mind getting other people into trouble. We are unlikely to care much for the supergrass whose orgy of squealing supposedly purges his responsibility for a decade of brutal robberies. And so we may feel admiration for the villain who, like a heroic agent caught behind enemy lines, refuses to make life easier for himself by naming names.

Of course the admiration is misplaced. There is no justified war in which the villain keeping shtum is on the side of right. There is no ideological divide between some presumed higher morality of the underworld and the pettifogging conventionality of straight society. Finding your home trashed and your jewellery and electrical goods gone is considerably more distressing than smelling a little nicotine or marijuana wafting over the fence. The school sneak reporting the bad lads smoking behind the bicycle shed doesn't make life any the better or worse for the rest of the school. The reformed thief who shows the police how to find a quantity of loot and give society a rest from a gang of enterprising burglars saves innocent people from a sense of their privacy and personal space being violated. He may help victims recover some of their property and even some of their sense of security. And he does his bit to keep down insurance premiums for the rest of us.

Dave Courtney, a fine showman who capitalizes on his past occasional criminality, actually calls TV programmes like "Crimewatch" grassing. Like a latter-day Jimmy Saville (and Sir Jimmy seems quite as much a role model for Dave as the Frankie Frasers and Freddie Foremans he acknowledges) he is beautifully attuned to knowing just how far he can go to shock the public while retaining his balance. After making his attention-gathering ripples, he grins and ensures that he never looks worse than a bit of a bad lad.

In fact, cursory examination of the criminal ethos quickly reveals its central weakness. It is childish to the point of being infantile. The crucial physical courage is only carrying into adult life the maxim, "Big boys don't cry". An excellent behavioural guide for three-year-olds. A way of life which can produce true heroism in extreme situations. But extreme situations, by definition, rarely occur. Only infants expect a life in which they will constantly face pain and feature heroically. The sensible, adult, law-abiding citizen is accustomed to avoiding unnecessary danger. If it comes upon him uninvited, he will promptly and sensibly inform the police and trust them to bring about reprisals. Gangsters know this, which is why protection racketeers need an extremely secure base in society before they venture to threaten honest and law-abiding people who have socially approved occupations and no unscheduled debts.

Gangsters, with an infantile approach to the world, are looking for adventure. This is the positive, childlike vitality which has given them popular appeal since the days of Robin Hood. Most healthy small boys have enjoyed going into forbidden places, be they orchards for scrumping or derelict houses for non-larcenous exploration. (Given perfect opportunities, the latter pleasure, in my personal experience, has lasting appeal into respectable middle age.) Small boys like to fight, and can be unbearably cocky when they win. They usually grow out of this in adolescence, not because they are afraid of being hit, but because they outgrow the puppyish need to test their strength against each other and they see the pointlessness of this way of settling disputes. Gangsters seem not to do this piece of growing up. Like infants, their sense of competitiveness overwhelms their sense of generosity or fair play. ("I'm not cheating I'm winning," explained my four-year-old niece, caught shifting her piece illicitly in a board game). And so they tool up or bite or do whatever it takes to win a fight.

Infants can't easily accept adult notions of fairness and socially correct behaviour. Right behaviour for the infant is that which satisfies it. Yet the adult world declares all sorts of things "naughty" that are obviously satisfying. Spooning jam out of the pot in the larder. Getting muddy, fishing tadpoles out of the stream. Playing doctors and nurses with the little girl next door. There is manifest injustice in these being forbidden. Grown-ups can eat what they like when they like. They can go up to their thighs in rivers catching salmon. There can be humbug, too. Mummy and Daddy may pretend that playing doctors and nurses is disgusting and something they would never do themselves.

The child who is lucky has parents who explain and put things in a social context that can be understood. Little tummies don't eat their nourishing supper if they fill up with sugary jam, but grownups know how to balance their diet. Daddy's waders keep his clothes dry when he goes fishing, so put on your old jeans and wellies before going to the stream. Selina's mummy and daddy wouldn't like her to be playing that with you, you'll just have to wait until you're older.

Unlucky children never get taught the difference between proper ethical training, formal etiquette, and convenient domestic regulations. "Don't speak with your mouth full" comes down with what seems to be the same moral force as "Don't steal". The child normally develops two strategies to ease the pressure and preserve self-esteem in the face of constant criticism. The first is lying. The second is writing off all adult rules and regulations as a silly and unjustified nuisance. If you can't remember lying to get out of trouble as a child, then you have simply repressed a memory about which you feel undue guilt. It is equally certain that you appropriated other people's property, from sweets to small change. But if when you're grown up you still lie, you don't tell the shopkeeper when he's given you too much change, and you still discount social rules that get in your way, well, it doesn't mean you are a criminal. "All men are liars", as the proverb says, even if only to spare others occasional embarrassment. "Are you scrupulous in your dealings with the Inland Revenue?" was one of the moral queries with which Quakers were required to examine themselves monthly until very recently, testimony that some of the most scrupulous people are well aware of the constant temptation to petty dishonesty. And most of us practise some rationalization at least some of the time to make our less savoury activities palatable.

But the criminal ethos takes habitual lying for granted (There can obviously be advantage to villains in mendaciously asserting with genuinely pained sincerity that they weren't there and couldn't have done it). It is blithely unconcerned about the pitfall awaiting habitual liars – that they may come to believe their own most frequently repeated whoppers and so distort their own sense of reality. Self-justification can backfire even more easily. It may start out from an almost acceptable set of independent moral markers. It has been observed that East End villains and detectives share a number of street-smart entrepreneurial and moral standards. Most thieves, fraudsters and drug dealers would approve the alleged limits to the tolerance of Detective Chief Inspector Alec Eist, variously described as the most corrupt or the best informed mid-20th-century Metropolitan Police detective, who reputedly offered a sliding tariff of payments for which he would drop or reduce criminal charges. But he would never interfere with proceedings for murder, rape and stealing from old people. Nearly all professional thieves pride themselves on never harming the old and helpless. "Granny-bashers" are only less despised than child molesters in criminal circles. And the most likable thieves insist that they only rob either institutions or victims whom they know to be well insured. A gang nicknamed the "gentlemen thieves" in the early 1980s even invited victims who happened to be unfortunately on the premises when they visited, to identify a few objects of special sentimental value to them, which they did not take.

Yet, as at least one of them subsequently realized, this self-justification blinded them to the fact that they were savagely invading people's privacy. Adventure for the thieves was real distress for their victims. Simply perceiving such a fact and acknowledging the normal social perception of crime lies at the heart of the "remorse" parole boards so often demand from criminals. Uriah Heep-like protestations of penitence and regret are of no value to anyone. But acknowledgement that one's own self-gratifying little games of villainy mean genuine suffering for others shows a mind that is growing up and appreciating the world in the way that the rest of us do.

At its very worst, habitual self-justification becomes a despicable whinge. I once encountered a housebreaker, just released from prison, who had drunk and whored away his £75 gate money in less than 12 hours and was lying, drunk, on the floor of a railway station waiting-room. He complained to me that the measly grant of £75 and a rail pass to his home in Cornwall left him with absolutely no alternative but to start robbing houses immediately. This, he felt was a terrible grievance. Since many of my friends in the guided walks business at that time regarded £75 as a very good weekly take in the off-season, and they got on with their work without moaning, let alone supplementing their earnings by theft, I found the man merely contemptible.

So the warnings to anyone from straight society investigating the world of gangland must be, look out for persistent self-serving lying and don't accept villains at their own valuation.

In the meantime one notices the trend since Billy Hill for villains to write self-glorifying memoirs. In earlier centuries a reformed slave trader converted to Methodism, John Newton (author of the hymn "Amazing Grace"), wrote penitently of his wicked past. But when the Kray twins emerged into the criminal world, repentance was hardly the fashion. Jack Spot in England and Joe "Bananas" Bonanno in America would boast in print about their standing in the underworld and various Mafiosi and other villains would tell packs of lies about notorious crimes. In the London gangland of the 1950s and ''60s, Frank Norman turned from thief to writer after accepting Victor Gollancz's somewhat patronizing publication of his first book of memoirs, which faithfully reproduced his spelling and grammatical errors. And thereafter, Sparrers did sing.

Which brings us to one of the biggest lies and pieces of criminal self-deception, which is that all real villains never, under any circumstances, grass anybody up, much less stitch them up – the great unwritten code of the East End, according to sentimental and self-interested crooks' memoirs.

But a concept that is true and which is given almost Arabian Nights formulaic recognition, is "taking a liberty" and its opposite, "showing respect". Like an Elizabethan gentleman feeling obliged to draw his sword should someone "give him the lie", the East End villain felt honour-bound to react with violence should anyone "take a liberty". The concept was appropriately vague about what constituted it and, while it would certainly include sleeping with a man's wife while he was in prison, it could include something as trivial as being in a pub that the offended party considered his territory, or knocking someone's coat from its peg to the floor. Thus far we are simply in the mindset of the playground bully. Anything which infringes his sense of proprietorial rights is an outrage to be avenged. And such revenge is morally acceptable, even admirable. Arthur Harding, compelled in the self-serving "memoirs" he dictated in the 1970s to admit that his admired Blind Beggar gang once got into trouble for manslaughter, dresses up the story considerably. He makes the legal result an acquittal with a glorious celebration instead of the conviction and long term of imprisonment recorded by history. And he changes the origin of the offence from the unprovoked bullying of a harmless couple on the underground that actually occurred into the discovery that an uninvited group of people had taken up the gang's favourite place in the Blind Beggar. Manslaughter as a response to the latter, Harding implies, would be perfectly acceptable. Not even he could expect to persuade us that shouting anti-Semitic insults at an elderly couple, pursuing them down the pavement and stabbing at them with umbrellas, accidentally pushing the ferrule of one through the man's eye, constituted an admirable exploit.

A villain who takes a major professional liberty in the interest of self-aggrandizement is demanding and, hopefully, commanding respect. It is taking a liberty to challenge another gang's control of a racket or a piece of territory. A fight is welcomed and seen as justified. The hope is to take over and, by successful liberty-taking, increase wealth and respect.

Respect may be an elaborately oriental courtesy, at least in words. "If it wasn't for respect for you, Ron, I would have shot him," said Chris Lambrianou to his gang boss, when a rival gangster called Webb made a rude remark in a pub where they were all drinking. The liberty demanded revenge. The presence of a weightier member of gangland demanded that respect allow him to determine if and when violence should ensue. The literal threat was mere verbiage; time would prove that big, bullying Chris Lambrianou was completely without murderous impulses.

The concept of respect, like *omerta*, derives from Sicilian banditry. The senior Mafioso considered himself *"un uomo di rispetta"*, a man of respect. Curiously, the self-serving and selective memoirs of Joe "Bananas" Bonanno clarify the strange preservation of this concept – after a lifetime of lying, stealing, bullying, stabbing and shooting. From the old Mafia tradition of making occasional small hand-outs to needy peasants, and using his bully's power to exact vicious revenge for wrongs done to them (especially sexual wrongs to their daughters), a "godfather" came to see himself as the necessary popular administrator of justice and protector of the peace within his fiefdom, after the manner of an old autocratic monarch. Darby Sabini was London's proudest and greatest "godfather", obeyed in Clerkenwell where his rule was law and where he was genuinely loved by some people who felt he protected them against anti-Italian tormentors.

The principle is very loosely true. We accept an absolute monarch who maintains the land's one army. And, since 1829, the civilian police force, brought into being by Sir Robert Peel as a protection against the "drunken women and vagabonds" who ruled the streets at night and robbed with impunity. Sensible people in law-abiding occupations rely on the police (or properly licensed security firms), with all their faults, to protect them against racketeers. Silly or dodgy folk suffer or encourage the backstreet hoodlum to imagine himself a sort of public benefactor, supplying minders or bouncers and pretending that the protection racket is the commercial supply of security.

Joe Bonanno crazily imagined his empire of extortion and murder made him into a cut-price Alfred the Great. Darby Sabini's men were allegedly used by Scotland Yard's "Charlie Artful", the famous Superintendent John Capstick, to help hold off other gangsters while he arrested and humiliated a brutalizing pimp they all hated. But the little 1960s colony of London thieves and bullies who imagined that their imitation of American gangland gave them "respect" only basked in the admiration of callow juvenile delinquents. Freddie Foreman, a generally successful thief who is unashamed of having literally got away with murder, entitled his memoirs *Respect*. His publishers described him as "the managing director of English crime", apparently in admiring imitation of Frank Costello, America's "Prime Minister of crime" throughout the 1940s and early 1950s. Not that Freddie ever had in his pocket the kind of important range of judges, legislators and law enforcement officers (allegedly up to and including J. Edgar Hoover himself) that gave Costello his power and influence. Nevertheless, Foreman was intelligent and capable and sensibly maintained a low public profile while active as a criminal.

If such a man could be dazzled by the false glamour of gangsterism, how much more vulnerable were those criminals who were less intelligent, less competent, and more in need of the quick fix of public admiration. The element of brash, high-spending notoriety peaked in the gangland of the 1960s, encouraging the next generation's court jester of crime, Dave Courtney, to exaggerate and parody the image of the overdressed, high-profile, self-indulgent villain. And as one of their lieutenants has remarked, Britain's best-known gang leaders, Ronald and Reginald Kray, were the biggest of all suckers for gangland glamour.

3

THE TERRIBLE TWINS

They were born to the north of Hoxton and east of Beauvoir Town on 24 October 1933. The birthplace was number 68 (not 64) Stean (not Stene) Street, between and parallel with Kingsland Road and Queensbridge Road, one of the flat repetitive terraces of cramped sooty brick dwellings that made the East End monotonous. Their births were registered by their mother, who reported that Reggie came into the world first, followed by Ronnie ten minutes later. Their horoscopes may be calculated precisely, if anyone wishes to do it, because their birth certificates, as is the case with all British twins, give the precise times of their birth. Without being quite so laboriously committed to the non-science of our ancestors, we may note that they were Scorpio. Certainly they could sting.

Hoxton was Kray territory, the family's unusual name believed to mark their Austro-Hungarian and Romany extraction. The twins' grandfather, "Mad Jimmy" Kray was a stallholder who peddled old clothes and shoes in the weekend market in Brick Lane. A noted local drinker and fighter (the sobriquet "Mad" acknowledged his fiery temper) he was, in his day, a dressy man who wore a white stock. Mad Jimmy married a housemaid from Highgate and their elder son Charles, a brighter and better businessman, went round the suburbs and the countryside "pestering" on doorsteps for cast-offs and any unwanted bits of old gold or jewellery. He worked with an Irish partner called Sonny Kenny and by judicious use of courtesy, deference and an appearance of only the most casual interest in the precious metals, ensured that his gold-weighing scales earned him something in the region of 17 shillings a week – more like £70 at today's values. It put the Krays in the better-earning brackets of the East End.

But Charlie Kray, a dapper snappy dresser like his father, also liked his daily drink and his daily bet. His earnings never accumulated into wealth. His slicked-back hair and smartly polished shoes marked him out as a cut above the average totter and the Chrysler car that took him on country forays was a far cry from the rag-and-bone man's horse and cart. His face wore a perpetual expression of mild anxiety, believed by some people to be a mark of gypsy wariness. It was inherited by his second son, otherwise one might suspect it was a result of his vaguely unstable lifestyle, which increasingly became a matter of running and hiding. But it didn't stop him from captivating one of the prettiest girls living east of Aldgate pump. Violet Annie Lee was one of three sisters whose family dominated the Bethnal Green end of Vallance Road. Known as Baker's Row in Jack the Ripper's day, it ran down to a point between the sites of his first two murders at its Whitechapel end. Renamed for a parochial Bumble whose unlovely reputation was for keeping Poor Law assistance doles rigidly within budget, this long, drab residential street has now been pulled down. Where the Lees knew rows of Victorian artisans' dwellings with outside privies in the back yards, there is now a long strip of waste land broken only by a curiously preserved local monument, Mary Hughes' former Dew Drop Inn. In the 1930s, the Quaker daughter of the author of *Tom Brown's Schooldays* ran this teetotal pub as part of her high-minded adoption of the life of the slum-dwelling urban poor. More famous today is the memory of 178 Vallance Road, the house Charles and Annie Kray moved to in 1939 and which their sons made infamous as "Fort Vallance".

At the Bethnal Green end, Vallance Road led into the heart of British Fascist territory, where Mosley recruited thugs in the '30s and their politically illiterate descendants distributed their newssheets in the '80s. Violet's father Johnny "the southpaw Cannonball" Lee was one of its most colourful residents. A former lightweight boxing champion and active bare-knuckle fighter, he had a powerful left hook that he kept in trim by beating a mattress hung over a washing line in his back yard. As a young man he built up a fleet of pony carts. No great businessman, he lost that business to bankruptcy. But, nothing daunted, he quickly mastered the art of licking white-hot pokers (which he saw a black man do in fairground sideshow) and added to it the feat of walking with his little son balanced on a five-gallon bottle on his head. As a finale he performed his famous "bottle-walking" stunt. For this, he placed a row of lemonade bottles upside down leading to a stepladder with more inverted bottles standing on its rungs. He walked the bottles without knocking one over, and dived from the stepladder into a barrel. And he offered onlookers £50 (an enormous sum of money for a working man in the inter-war period) if any of them could copy him. It had taken him four years to master the trick and he never had to pay out. Instead, he travelled the country performing at music-halls, until his age made his balance less certain, whereupon he returned to his Bethnal Green base and worked as a market porter.

His perfect balance was partly due to his strict teetotalism. That had been encouraged by the sad spectacle of his own father, "Creecha" Lee —who spent the last 17 years of his life in Claybury Asylum suffering fits brought on by alcoholism — and of an uncle, "Jewy" (whose nickname marked the Jewish blood mixed with the Lees' Irish and gypsy heritage), who was another incapacitated and incarcerated victim of the demon drink. Perhaps it is unsurprising that the Cannonball became a model of patriarchal discipline and propriety, forbidding alcohol in his house and bringing up his three daughters and two sons to fear and obey him.

Violet revolted. She was 17 in 1926 when she ran away from home to marry Charlie Kray, the handsome "wardrobe dealer" (as a doorstep clothing pesterer is officially entitled). She invited Cannonball's wrath, and she incurred it. Her register office marriage in Kingsland Road was not a "proper" wedding. She was banished from her father's house and felt this as a genuine punishment, for she quickly found Hoxton, although barely a mile away, to be a poor exchange for Bethnal Green. But Charlie was a hard worker and a good earner. Unlike many East End wives, Violet never had to go out to work until after he had retired. She missed her sisters, however, and she longed for reconciliation. It was not to come immediately, although her mother paid quiet visits and brought meat or cheese to help with the housekeeping.

When she became pregnant, Violet was told she might be expecting twins, but in fact produced a single infant, Charles David. Cannonball relented a little and began to speak to her again, but she was not yet readmitted to his house. In 1933, when Violet thought she was expecting a single infant, Reggie and Ronnie were born. She knitted them little angora outfits and placed them in the double pram Charles's earnings easily afforded. While they were toddlers she let their hair grow to Christopher Robin length, like their brother's. That was most unusual before the mid-1960s. But it made the kids look very sweet. Cannonball's heart melted. He and grandma Lee became adoring grandparents and Violet was restored to the fold, feeling herself to be special among mothers. Her sisters, Rose and May, were thrilled with their little nephews. Her brother John, who ran a small cafe opposite the family home, was, too. Her brother Joe, who carted fish to Billingsgate market, looked forward to having two stout young helpers. Shortly before the war broke out, Violet moved her family back to "Lee Street", as neighbours called the section of Vallance Road where her sisters lived in adjoining houses, opposite their brother. Their parents lived round the corner. When number 178 fell vacant, the Kray family snapped it up, the third adjoining house, next to Aunt Rose's. It was a little larger than number 68 Stean Street and although Ronnie would later recall it as "a dump" and disparage its cramped interior and outside privy, it was felt to be a move up in the world. The nickname "Fort Vallance" stuck to the house, showing the sense of security the Kray boys felt there. Charlie and Violet would continue to live at number 178 until the street was marked for demolition.

Before Violet's happy return to Bethnal Green, the twins suffered a trauma. They were three years old when they contracted diphtheria complicated by measles. They were seriously ill, Ronnie especially. According to his brother Charlie, he was also suffering from a hernia. And tuberculosis may have been feared. The doctor had them placed in separate hospitals, Reggie in St Anne's, Tottenham, and Ronnie in Homerton. Within a couple of weeks Reggie was on the mend. But Ronnie was evidently pining for his twin. Violet made a decision. She discharged the boy and brought him home to nurse him herself. It saved his life, the family believed: he would not have survived continuous separation from Reggie. But, at the same time, the illness may have done him long-term damage. Previously the twins had seemed identical in personality as well as appearance. Subsequently, Ronnie was a little slower, a little less apt at mastering speech; seemed to grow a little heavier. Reggie had natural charm. Ronnie had to compete and manipulate to win the attention and approval both craved. If he could not outshine his brother, he would undercut him. Both boys grew to admire grandfather Lee intensely and certainly learned from his example that cutting a public figure was its own huge reward.

The two fought fiercely and inseparably from time to time, their savage rage ending as quickly and inexplicably as it began. They had in full measure "the twin thing". They understood each other without needing language to explain what they were feeling. If one suffered pain or discomfort, the other felt it sympathetically. When far apart, they felt they sometimes knew when one was undergoing some crisis and there is substantial anecdotal evidence to support this. In East End society family ties were deeply felt and siblings referred to each other as "my Tony", "my Chrissie", "my Nicky", (as Yorkshire siblings would say "our lad", "our lass", "our kid"). In a gangland where families of brothers were the commonest mutually supportive bases for "firms", (the Sabinis, the Nashes, the Richardsons, the Haywards, the Millses, the Lambrianous, to name at random), the Kray twins were exceptionally strongly tied to each other. And as Ronnie developed the habit of forcing his way into prominence and attention, he dragged the slightly easier-going, more charming Reg with him.

Big brother Charlie was firmly pushed into the background. Many people have commented on his good nature and charm. And this was perhaps never more clearly demonstrated than in his tolerant acceptance all his life that his little brothers took the limelight. Once the family had moved to Vallance Road and the Lee sisters were reunited, the twins were assured of their adult world's love and approval, provided they remained sweet and fetching. Violet didn't believe her lovely little boys were capable of bullying and violence. Her sister Rose did. She was a fighting woman herself. Her son Billy Wiltshire, five years older than the twins, taught them rough street games. He raced them in a soapbox go-cart fitted with a spike to ram other kids' carts. He rolled them in a barrel along cobbled streets. He climbed over the screens to duck them when they were sent to the public baths in Cheshire Street. He took them camping in Chingford, pulled the tent down about their ears and forced them to travel back to London in the thick dust under the train seats. The twins didn't mind deeply. They were being toughened up and it was worth it. Some resentment lasted, however. They saw Billy's failure to visit them in prison as a black mark, perhaps indicative of his poor character.

They loved Aunt Rose's toughness, her willingness to fight strange women and deliver socking punches to the jaw. And Aunt Rose knew more than the Lee grandparents or Violet about her nephews' increasing scrapping in the streets. Bullies, other kids' parents might call them. The terrible twins. But the Lees stuck up for family, come hell or high water. And the twins learned that being polite and charming at home gave them home's support when the outside world attacked them.

Home was more matriarchal than patriarchal in Bethnal Green. Charles Kray lost authority when he moved away from his home turf of Hoxton. The Lees stood together. Teetotal Cannonball did not much approve of his hard-drinking son-in-law. Charles Kray brought home the bacon too reliably to be henpecked, but his writ did not run unchallenged in his own house. At the best of times his authority had been intermittent, since travelling to knock on doorsteps could take him away for the mid-week. And after the manner of men of his time and society, he preferred his evenings to be passed in male company at the pub. Family life was not an ingrained habit.

In later life, Charles wondered whether his own failure to impose himself had contributed to the twins' disastrous lives. Had he been free to do so, he would have beaten them for disobedience and misbehaviour. But Violet, a rebel against her own heavy-handed dictatorial father, would not tolerate that. On the other hand, Charles' example was hardly conducive to law-abiding virtue. Not only did he stay out drinking night after night, and come in drunk from time to time, he cultivated the society of old rogues and villains. He introduced his sons to Jack "Dodger" Mullins, a grand old has-been of East End crime who had once lorded it over local street bookmakers, publicans and shopkeepers and who had been with Arthur Harding's gang when they signally failed to help the Brummagen

Boys put Darby Sabini out of business. By World War II, poor old Dodger was best known as someone who needed the protection of rogues like Billy Hill if he was to avoid the taunts of very young thugs on the rise. But the Kray boys were introduced to this sad old man as a legendary one-time "King of the East End". They were impressed by Dodger's contemporary, Wassle Newman, who reputedly threw bricks in the air and punched them to harden his hands. Charles Kray's chosen associates were not as reputable as Cannonball Lee's and Violet's and Aunt May's, though Aunt Rose, the wild one, would have understood. And Charles was not a model of rectitude. Visiting houses and collecting cast-off clothes and valuables for resale, he was not adverse to a bit of shady dealing. His children would have felt no inherited distaste for receiving stolen goods or picking up any property its owners left carelessly lying around.

The twins' relationship with their father immediately demonstrates the difficulty of assessing habitual liars' accounts of their lives. Commentators agree that Ronnie in particular disliked having a more severe standard of discipline imposed when Charles Kray came home for the weekend. Nevertheless, "Despite what has been written about us in the past," says Reg in his autobiography, *Born Fighter*, "it is not true that Ron ever struck the old man." Ron's story is rather different. "I don't have quite such happy memories as Reg about our father," he says in *Our Story*. "I used to think that one day when I was bigger I would give him a bloody good hiding – and I did." Revising and improving his account in *My Story* five years later, Ron dropped the two sentences and simply described his father as a man who was good at his job, a parent who joined Violet in teaching his sons to pray and to be kind to animals. It was characteristic of the twins to try to use later books to repair damage they spotted done to their own image in earlier ones. Their official biographer John Pearson, apparently reporting Charles' personal remarks to him, says that after they were 15 the twins picked on their father and sometimes hit him. Pearson's account commands immediate credence. But which Kray was telling the truth, Ronnie, Reggie or their father? The only test we can apply to these stories is *cui bono*, if this is a lie, whose interest is served, and how? One can see that Charles Kray would be unwilling to admit to having received "a good hiding" from one of his sons and may be minimizing the violence he suffered. Reggie, the "charming" twin with a real (and maybe sociopathic) awareness of what is and isn't acceptable, blandly denies unfilial violence on his brother's part, seemingly eliminating himself beyond question. Ronnie, seriously mentally ill and not always capable of understanding how the world sees things, made a boast that probably came closest to the truth. But the fact that Ronnie's madness was known and understood in the family would also have given Charles a valid excuse if a beating from his paranoid son was the only violence he had ever suffered at the twins' hands. So his allegation that Reggie used at least some violence against him looks valid.

The biggest blow to whatever sort of paternal authority Charles Kray tried to impose on his family was the war. A man who prided himself on never having worked for a guv'nor could easily appreciate that a sergeant-major with the royal warrant as his authority constituted the worst possible guv'nor for any independent-minded man. And although the whole Kray family has always shown itself admirably free from any taint of racism, rejecting Mosley's homegrown cut-price Fascism didn't mean perceiving Chamberlain and Halifax as nobler and more admirable figures than Hitler and Mussolini. The war that the "men of Munich" stumbled into so ingloriously was not one that automatically invited the patriotic support of gentile East Enders. The dictators, for example, were not in the habit of dismissing as absurd the idea of giving baths to the working classes on the assumption that they would only keep coal in them. Rather, they offered the workers healthy open-air holidays at cheap prices and urged them to keep clean, fit and proud of their bodies, a regimen the Kray men followed.

Charles Kray was one of many urban working men who quietly but definitely declined to be conscripted into fighting for a king and country that had shown considerably less willingness than either Adolf Hitler or Franklin Roosevelt to see that the financial profiteers whose greed brought about the great slump were made

to do something about the massive unemployment they had created. His family and in-laws were so supportive of those who refused
conscription that "Lee Street" now became known as "Deserters'
Corner".

But this meant that from 1939 until 1952, the father of the Krays
was a man on the run. Now his visits were even more sporadic, and
they were punctuated by fears of a visit from the police. The twins
quickly learned to hate the constabulary as enemies. Ron earned
praise for his quick remark, "You don't think he'd be fool enough
to hide in there?" when a policeman was about to open the cup-
board where his father cowered. None of the family seems to have
been bright enough to grasp that some of the police, working
people like themselves, were quite sympathetic to men who did not
see why they should enlist for possible death or mutilation, simply
because the governing classes were incompetent and the Versailles
Treaty, as predicted, had brought about renewed warfare after 20
years. When a searching copper remarked loudly beside the outside
privy where Charles Kray was hiding, "I doubt if he would be in
there," the Krays assumed the old man had enjoyed a lucky escape.
But it was more likely to have been a break deliberately granted.
The implausible stagy aside suggests an amiable copper's advice to
Charles not to cut and run, which would have meant he had to be
arrested.

Nonetheless it is not conducive to respect for one's father if he is
habitually skulking and hiding. This was something the twins
watched from the time they were six until they were 18. Charles'
preferred safe house was in Camberwell with an old pickpocket
called Bob Rolphe. Violet would take her boys to visit their father
there, further confirming the impression that crooks were goodies
and cops were baddies.

By the time the twins were 15, their father already admitting he
had lost control of them, they had swallowed the skewed "morality" of the underworld. "Fair is foul and foul is fair, Hover through
the fog and filthy air." The police were the enemy, pure and simple.
Law-abiding folk who had nothing to do with crime were mugs.
Theft and receiving were approved ways of acquiring property.

Violence was a proper means of establishing superiority and imposing one's will on others. The twins were part of the post-war tearaway generation.

The positive morals the twins absorbed from their parents were interestingly individual. Charles taught them to respect the Royal Family who had been born into their station and hadn't chosen it and who, he insisted, had much less happy lives than free East Enders. He also taught them not to resent the rich and the upper classes. The Kray twins would have a peculiar love-hate relationship with the Establishment, using it and basking in its approbation whenever they could, while proudly aware that they were self-made kids from the slums.

Violet was a model of curious respectability. On learning that Ronnie's childish contribution to the war effort was praying that Adolf Hitler might be knocked down by a bus, she gently reprimanded him and told him that wasn't the sort of thing he should ask God for, no matter how bad a man Hitler might be. She instilled in all her sons the strong belief that eschewing strong language was a vital mark of gentility. In later life, all three boys would bitterly resent the film *The Krays*, largely because Billie Whitelaw's wonderful portrayal of their mother as a strong, vibrant cockney personality was scripted to let her use the occasional word like "Bollocks!". When he was seventy years old and caught trying to cut drug deals, Charlie junior was deeply shocked that his tape-recorded conversations proved beyond doubt that he was up to as much effing and blinding as any other villain. This seemed a far more embarrassing revelation than the exposure of his utter stupidity in offering millions of pounds-worth of cocaine to a wired-up covert police officer!

Obviously the twins, like almost everyone else of their generation, suffered educational disruption from the war. They left their primary school to be evacuated to the country, first to Hampshire, where a doctor's family found them too much of a handful, and then to Hadleigh in Suffolk. Violet, a supportive – perhaps possessive – mother, accompanied them, so they did not suffer the sense of desertion felt by many little evacuees. In Suffolk they discovered a love of the countryside that was to stay with them for life. It is one of the oddest things about the Kray twins that their characters were indelibly marked with a strong sensitivity that could at times deteriorate into extreme sentimentality. Indeed, as we shall see, they provide a perfect example of the paradox that sentimentality can co-exist with brutal cruelty. Their immediate and genuine love of country life, however, was not enough to overcome Violet's yearning for the company of her sisters and the setting of grimy cafes and city pavement conversations that she had always known. Perforce the twins were dragged back with her to become little townees, picking up lice and scabies from playing on verminous bomb sites and learning street-smart ways that would have far more damaging consequences than the poaching and scrumping that would probably have engaged their youthful love of mischief had they stayed in the country.

Back they came to London, to face the doodle-bugs and the V-2s. Wartime memories included the old Cannonball's success in entertaining the evening crowds gathered in the improvised air-raid shelter under the railway arches at the top of Vallance Road. He sang and recited his own patriotic doggerel verse. Back at home he told his grandchildren stories of local heroes. Ted "Kid" Lewis, boxing champion at several weights, who still lived round the corner. Jimmy Wilde "the Welsh wizard", who took the Lonsdale Belt at granddad's own flyweight level. By the firelight in winter, he would tell tales, too, of the great murders of the 1880s. The mysterious Ripper who disappeared into the darkness leaving mutilated streetwalkers on the pavement just round the corner from home. John Martin and Jim Baker, who went up to Netherby Hall in Cumberland with their friend Tony Rudds to steal Lady Graham's diamonds, an adventure that went sadly awry when they were accosted by three policemen in Carlisle. They shot and injured two of them and gave the third a terrible kicking, before shooting and murdering the village bobby in Plumpton. Trapped in a coal truck on the railway trying to escape back to London, the three went to the gallows. Ronnie had reason to be interested in the gallows. When he asked his gypsy Aunt Rose why his eyebrows met in the middle, she told him affectionately it meant that he was born to be hanged.

With schools closed because of the blitz, kids ran free. And now it was that, toughened by playing with Billy Wiltshire, the twins started to be a real terror among their own age group. The "terrible twins" who would fight anyone for any reason, and whose mother and grandfather would always back them up and insist that they had done no wrong.

Elder brother Charlie had gone into the forces and, first as a naval cadet and then as a naval rating, he developed his passion for sport. Always a keen footballer and boxer, he rigged up a bedroom in Vallance Road as a miniature gymnasium. He put in a kitbag stuffed with old rags to serve as a punchbag, suspending it from the ceiling and fastening it to the floor with a meathook. When the old man climbed in drunk one night and ran the hook into his stockinged foot, his lack of authority was mercilessly underlined as the whole family simply laughed at him. But both Charlies, father and son, made generous contribution to the only real education the twins would get, their training in boxing. Charles junior helped his brothers train in the home gym. He would go down on his knees to show them how to position themselves. He would mock spar with them. Charles senior gave all his sons first-rate kit, good leather boxing boots, silk shorts with their initials on, gloves, bandages, the necessary array of guards. He supplied a speedball. He took the twins to Robert Browning's gym in south London, where their skill and style at a tender age made an instant impression. One of the best-known stories about them is the incident when they were about ten and went to see Alf Stewart's boxing booth at the annual fair in Victoria Park. When the cauliflower-eared bruisers had run out of contenders for the five pounds to anyone who could last three rounds, everyone was amused when Ronnie volunteered to get in the ring if no one else would. Where would they match his weight, Alf Stewart wondered into the loudspeaker? Reggie, egged on by Ronnie's implicit dare, stepped up. And the two fought stylishly for three rounds, whereupon the showman declared it a draw and rewarded them with payment later recalled variously as half-a-crown or seven shillings and sixpence. Either way, it was a fine prize for kids at that time and they went home proud of having started on the career that offered the most promising route out of East End poverty. Cannonball Lee was proud of them. Violet would rather they hadn't fought each other, but it was inevitable, coming in at the same age and weight, that they would do so from time to time. Their occasional confrontations in the boxing ring, however, were never the insensate mauls of the kind falsely suggested in the highly imaginative film version of their lives.

When the end of the war made schooling permanent, they accepted it without any serious rebellion. Daniel Street School, off Brick Lane, had a good football team and it encouraged them to box. This, coupled with sensible schoolmasters who had no unrealistically high expectations of them, made their schooldays far pleasanter than might have been anticipated. They remembered with especial pleasure Mr Evans, a Welshman who himself recalled them as being no problem, if you knew how to handle them. Of course they rejoiced in the identical twin trick of standing in for each other to let the one wanted for discipline make good his escape. But most reasonable people found the trick fascinating, and harmless.

The adult Krays and Lees had combined to instil into the twins one lesson that would prove invaluable for a lifetime. While Ronnie and Reggie were very obviously normal, cheeky, high-spirited lads, they enjoyed the added charm of beautiful manners when in the company of elders they respected. Father Hetherington, the priest at St James' church in Bethnal Green Road, remembered them with the greatest warmth and affection. They were kind, polite boys who would do anything he asked them (except come to church!). He was a willing and honest character witness for them in due course and in all fairness they had earned his testimony. If Violet, granddad, the aunts, and perhaps the two Charleses (in that order) insisted that some adults merited polite and respectful conduct, that is how the twins behaved towards them. And this attractive deference to worthy old age stayed with them for life. In 1964 there was a sort of triumphal street party in Vallance Road to welcome them home from dubiously deserved acquittal in the authorities' first serious attempt to bring them to book. It was an occasion when they might have been expected to crow a little and show off. Photographs of the occasion, however, show the old Cannonball bursting with pride in his grandsons, while they shake hands with their neighbours with really becoming modesty. More than any other picture of the twins, it explains their lasting popular memory in the East End and the extraordinary willingness of Bethnal Green to swallow the myth that they were benevolent protectors of the weak who are sadly missed in today's age of muggers and rapists.

Polite little boys may still strike petty officialdom as little terrors. The twins' first confrontation with jacks-in-office came when they were 12. They had been on a picnic to Chingford and in the train on the way back Reggie fired an airgun out a window. Not the most heinous of offences. But the guard locked him in his van before handing him over to the police, who upset Violet by deciding to make a juvenile court appearance out of it. Father Hetherington spoke up for him. The magistrates were sensible, and gave him a warning. But the general overreaction led Reggie to feel that the authorities were personal enemies rather than just a threat to his old man. And what Reg felt, Ron felt. It was "the twin thing".

They were starting to earn a little in areas where the family worked, even before they left school. They went out totting with their dad's great friend Harry Hopwood and his brother George. Harry had been best man at Charles and Violet's wedding and would play a significant part at the climax of the twins' career. They went on another cart with their mother's brother Joe to help him at Billingsgate market. When they left school at 15, they made a tentative start on work as market porters or trainee fish salesmen. It didn't suit, and in the summer they gave it up and went fruit picking with Violet, the traditional cockney working holiday in the country. After which they went back to totting with their father and his younger brother Alf, who had taken over "Mad Jimmy" Kray's street stall, and sold off the old clothes they gathered in Cheshire Street and in the Petticoat Lane Sunday market. An account by a bitterly hostile enemy, which nonetheless seems persuasive, suggests that Reggie worked fairly hard, if not always successfully. But Ronnie was lazy and would hurry back to the car and put his feet up, claiming to have knocked on all his allotted doors and received no answer and no clothing. Charlie trained his sons to stand well back and speak in a soft voice so as never to intimidate the housewives who came to the door. This may have been the genesis of the way the twins spoke, at first sinister and threatening but subsequently somewhat camp, that many gang-members later associated with them.

But the twins' ambition at this time was to be boxers. Before they left school they had collected a number of local titles in their age- and weight-groups and Reggie, to his justified gratification, had won the London Schoolboys' Boxing Championship in 1948, after Ronnie had beaten him when they faced each other in earlier rounds the previous two years. All observers agreed that Reggie had the makings of a fine boxer, stylish, observant and intelligent. Ronnie was more of a raging bull rushing in to attack with fury, going for the knockout but too often walking blindly on to his opponent's best punches.

Brother Charlie had secured a number of welterweight titles after going into the navy during the war and turned professional on his demob. He was a useful technical boxer, able to take care of himself but never showing what it takes to make a champion. He went on to a very respectable professional career winning 18 of his 21 bouts.

Following his example, and coached by Charlie Simms at Browning's gym, the twins quickly made a name for themselves. The peculiarity of identical twins appearing on the same bill and picking up titles here and there naturally interested the papers. It was the sort of "positive" news that local journalism welcomes, but Father Hetherington felt that having their photos in the papers from an early age turned their heads and made naturally lively lads into self-important show-offs and bullies. Certainly it may explain Reg's claim that they started to become "famous" in their generation in north-east London.

Like most boys their age, the twins belonged to a gang. "Laddish" rather than criminal, the harmlessness of the Krays' early adolescent gang is indicated by the membership of Kenny Lynch and other kids who went on to perfectly respectable careers. In later life the twins would be proud of their early friendship with the successful black entertainer which, as usual with them, was free from racial prejudice. Unlike some more foolish showbiz personalities, Kenny Lynch saw no glamour in cashing in on his schoolboy association with two top crims.

If the Kray twins were "famous" East End fighters, other young scrappers who wanted to prove themselves would willingly take them on. (It is a mark of the puerility of American Mafiosi that they continue to fight and kill for the silly title of "capo di tutti capi", boss of all bosses.) The spotty youths put on their dark suits of an evening, and made for the dancehalls. They would eye each other over. They would eye over the girls. Young male hormones struggled with young male inhibitions. Dared they fight? Dared they risk scornful rebuff if they asked for a dance? There was safety in numbers, either way. Enough cold-faced youths could stare another gang into silence. A gang of yobs could jeer at and embarrass pairs of girls who, when not outnumbered, could use feminine scorn to reduce individual hobbledehoys to blushing bashfulness.

Dancehalls. The Royal Ballroom in Tottenham. Barrie's in Mare Street, Hackney. Eugene Grey's Dance Academy in Finsbury Park. These were the places where East London youth gathered to play Montagues and Capulets and watch with envy those who actually knew how to dance and so stood some real hope of getting off with the girls.

In the Krays' early days, threats and stand-offs were more likely than regular fights. A few years later the press-hyped cult of the teddy-boy, coupled with Leonard Bernstein's glamorization of the city rumble in *West Side Story*, meant that there were likely to be fights outside the dancehalls every Saturday night. Often just fisticuffs and kickings, a toughening up process, much like the infant Krays' experience at the hands of their cousin Billy. But the most determined juvenile delinquents brought weapons to the affrays and did some serious damage. And Ronnie Kray had started his lifetime obsession with weapons, hiding knives and coshes and his first pistol under the bedroom floorboards. As the police worried about the increasing savagery and danger of youthful street fighting, Ronnie and Reggie supplied the opportunity for an exemplary prosecution.

The twins were 16 when, in an alley off Mare Street, the police found another 16-year-old, Roy Harvey, lying in pools of clotted blood. Severe contusions around his neck and chin had evidently been caused by bicycle chains that had been dropped beside him. Once he had been laid out, he had been savagely kicked all over. Roy went to hospital, where he said who had done it. The Kray twins had set about him and his friends Dennis Seigenberg and Walter Birch. There were independent witnesses, too. A 19-year-old girl and an insurance clerk had seen the fight and could recognize the culprits. The north London magistrate remarked that "beasts" capable of this violence evidently thought themselves above the law and needed to be taught a lesson. The twins were sent on to the high court and appeared at the Old Bailey before Mr Justice McClure, charged with causing grievous bodily harm to Birch, Seigenberg and Harvey.

But by that time friends had rushed into action. Somebody approached the witnesses. The twins later denied fervently that they had ever threatened to mark the girl with a razor. It was an essential part of their legend that these verrai parfit gentil knights never threatened women, children or old people. (And quite probably they never did threaten children.) Perhaps they didn't make the threat personally. But, like the clerk, the girl withdrew her evidence. Somebody visited Roy Harvey in hospital and he was persuaded that "the code of the East End" was rather more important than the Ten Commandments. He ceased to be sure of his assailants' identity. Father Hetherington turned out again to give character evidence. The case was dismissed for lack of evidence.

"Don't go thinking you're the Sabini brothers," Judge McClure warned the twins. He was wasting his breath. Ronnie, remembering the case years later, believed that he had ultimately grown greater than Darby Sabini had ever been, and ruled London's underworld more absolutely. Of course, Ronnie was schizophrenic and prey to delusions.

Whenever they recalled the case in later years, Ronnie and Reggie never failed to remark that Dennis Seigenberg later changed his name to Dennis Stafford and was convicted of murdering a fruit-machine salesman. They tut-tutted over this delinquency – with total unconcern that two brothers named Kray each scored similar convictions. But gross humbug is a keynote of most under-world morality. Reggie's insistence that this was just an ordinary evenly matched adolescent dust-up that should have been written off with the view that boys will be boys, can be absolutely dis-counted. As will be seen when we discuss Flossy Forsyth, Reggie had the happy knack of seeing things in whatever light suited him, without being distracted by troublesome irrelevancies like facts.

The twins were lucky to escape conviction. For that year they made the important break and became professional boxers and they might not have been given licences had they acquired a record for violent crime. They were still luckier not to lose their licences as soon as they were granted. For they were up before the courts again one week after their first professional bout. PC Donald Baynton had gone to investigate a reported fight outside a youth club near Bethnal Green Road. When he questioned a group of yobs loiter-ing outside Pellicci's Cafe they gave him some lip. When he pushed one in the stomach twice, telling him to move on, he got a clip on the jaw. It wasn't very serious, and after a quick chase Baynton arrested the youth, who came quietly to Bethnal Green police sta-tion where he was charged. The boy was Ronnie. I see no reason to doubt the Krays' insistence that he was beaten up in the cells before being returned home. The smiling face of "Dixon of Dock Green", lovable copper of the 1950s, concealed an amount of violence and "noble cause" corruption that would not be tolerated today.

It didn't end there. Baynton returned to patrol and came across Reggie. Words were exchanged in which, according to the Krays, Baynton boasted of having given Ronnie a hiding. Reggie prompt-ly thumped Baynton and ran off. Baynton turned up at Vallance Road with an inspector and the situation was negotiated into a compromise. Reggie was charged with assault alongside Ronnie. But the Krays were guaranteed that the police (supported by the usual Father Hetherington) would not make the case too hard for them and they could be reasonably certain of getting off with probation. The police further guaranteed that Reggie would not be beaten up at the station. They also hinted that if the Kray family didn't play ball, they would start a heavy pursuit of runaway Charles senior. Playing ball meant making no public protest about Ronnie's beating. The agreement worked well for everyone, except that the magistrate described the boys' attack on Baynton as "cowardly", something their enemies were able to dredge up in future years. But on the plus side, Baynton was transferred to another division shortly afterwards, so the family did not have a uniformed enemy stationed in the neighbourhood. And the probationary sentence did not affect the twins' boxing licences.

They did well in their first six professional bouts, Reggie winning all of his and Ronnie winning four. This brought them to their crowning achievement, an appearance at the Albert Hall on the same bill as brother Charlie, according to whom it remains a record for any boxer to appear in that Mecca of fisticuffs after only six professional fights. Charlie himself, married and developing ramifying small business interests, was actually almost retired from the ring. He had given up regular training, but was lured back for one last bout by the promise of a £25 purse and the satisfaction of seeing three Krays on one bill.

In the event, only Reggie covered himself with glory, skilfully outpointing Bobby Manito of Clapham. Ronnie twice knocked down Bill Sliney of King's Cross (whom Reggie had defeated in a previous encounter), but was subsequently out-pointed when a cut over his eye robbed him of vision in the later rounds. Charlie was comprehensively beaten by the future champion Lew Lazar, but won admiration by his game attempts to keep on rising from repeated counts of eight. The Krays went home happy in the knowledge that they had fought well and the two who had been beaten had been beaten by better opponents on the night. Where boxing is concerned, all the Krays were capable of generosity and objectivity that eluded them in other fields. Old man Charlie had thoroughly enjoyed watching his sons, but Violet remained at home. The spectacle of men knocking each other about didn't appeal to her and was absolutely unacceptable if some of the men being knocked about were her boys. But she had enjoyed the presence of her sons' friends in the little mock-up gymnasium at Vallance Road in the early days. And she took pride in the twins' achievements.

They, meanwhile, enjoyed meeting celebrity boxers at the various gyms around London where they trained and sparred. At the most famous gym of all, Jack Solomons' in Great Windmill Street, they met the most famous English boxer of the day, Freddie Mills. Neither he nor they could have imagined the way in which their names would be linked years later. At this time they were just deferential young novices, proud to carry out any errand for the one-time world light-heavyweight champion.

While their professional reputation in the ring climbed, their street cred climbed, too, in a succession of fights with other gangs. Their brother Charlie's memoirs claim that they always won, often against severe odds. Their hostile acquaintance Billy Webb maintains that they and their closest ally Patsy Aucott never fought unless they had the backing of a strong mob. There can be little doubt, however, that it was at this time that the Krays first fought with and made lifelong enemies of the tough Irish docklanders known as the Watney Street gang. These silly adolescent gang brawls take on their only real importance from the fact that among the Watney Streeters were a pair of brothers called Myers one of whome, George – according to Billy Webb – gave Ronnie Kray a savage beating in a pub called the George and Dragon. George Myers later changed his name to George Cornell.

Perpetual brawling and bragging didn't bring the twins before the law again. It was not general criminality that lost them their boxing licences. It was National Service.

There are a host of legends about their finally successful attempts to get themselves dishonourably discharged from the army. Most of them come from the twins themselves and paint them in a splendid light as tough but cheeky cockney chappies who feared no sergeant and always had a quick repartee when Authority used Superior Force to Impose Discipline. Such tales had better be taken with a pinch of salt. No doubt the two did go AWOL on their first day, after reporting to the Royal Fusiliers in barracks in the Tower. No doubt one of them did knock down – perhaps even knock out – their corporal on the way. But it was silly bravado to go home for tea, pass an evening at the Royal Ballroom in Tottenham and suffer inevitable arrest the following morning when the Military Police came looking for them at their home address.

That one night AWOL got them seven days in the guardroom. They went AWOL again, this time for a few weeks during which they took a trip to Southend from where they sent a cheeky postcard to their CO, but where they were so bored they returned to London within a day. A longer spell in detention followed after PC Fisher spotted them visiting Vallance Road and arrested them. The army attempted to control them by separating them, keeping Ron in the Wellington Barracks at the Tower and sending Reg to the Fusiliers' punishment cells at Purfleet. During this time Reg had a few scraps with NCOs and Ron started the very dangerous game of pretending to be mad. His actions were harmless enough – only shaving half his face, or refusing to put on his uniform. But the mental effect on a young man whose personal insecurity always encouraged extravagant role-playing was devastating. Within a few years Ron Kray really was mad.

The twins were reunited for a month in Colchester military detention barracks; absconded again into the East End when they were returned to the Tower for regular duties; and spent autumn on the run hiding out part of the time in a rented flat in Finsbury Park and part of the time south of the river, until Police Sergeant Silvers recognized them slipping back to Vallance Road again.

More cells. Another break for freedom, which ended when PC Fisher once more spotted them in the East End, this time at the Orange Cafe in Mile End. He amiably refused their request that he cast a blind eye and let them stay out for Christmas at home, so they pushed him over in the road and scarpered. That put the kybosh on Christmas with the old folks. They were wanted for "assaulting a policeman" and the Bethnal Green police knew just who they were looking for. When the twins were arrested in Hackney at the beginning of 1953 they got a civil sentence of one month, which they served in Wormwood Scrubs.

Release from the Scrubs merely meant a transfer to the Howe Barracks' guardroom in Canterbury. Here they spent three months under close arrest awaiting trial for repeatedly absconding. They enlivened the time with the various silly antics by which prisoners try to persuade themselves that they are better than their guards. They fought with individuals who annoyed them. They refused to wash or shave. They both play-acted madness. They threw a full chamberpot over a guard. They climbed on a roof and played the mouth organ with their friends Dickie Morgan and Ted Bryant. Ron swigged the medical officer's coffee. Reg threw the NAAFI keys down the drain. Petty tyrants foolish enough to fall within arm's-length of the twins suffered schoolboyish revenge. One found himself handcuffed to the bars of their cage for an hour. Another was debagged and tied to a pillar while the Krays and Dickie Morgan lit a fire of newspapers and danced around him. These were just boys at the end of their teens and their behaviour in the main was simply cheeky and boyish. But according to one acquaintance it could be nasty in an unbalanced way. He claims that when they had a guard temporarily in their power, Ronnie masturbated over him.

Imperturbable style and maturity impressed them. The adjutant, with a languid Eton and Sandhurst manner, told them he didn't care what they did, but he wished they wouldn't frighten the horses. They envied his sang-froid and, with a mental tug at their forelocks, obeyed this toff whom they would have loved to emulate. Corporal Ted Haines who had seen it all before wasn't impressed and quite genuinely invited the boys to make their time easier by not knocking themselves out for punishment. They in turn respected him and gave him no trouble.

But come Easter, they wanted another home visit. Their father, ironically granted amnesty for his own wartime desertion while his sons were themselves deserters, arranged with his old friend Harry Hopwood and Harry's brother George to see them safely out. The Hopwoods and Charles drove down to Canterbury, parking their van around a corner of the prison. The twins, Dickie Morgan and Ted Bryant broke through the guards' mess and out, thanks to the element of surprise, but went round the wrong corner, missing the van. An inglorious hurry away through shunting yards, the theft of a clapped-out truck that broke down on the main road – and the great escape came to an end in Eltham where a police motorcycle patrol was waiting for them. They went back to the army, were court-martialled and served nine months at Shepton Mallett army prison before winning their dishonourable discharge in 1954.

Like most young men of their generation, the Kray twins had lost two years' freedom for virtually nothing. Worse, where others usually acquired some useful skill, they had spent more than half their service banged up. Had they the sense to learn from it, their marksmanship training proved conclusively both were and would always be lousy shots (They were short sighted). Their brother Charlie thought it a tragedy that they had not been allowed to become PT instructors, in which case he believed their National Service would have been useful to them. He could see clearly enough that two years of childish and violent bad behaviour and well-merited punishment did not warrant the twins' cocky self-deception that they had tested their mettle against a great institution and won. The only "result" (ie decision in their favour) was that Reg was able to claim that their offences might have deserved much longer than nine months in Shepton Mallett. Their civil crime and month's imprisonment in Wormwood Scrubs should have meant they lost their boxing licences, but PC Fisher magnanimously wrote to the Boxing Board of Control saying that his refusal to "negotiate" their continued freedom over Christmas was probably provocative. And he won them a provisional temporary right to box again. They took no advantage of this unlooked-for kindness.

Army diet and exercise had filled them out. Inducted as spare, athletic and mildly delinquent lads, they had grown into physically strong young men and they came out, accepted by the criminal acquaintances they had made in the army's jankers and in the Scrubs as up-and-coming villains.

4

THE MAD AXEMAN AND OTHER PLAYERS

Accused of absenting themselves without leave and striking a corporal in the performance of his duties on their first day in the army, the twins accepted the first charge and played the identical twin game to escape the second.

"Not me, sir."

"Not me, sir."

"Which of us are you accusing, sir?"

The corporal couldn't be sure. Seven days in the guardroom was a mild punishment for the Krays' outstandingly bad start to a military career.

Into the guardroom shuffled their first introduction to the real world of criminality. Dickie Morgan was a grey-faced young thief from a family of thieves. He had just spent four years in Rochester borstal where his elder brother Chunky had distinguished himself in a riot. And that riot was arranged by a strapping, handsome but backward young rascal called Frank Mitchell (not yet Frank "the Mad Axeman" Mitchell), whose name would be forever linked with the twins.

Chunky Morgan, meanwhile, had graduated from borstal to Parkhurst. His and Dickie's father had just been sentenced as the inside man in a robbery on the warehouse where he worked as night-watchman. The professionally crooked Morgan family represented a new experience for Ronnie and Reggie who had grown up under the aegis of the non-thieving Lees. Their father's friendship with pickpocket Bobby Rolphe and social acquaintance with the old has-beens Dodger Mullins and Wassle Newman had been their closest contact with the mainspring of criminality. Now they were meeting the real thing on equal terms. Crime offered the fast track to what they both regarded as "the good life", acquiring money quickly and easily and spending it with equal facility.

As soon as the week's jankers was over, the Krays and Morgan absconded together, making for the Morgan home in Clinton Road beside Mile End underground station, parallel with the canal. Motherly Mrs Morgan happily added Reg and Ron to the list of "wanted" men who habitually dropped in for a night's kip and a quick breakfast. "Deserters' Corner" had never been quite like this clearing-house of crime.

The runaways needed money. The Morgans were in touch with Billy Bellamy, an experienced thief from Dalston. He took Dickie and the twins to help him raid a cloth wholesaler's in Clerkenwell. For the first time the Kray twins made some money from crime.

They couldn't stay at Vallance Road for any length of time. The civil and military police knew that address. The same objection ruled out Clinton Road. Billy Bellamy's home in Kingsbridge Road was an occasional refuge and the twins also stayed from time to time with a rival who was another deserter from National Service. Billy Webb was one of the "crazy" gang from Tottenham, notorious for proving their fortitude by inflicting cigarette burns on themselves. His memoirs are filled with recollections of facing down the twins, just as Krayite reminiscences describe the twins' various triumphs at Tottenham, and the occasion in the 1960s (agreed on all sides) when the Kray gang outnumbered and beat up Billy and his brother Ron at the Old Horns public house in Bethnal Green.

But in 1952 and 1953 the Krays and Webb were neophyte rogues together. They hung out in Lyons Corner House on Oxford Street, the Vienna Rooms opposite Edgware Road police station and a variety of East End caffs, all frequented by crooks and runaways, prostitutes and homosexuals. In these surroundings, Ron Kray started to reveal his homosexuality to his contemporaries. He fancied boys. By one account he was intensely turned off women, saying, "They smell bad and they give you diseases". Despite that particular piece of nastiness, in general Ronnie deserved praise for the dignity with which he accepted his sexual orientation. He neither denied it nor flaunted it. He was no pansy; no raving queen. But if he felt he could trust you, he would simply and plainly declare that his sexual preference was for boys. He would quietly eye over and comment on "a nice little bum" if he saw one. Sometimes, when Ronnie spotted a nice "prospect", Reggie pretended to some homosexual fellow feeling, to spare his twin any feelings of isolation. But Ronnie was not ashamed of being homosexual. Nor was he intimidated by the law calling his natural sexual practices an offence. Toward the end of his life he tended to describe himself as bisexual and while in Broadmoor he married twice. But this was probably a calculated pose as the end of his recommended minimum sentence drew near; everyone knew that parole boards look favourably on married prisoners whose wives promise a stable home life if they are released.

To brother Charlie's surprise and bewilderment, and the covert amusement of hostile rivals like Billy Webb, Ron Kray now started the practice of collecting a small entourage of good-looking youths who accompanied him, one or two at a time, as trophy wives and supplementary girlfriends might hang on the arms of a movie mogul. It was short-sighted of those who sneered at Ronnie's boyfriends. He used them as a far-ranging spy network, keeping him informed about underworld rumours and rivals' movements.

Not that the Krays were mature leaders of villainy at this time. On the run from the army, they were themselves only in their late teens. Their recollections of their exploits may give an impression of wily street-smart young men. In reality they were often very unsure of themselves, very much in need of a substitute for the close family support they had always enjoyed. They were remembered sitting in shy silence (which could seem sinister) as they and other runaways passed whole days eking out cups of tea in Lyons Corner House.

In the Vienna Rooms they glimpsed the great Jack Spot. And they made themselves acquainted with his sidekick, Moisha Blueboy, from whom they tried to learn the ropes of criminality. They were with Moisha when he won a large sum at cards off a country mug called Jeff Allen. And they (like Moisha) were impressed when Allen, having left "to fetch the money", telephoned to say that he knew he'd been cheated and warned that he'd be waiting with a shotgun if anyone came to collect. The twins became friendly with Allen, who went on to become a substantial property dealer and come to grief when the law took an interest in fires that burned down houses he couldn't sell. But on the upswing he was an associate who helped the twins when they were able to go some way toward gratifying their yen for country-house living.

The twins could be sure of widespread East End support for resisting National Service. Although they were never sufficiently articulate to express the sentiment adequately, many of their contemporaries and elders saw conscription into the armed forces as a diabolical liberty. Why should working-class lads be turned into cannon-fodder to enforce their rulers' foreign policy, or drafted to hold down the far-flung empire that didn't seem to be any of their business? Billy Webb likened the military conscription of would-be civilians to the 18th-century press-gang. And it is hard to refute his analogy.

Neighbourhood sympathy, however, could not provide a network capable of maintaining the lads at liberty. For that it would be necessary to make contact with formal criminal organizations. At this point, the twins and Billy Webb put themselves under the protection of Tommy "Scarface" Smithson. The ill-fated loner had a billiards club in Archer Street, Soho, where the young villains-in-the-making were welcome to pass the night. The twins slept on billiard tables while Webb slept in a chair. Once Ronnie took a favoured young boy on the table with him and kept Webb awake all night with murmured conversation. Neither the Krays nor Billy Webb would ever forget Smithson's kindness. The Krays were also impressed by another pair of freelance loners, ex-boxer Tony Mulla and his friend Alf Melvin. Mulla had been seriously striped by the Maltese whom Smithson had crossed, saving his face and his wife by literally offering up his arse to the razors. A few years later Mulla and Melvin would make a fresh start as Soho strip club operators. And just as they were starting to succeed, they quarrelled. Melvin shot Mulla dead, and then killed himself. The twins' choice of these criminal losers as role models, and their pretended indifference to Jack Spot who really ruled the West End at the time, was a sad pointer to their future poor judgement of people.

As army deserters, the twins could not box under the auspices of the Boxing Board of Control. But street fighting remained a possibility. The rough, tough, gouging and butting fights at which old Cannonball once excelled could still draw a crowd, who would have preferred it had the Marquess of Queensberry restricted his reforming activities to suppressing Oscar Wilde. Ex-boxers like Johnny Hudson and the ganglords' elegant follower, Bobby Ramsey, put on unlicensed fights at which the fighters were paid peanuts and the crowd was even more bloodthirsty than an audience at Harringay.

The twins met a splendid old heavyweight bruiser called Tommy Welsh. In his youth he had been a sparring partner for Tommy Farr, the immensely popular miner boxer who was considered unlucky to have lost a world title fight on points against the great champion Joe Louis in 1938. Welsh was nicknamed "Tommy the Bear" and preferred to be known as Tommy Brown. He and his wife were immensely kind to people who were down on their luck and he encouraged the deserter twins to keep fit and train with him at various gyms. He also introduced them to Bobby Ramsey. Reg fought his last professional fight in a little hall next to a pub in Tottenham. He knocked his man out in round three and accepted a fiver from Ramsey's elegant yellow-pigskin-gloved hands. He and Ron were both booked to fight for Johnny Hudson in a Christmas tournament in 1952, but this coincided with their mild assault on PC Fisher and fearing police attention, they scratched at the last minute. Neither would ever box in a ring again.

Their spell in Wandsworth confirmed their acceptance as professional villains in the eyes of older and more experienced offenders. Their trips to army jails introduced them to kids of their own generation who were preparing for lawless lives by offering the army national disservice. Most notable among the crooks of their era that they encountered in detention at Shepton Mallett were Charlie Richardson, whose rivalry would herald their ultimate downfall, and Johnny Nash who, with his brothers and their Islington based north London mob, would always remain on good terms.

They were only 21 when they came out of the army. Ronnie especially had acquired a taste for sitting around in billiard halls doing nothing rather than buckling down to hard work. They made a half-hearted attempt to go totting again with their old man. It was clear this would not be their career. Charlie junior was setting himself up in small business ventures and through Stan Davis, an East End receiver with a lock-up in Old Ford Road, he met an up-and-coming south-of-the-river thief called Freddie Foreman. The two took to each other and remained friends even after Freddie broke with Stan Davis, suspecting him of having grassed up his brother George, leading the law to find a quantity of stolen kitchen knives that Stan had supplied in George's flat. When Freddie Foreman became a friend of the Kray family, a man with a big future as a very successful villain with a low-profile had started his association with a pair who would become unsuccessful villains with a very high profile.

It is the more strange that Charlie Kray should sound all hot and bothered about his little twin brothers getting pally with Bobby Ramsey, by this time a minder for Jack Spot. If Ramsey was likely to lead the lads into trouble, as he feared, Foreman was hardly likely to redirect them to the straight and narrow.

Ramsey became an occasional visitor at the twins' first successful business venture, the Regal billiards hall in Eric Street. This dismal urban business venture was a former cinema, a cheap hang-out furnished with billiard tables for the evening entertainment of local layabouts off the Mile End Road. The favourable Kray story is that the twins realized the manager would never make it pay its way because he was too fond of playing billiards and bending the elbow and did not have the gift for dealing with troublemakers. The twins offered the owner their services for £5 a week, borrowed money from Charlie to refurbish the place, and, lo and behold, the 21-year-old tycoons had a success on their hands.

Well, that's their story.

Less starry-eyed observers remark that the twins started frequenting the Regal so that Ronnie could indulge his favourite activity of chain-smoking and doing nothing. But as their attendance became regular, so, mysteriously, did the arrival of troublemakers who created rows and threatened to cut the cloths. Indeed, it was the greatest good fortune for the owner that just as the hall threatened to get out of hand, two young men capable of taking over the management and bringing it back in line fortuitously started to visit the place.

And management (culminating in ownership) of the Regal was further marked by historic fights which were described over the

East End and in which, no doubt, the twins' prowess against mighty odds grew ever greater with each retelling. They drove out would-be Maltese protectionists with a sword that hung on the wall. They handed out a savage beating to four Poplar dockers who expressed contempt for their youth and who were widely expected to massacre them. Charlie thought they had the Midas touch and made everything they took up pay. They were probably as much, if not more, interested in the fame that came with success. Ronnie especially seems to have had almost no central sense of identity and desperately needed the recognition of an audience and some easily identifiable role to play. Once other people perceived him as a particular type of person, and he could see himself dressed for and acting the part, he could accept that he really had the attributes he was assuming.

The twins' instant success didn't seem quite so gratifying to Charlie as it was to them. Their elder brother was shocked by the presence of large numbers of young tearaways and thieves, mostly acquaintances Ron and Reg had made in the glasshouse at Shepton Mallett. Charlie had little doubt that the reason the young club managers, who had started on a weekly £5 wage, were prospering so remarkably had something to do with the crooks and ex-draft dodgers hanging about. But was Charlie really as primly innocent as he claimed? He was always good at "not knowing" just how his brothers' "business" capers worked. The three were advised that it was well worth their while to have one brother completely ignorant of any criminal activity who could present the honest front. And affable, good-natured Charlie was obviously the best suited for this role. The "twin thing" wouldn't have allowed Ronnie and Reggie to be happy if one kept dark secrets from the other.

Charlie was very happy "not to know" that, under his brothers' management, the billiards hall was widely recognized as a good place to stash stolen goods before they were fenced. He did not want to be told that the twins were happy to look after weapons at such times as their clients did not want to be tooled up. That they charged high fees for these services and so had already started living off the theft industry without actually running the risks of thieving.

They had discovered in their days on the run that they really weren't especially good at "jump-ups" – breaking into lorries parked on bomb-sites to steal cargoes of cigarettes and suchlike resalable merchandise. It seems odd that Charlie should have retained such a naive outlook when he was introducing to the family the south Londoner who would one day prove one of the best thieves in the capital. It is ironic that Charlie objected so strongly to the twins' friendship with Bobby Ramsey, a mere strong-arm minder who might threaten or beat people up, when his friend Freddie Foreman would one day confess to having little regret about two murders, one a favour for a friend, the other a private revenge.

But Charlie was right to fear that Ramsey would prove a poor role model. It was flattering that Bob should seek the twins' support at Epsom for Jack Spot; wildly flattering that Spot himself should visit the billiards hall to recruit them in 1955. It is the wildest of paranoid fantasies on Ronnie's part to have suggested later that they only went to Epsom to show that they were poised to take over rule of the underworld. Attention from Spot fed their vanity and Ronnie especially began to indulge in dreams of ganglordship. His boyhood heroes had been General Gordon and Lawrence of Arabia, lone homosexual adventurers in imperially dominated oriental worlds. Not long after he came out of the army, a street fighter called Curly King, "the king of the teddy boys", nicknamed him "the Colonel". Ronnie adopted the title with enthusiasm and so referred to himself until his death. At the same time he came increasingly to admire Al Capone. And with quite remarkable emotional immaturity he would spend the rest of his life trying to "live up to" the image of the bestial, hypocritical, vain and syphilitic thug who ordered the St Valentine's Day Massacre. In the mid-1950s, Ronnie hoped for a gang war between Spot and Hill in which he and his brother might distinguish themselves and become notable gangster soldiers. He was deeply disappointed when, after Frankie Fraser and Bob Warren slashed Spot's face, the rival underworld leaders tacitly agreed that enough was enough, and retired. The Krays were too young and inexperienced to know how to take over the vacant throne of the West End. They were alarmed when it was reported that Albert

Dimes and the Italians were cutting everyone who looked likely to challenge them and for a week or so they retreated into Fort Vallance. Then they sallied out, issuing a challenge to Fraser and Hill's other former young muscle. The challenge was contemptuously ignored. Ronnie marched into a Clerkenwell pub and fired a Mauser vaguely in the direction of some Italian "enemy" drinkers. Nobody did anything. The would-be kings of the underworld had to return to being kings of the Regal Billiards Hall in Eric Street.

Over the next year they played their cards very well indeed. They had spent their adolescence visiting the dancehalls of Finsbury Park and Hackney and making themselves known across a wide swathe of the East End. Now they continued to win friends and influence villainous people by their charitable concern for the "aways", criminals who had been caught and convicted and were serving prison sentences. The Krays collected for them. They would simply go into a pub or club and announce that they were taking up a collection for the "aways", and contributions could be put into the pint glass they put on the bar. There might be an implicit threat in the invitation to subscribe. But the money came in. And Kray henchmen (always going in pairs so that there could be no suspicion that they wanted any hanky-panky) would deliver cash gifts to wives who struggled to make ends meet while their husbands were in Strangeways or Pentonville or Albany. "A present from the twins" was remembered with gratitude. So was the advertised fact that "aways" who came out of gaol and found themselves penniless on the street were usually welcome to go to the Regal, or to whatever pub Ronnie and Reggie were holding court in, where they would be given a useful sweetener to be going along with.

Not yet 24, the twins were starting to assemble a network of grateful and informative clients who let them know just what was going on and who was prospering in the world of theft. Which allowed them to know who could be "nipped" for a contribution from a haul. Thieves' poncing was starting as "the firm" spread out across Bethnal Green and Bow, Mile End and Stepney, Whitechapel and Shoreditch, Hoxton, Hackney and Stoke Newington. Their territory abutted Islington, but they left the Nash brothers secure in their north London manor. And they didn't cross the river where Charlie's friend Freddy Foreman was their contact, although he was a "legitimate" thief rather than an extortionist. The West End was a confusion of Italians running the gambling and drinking clubs and Maltese running the porn and prostitution. The Krays' way into that rich treasure-ground, they hoped, would be through protection and club ownership. Their entourage of minders and heavies were the first to be given the title "the firm" (a title that ultimately became applied to any coherent criminal mob). Some people felt that their crew members in the 1950s were the best they ever had: "Tommy the Bear" Welsh (aka Brown) and Big Pat Connolly as the heavies; Johnny Squibb, scion of a great family of late Victorian East End thieves, and Ronnie's childhood friend, Checker Berry, as henchmen; with Uncles Alf and Billy Kray, their father's brothers, as older if not immensely wiser heads. "Limehouse (Alf) Willey", Checker's brother Teddy Berry and Billy "Jack" Frost were their drivers, an army of lesser men were gofers.

The inner circle of "pensioners", drawing a weekly wage from the firm were well cared for. Generous "pensions" could be supplemented by "nips" from the clubs, pubs, spielers and car dealers that, willingly or unwillingly, enjoyed the firm's "protection". A nip could be free drinks or gratuitous gifts of merchandise as pioneered by Jack Spot. Or it could be a "loan" whose return was never seriously intended. When Kray employees grew too old for active work on the streets, they were found suitably quiet, stationary jobs. Limehouse Willey was installed in a pub, and Billy Kray and Teddy Berry managed spielers in the 1960s, with Teddy ending up as the publican of the Horns in Bethnal Green Road

The twins always needed drivers. Ronnie could not drive and, colonel-like, was content to sit in the passenger seat and be chauffeured. Some grave error on the part of a driving test examiner granted Reggie a licence. He refused to wear the spectacles his short-sightedness required and he was always more likely to run a brand-new car into a tree or a lamp-post than take it to his intended destination. Mind you, he knew just how to deal with such a mishap. Abandon the car immediately. Go home, and report it stolen. Then claim on the insurance.

They had come a long way. They had moved into the gold-watch-and-tailored-suit bracket. They commanded men many years older than themselves and were reckoned good guv'nors. The threat to their prosperity lay in Ron's flaky personality, his silly tuppenny-blood ambitions and his capacity for raging bull violence. And "the twin thing" that meant Reg would not always avoid the contamination.

A straight car dealer gave Ronnie Kray his first opportunity to put his growing gun collection to practical use and fire a bullet into human flesh. The twins found car dealers useful. They could be intimidated because their stock was vulnerable to attacks with paint stripper and axes. They could sell new cars on hire purchase agreements that the twins might run for two years without payment before the finance companies could complete the legal procedures for repossessing them. This particular dealer had been threatened by an angry Bermondsey docker who had bought a dud vehicle from him and declared his intention of coming back in the morning mob-handed. Delighted to fight off such "invasion" of his territory, Ronnie donned his Al Capone overcoat, packed a Luger, and had himself driven down to the car site. The docker was inside talking to the dealer. Ronnie strode in, pulled out his pistol and shot him in the leg. And strode out again.

The appalled face of the car dealer told Ronnie's driver the truth. The docker had come in to apologize for his conduct the night before and the car dealer had reciprocated. The would-be great gangster had pumped lead into a man who had committed no offence and uttered no provocation.

The twins' permanent way of dealing with such crises promptly came into action for the first time. Reggie delivered a tirade about Ron's stupidity and took on the task of cleaning up. Ron, smugly satisfied at having shot to injure, went to lie low in a safe house in Walthamstow while Reggie destroyed his clothes and got rid of incriminating evidence. Reggie let himself be arrested in Ronnie's place and picked out at an identification parade, only then revealing his identity and thus "spoiling" any future identification evidence. "Red Face Tommy" Plumley, a Brick Lane stallholder who knew everyone in the East End and how to buy their favours, was called in to help. It was the start of a long association in which Plumley would negotiate the gifts and agreements that opened hospital doors or exposed the state of police enquiries. The car dealer suffered a sudden loss of memory and was quite unable to recount the events of the morning of the shooting. The injured docker, whose leg would be permanently shortened, disabling him for work, was made an offer he couldn't refuse. A substantial gift of money bought him a little sweetshop, satisfying a long-held ambition to retire from the docks. The car dealer, of course, paid. The whole business of bribing and fixing and straightening cost him over £3,000. And throughout it all, Ronnie Kray sat in Walthamstow listening to records of Puccini and soothing himself with the game of "wanted man on the run", which had proved a solace in National Service and would become a long-term retreat from reality.

As for the East End, it now suffered the petty tyranny of a pair of criminal masters who thought that shooting people in the legs was a safe and reasonable way of expressing their displeasure.

In August 1956 Bobby Ramsey led the twins into the trouble Charlie had anticipated. He had introduced them to his friend Bobby Jones, who ran The Stragglers Club off Cambridge Circus. The Stragglers was suffering from a disorderly clientele and the twins were recommended as minders or bouncers. As this was a simple route into the West End, they jumped at the chance. Reggie had perfected his "cigarette punch", offering a victim a cigarette from a packet with one hand while delivering a cross to the jaw with the other as his attention was distracted. It produced a lot of instant broken jaws and it calmed life at The Stragglers.

Then Jones, who lived in the docklands, had a quarrel with a Watney Streeter called Charlie Martin. And violence escalated. Martin beat up Jones. Ramsey drove down to the East End and beat up Martin. Martin and a mob of Watney Streeters caught Ramsey in the docklands pub The Artichoke, dragged him outside, and beat him severely, Martin finishing the job with an iron bar.

When he was recovered, Ramsey wanted revenge. And the twins were ready to help. Charlie Martin had been running a little scam with relabelled postal packages and had proved unreliable in paying over a cut to the thieves-poncing Krays. Military minded "Colonel" Ronnie took over operations. His spy network watched the Watney Streeters until, on a Saturday night, they reported that Martin and another of Ramsey's assailants, Jimmy Fullerton, were drinking in a pub called the Britannia. Two cars roared away from Eric Street. Jones, Ramsey and Ronnie were in the first, Reggie and some hand-picked henchmen in the second. Ramsey had tooled up with a bayonet, a machete and a crowbar. Ronnie had taken a loaded revolver.

But either the spy system was faulty or Charlie Martin had got wind of the approaching army. When the Kray mob reached the Britannia, the only occupants were Charlie's young brother Terry and three other lads with whom he was playing gin rummy. Crass brutality and stupidity took command. The gang dragged Terry Martin out onto the street, where Ramsey was given a free hand to beat and stab him. He felled Terry with two bayonet thrusts to the back of the head, and then, according to John Pearson, stabbed him in the shoulder. Charlie Kray, less concerned with decorum, says Ramsey stuck the bayonet up his backside. After which the gang fell to kicking the fallen lad until Reggie called them off. They were all lucky he was not killed.

Instead of driving home, satisfied with the night's squalid brutality, Ronnie and Ramsey decided to drive around looking for the real Watney Streeters to exact a more proper revenge on somebody more their own size and weight. And with exquisite folly they let themselves be picked up for speeding. Naturally, the police wanted an explanation for the bloodstained bayonet and other weapons, including Ronnie's concealed pistol.

Ronnie was stupidly confident. Red Face Tommy had cleared up the mess once. He would do it again. Only he couldn't. Terry Martin wouldn't play. He was young and innocent enough to see that the great "East End code" was an emperor with no clothes. If you're severely and painfully wounded for no reason at all, you'll squeal. It's a natural response. Terry was also old enough to perceive that the police were, in the long run, more numerous and better equipped than two well-dressed young tearaways, although older and stronger men than he would have felt that crossing the Kray gang was brave to the point of foolhardiness.

The police had found a bloodstained jacket of Reggie's and not even the old identical twins trick could make that go away. Reg offered to take full responsibility for everything, but Ron pointed out that the gun in his pocket meant that he would be charged whatever happened. And so the firm's best forensic efforts were devoted to getting Reggie off.

They succeeded. Reggie's claim that his bloodstained clothes might have been soiled when he was watching a boxing match created a reasonable doubt. Brother Charlie, always willing to tell a few whoppers in defence of the twins, remarks that Reggie was, "thankfully, justly acquitted", and claims that he hadn't even known about the attack until afterwards. When a Kray makes a straight and po-faced declaration of innocence like that, (especially if citing the judgement of the courts to give it weight), it is sensible to read it as proof of guilt. Brother Charlie overlooked the fact that John Pearson, given his information by the twins themselves, reported that it was Reggie who stopped the attack when it was going dangerously far. So Charlie's "afterwards" has to be capable of very flexible contraction.

But there was no acquittal for Ronnie. He, Jones and Ramsey all went down for causing grievous bodily harm to Terry Martin. Reggie later had the impertinence to claim that the Martin family "were responsible for getting Ron his three years", and cited this in justification of his organizing the fire-bombing of a spieler they opened in what he regarded as "his" territory.

Ronnie went to Wandsworth. As prison may do for second and subsequent offenders, it confirmed him as a professional criminal. His old deserter friend Dickie Morgan was inside, serving four years for the theft of a lorry-load of meat. Checker Berry was inside, too, and renewed the childhood acquaintance that would lead to his becoming a Kray driver. Other prisoners who did not know "the Colonel" personally had heard of his informal "Prisoners' Relief Association" for East End "aways". He slotted into prison life well up the pecking order.

And he made friends with another East End "away" who was very high up the order, a man who was making himself a reputation that would spread across the prison system of the whole nation. "Big Frank" Mitchell was not yet "the Mad Axeman". The exploit evoking that misleading newspaper sobriquet would not take place for another two years. But he was recognized as a serious mental case, although those who knew him best saw his weakness as a matter of intellect rather than emotional health and stability. In old-fashioned terms Frank was very backward. In euphemistic terms, "educationally challenged". He was a man in his 30s with the mind of a child of 13 or under. At times a rather nice child. Amiable and given to hero-worship. But also prone to showing off. And capable of childish temper tantrums if confronted with authoritarian pettiness or pernickety discipline. Two things in which prison specializes.

Frank was 27 when Ronnie met him in Wandsworth. He had been in trouble with the law since he was nine years old, when he stole a bicycle from a smaller kid. The Mitchells were a respectable working-class family from Limehouse. Frank's father decided he needed a lesson and took him to the police station for a serious telling off. The police, unfortunately, took matters into their own hands. Despite his obviously responsible attitudes, they did not regard the humble Mr Mitchell as the appropriate disciplinarian for his son and they had the child brought before a juvenile court, which put him on probation. Mr Mitchell and Frank's younger sisters never doubted that this high-handed action by police jacks-in-office was the start of all Frank's misfortunes. He learned instant mistrust of authority and made friends with bad company. He went through the rogues' formal education system of probation, approved school, borstal, prison. He was a ringleader in the Rochester borstal riot and rejoiced in the attention and adulation it brought him from fellow delinquents. He became a thorn in the flesh of authority, losing his temper and acting up if he felt the prison officers were "taking liberties".

So why did it matter if Frank lost his rag from time to time? Lots of other prisoners did. It mattered because he was quite exceptionally strong. Recollections of his height vary from 5ft 10ins to 6ft

4ins. His records show he was actually 6ft 1in. They can't show that, as he would have put it, he was built like a brick shithouse. Prison warder Derek Brisco later remembered him as having a 54-inch chest. Albert Donaghue said simply that his arms were like legs. He was a fitness fanatic and performed endless press-ups and sit-ups in his cell. He could pull himself up on a doorframe with one arm. He could lift up a fellow prisoner with one arm. Better still, he could lift two full-grown men, snatching them up by their belts. His limited brain was not going to win him esteem for his wit or perception, but he could win it for feats of strength. And so, like a showman, he put them on. Doing more press-ups than anyone else could manage. Lifting more weights than anyone else. Picking up people.

Frank's strength and his short fuse led to some very serious acts of violence against prison officers. He had been birched and he had been given the cat, punishments that were, mercifully, as unusual as they were cruel. They seemed particularly cruel when given to Big Frank, because he struck intimates as a classic "gentle giant". He had a sunny disposition, smiled a lot and had a big, infectious, guffawing laugh. Warder Brisco, who saw a lot of him in his last two years in Dartmoor, reckoned it was almost 100% certain that anyone who sat down and chatted with Frank would like him by the time he got up to go. During one of his short spells of freedom, he became friendly with a Poplar girl. She bore him a daughter. Frank's friends, fellow prisoners and his sisters didn't know about it. The Misses Mitchell appear to have thought that Frank's misfortunes included losing his only girlfriend to cancer. He did not even know of his fatherhood himself. The girl had no further contact with him, after he went back to prison, but like almost everyone who knew him in a private or domestic situation, she remembered him as a gentle person, "at no stage violent".

Yet violence made his prison reputation. He beat up one warder and cut another's face. He attacked a prisoner he believed had grassed him up, and was charged with attempted murder. He attacked Bruce Reynolds (before he was famous as the Great Train Robber) and knifed him in the showers - not as an act of rage but as an act of assistance to help Reynolds get into the infirmary as part of an abortive escape plan. Warders who knew Frank Mitchell only by reputation, or whom he did not like, regarded him as an incorrigible menace. It was quite easy not to know him well, for Frank was choosy about his friends and associates and spent a lot of time on his own in his cell where, like many other big men, he worked surprisingly deftly with his huge hands, mending watches or making little model cars, and where he bred budgerigars.

The Krays were always capable of voicing generalized liberal attitudes that contrast sharply with their more than illiberal violence towards anyone whose money or enforced respect they wanted. But Ronnie was genuinely concerned about the apparent injustices, or (as the Mitchell family put it), "bad luck" that Frank suffered. Ronnie saw him as a lonely "away", with few visitors. So he got some of the firm to write to Frank and visit him. Limehouse Willey and his wife became regular correspondents and visitors for the rest of Mitchell's life. And Frank, unaccustomed to concern that rose above the rough camaraderie of prison life, started hero-worshipping Ronnie Kray, his benefactor.

And then a new and liberal governor changed everything for the worse. Ronnie was transferred to Camp Hill, a less restrictive prison where men of good behaviour enjoyed a wider range of activities and sports in preparation for their discharge. It didn't suit Ronnie one little bit. Instead of admiring fellow professionals, he was surrounded by first offenders and amateur criminals. He had no interest in organized games. He became depressed and his near-catatonic withdrawal led the governor to send him to Winchester prison's psychiatric centre for observation. "Prison psychosis" was the diagnosis. A catch-all phrase recognizing that prison is a frustrating place in which stress quickly leads the unstable to violence or breakdown. Reggie Kray once remarked that after he had seen the extreme and extravagant behaviour of inmates in a prison infirmary, he was quite sure that he himself was not mad.

Ronnie went, literally, raving when his beloved Aunt Rose died. Told the news in a callous manner by an unsympathetic warder, he had to be strapped in a straitjacket and was certified insane. There is no reason to doubt his subjective feeling that the way his bereavement was given to him was traumatic and triggered his florid paranoid schizophrenia. But his irrational violence and extravagant role-playing ever since he entered the army, and his private delusional fears that he might unconsciously have grassed up his companions in Camp Hill, showed that the warder's unpleasantness landed in fertile soil. Early in 1958, Ronald Kray was transferred to a mental hospital.

Reggie meanwhile, in collaboration with brother Charlie, had been flourishing. Popular legend would have him a potentially good businessman and club owner unhappily lost to the world of crime because of his unstable twin. He blew away that legend himself in his second effort at autobiography. Shaking off the restraining hand of a professional writer-collaborator, he boasted in *Born Fighter* of fire-bombing rival clubs and spielers. Partly for revenge on the Martin family. Partly as an extreme version of capitalism's much-loved commercial competition. But most often to intimidate the owners into selling or making over their businesses to him. Reggie Kray was no natural businessman who unhappily found himself mired in crime. He was a vicious and violent villain who stole other people's businesses.

Except for his best business. The Double R Club in Bow Road was started quite legitimately when a tearaway called David Cohen recommended that Reg rent a well-placed vacant shop and turn it into a drinking club that might successfully compete with one run by Cohen's enemy, Joe Abrahams. Reg's clean and neat appearance and good manners made an excellent impression on the property's owner in Park Lane. And the young man borrowed (or perhaps "borrowed") the first three months' rent from a car dealer, cut his brother Charlie in as part-owner in return for the money to stock the bar, and set about redecorating. Naturally the absent Ronnie was third part-owner, the other half of the Double R.

The appearance was less than stunning. Flock wallpaper with little pink lampshades was the tarted-up decor that the twins had seen in the Stragglers Club, the fashionable nightclub look of the period that led the unhappy Ruth Ellis to believe her pimp had made her manageress of a really smart venue. But it was an immense improvement on the dirty, dusty, dingy settings of the East End's usual spielers and drinking clubs. It brought a touch of "Up West" to Bow. And Reggie had the vision to see a future for a local club that was almost a family place – at least somewhere you could take a wife or a lady friend. (Charlie takes no credit for this perception, though it seems altogether more his line of country.)

The Double R was an immediate success. Big Pat Connolly, and a veteran of the Krays' wars with the Watney Streeters, Bill Donovan, manned the door. Reggie assisted with his "cigarette punch" to make it clear from the outset that rowdies and troublemakers were not going to turn this place into yet another downmarket dump. Charlie ran the bar with an amusing homosexual called Barry Clare as his assistant, who was the compere for any cabaret. If necessary, Charlie would cross the bar to revive his boxing skills when the doormen needed help. Charlie's wife Dolly, who faced the difficulty that the rest of the family disliked her, was happy to give a hand, though Reg resented her attendance as a false assumption of proprietorship.

The Double R pioneered something that would become a mark of the twins' ventures, the cultivation of gangster-struck celebrities. First local notables and would-be starlets. Then Barbara Windsor, a local girl made good who was by no means slumming it as a gangster-struck outsider. She had known people who frequented East End spielers all her life. She became personally friendly with Charlie Kray and later married a well-known local villain, Ronnie Knight, who would be one of Freddie Foreman's partners in the biggest cash-snatch of all time. Barbara Windsor had risen to prominence with Joan Littlewood's renowned experimental theatre company at the Theatre Royal, Stratford, and starred in the cockney musicals written by East Enders Lionel Bart and reformed thief Frank Norman. Her stardom was part of the growing '50s and '60s cultivation of the East End. The Prospect of Whitby in Wapping had been a favoured pub to end the evening for some years. Now the Double R offered equally clean surroundings and longer drinking hours, and down from the fashionable West End came such notables as Joan Collins' sister Jackie (not yet famous as a novelist) and Richard Burton's wife turning ex-wife, Sybil. Danny la Rue dropped in. The drag entertainer's mix of swishy femininity and growly cockney masculinity had not yet brought him to national stardom, but he was professionally in tune with Queenie Watts, the traditional cockney and blues singer who gave away the fivers Charlie paid her to be spent on drinks all round at the bar. And after these celebrities came the deluge of others who wanted to show that they too knew the East End and had dipped their toes into haunts reputed to be frequented by gangsters.

They were warmly encouraged. The twins were as keen to be seen and photographed with celebs as the celebs were to pretend to acquaintance with "real" (criminal) life. Charlie even succeeded in getting the immensely popular boxer Henry Cooper to open the gymnasium he established above the club, though 'Enery of Bellingham had no wish to be associated with thugs.

This was the point at which Kray Bros might have become an almost respectable company. Charlie "didn't know" that his little brother's success in acquiring gaming clubs rested on firebombing and intimidation. He simply claimed that he and Reggie "saw the possibilities" in spielers, "acquired one" and later "opened two more". The underworld has always insisted that Charlie doth protest too much about his standing as an honest businessman who had no idea what his little brothers were up to.

After being certified insane, Ronnie was transferred to Long Grove Hospital in Surrey in February 1958. He was one of six patients sent from prisons and the hospital insisted that they were to be treated no differently from other patients. So his life was immediately made rather more comfortable. His parents thought good old Ron had again acted insanity and successfully pulled the wool over the authorities' eyes to get himself a cushier time. Reggie hoped somewhat anxiously that Ronnie was play-acting, worried that madness might be part of the genetic heritage. They all understood Ron's application to return to prison in May, once the anti-depressant Stematol started to control his troughs. As long as he was certified insane he could be detained forever, if that was the doctors' recommendation. If he went back to prison, he had less than a year of his sentence to finish.

Despite a general medical report on his improvement, the transfer was refused. And so in June the twins pulled their most celebrated identical twins trick. Reggie went down with their associate Georgie Osborne for the regular Sunday visit that two friends or relations always made. Only this time, another car full of gang members accompanied them, pretending not to know that there was a restriction to two visitors at any one time. The second car waited outside. By prearrangement, the twins wore blue suits, white shirts and dark ties, with Reggie also wearing a fawn overcoat. In the visiting room, the three men laughed loudly over an album of holiday photographs. When the attendants' attention was distracted, the overcoat passed from Reggie to Ronnie. Shortly thereafter the man in the overcoat went, ostensibly, to get some tea, as visitors (but not inmates) were permitted, walked out of the secure hospital into the waiting car, and away into the distance. After half an hour, the twin in the blue suit asked the attendant where Ron was with his tea. And showed, with his driving licence, that he was Reg. As usual, there was nothing that could be done about this trick. It wasn't a crime to lend your chilly brother a coat or to wait around half-an-hour for a cup of tea that didn't come.

The aim was to keep Ronnie out of hospital for six months, after which he would have to be re-certified. And to ensure that he wasn't, the family had him examined by a specialist under the name of John Lee, who wanted to marry but feared there might be hereditary madness in his family. Mr Lee was given a certificate of sanity which, it was hoped, would be Ron's ticket to completing his sentence in prison. In the meantime he was sent with a minder to live in a caravan in Suffolk. Although he enjoyed some country pursuits and learned to ride – a skill Reggie also acquired as the Double R and the spielers brought prosperity – he wanted more urban amusements. He resented the fact that the young men brought for his sexual companionship over the weekends always returned home after two nights. And he wanted to see and be seen in the Double R. Finally he persuaded Reggie to let him make clandestine visits to London.

These proved disastrous. He enjoyed to the full his role of "gangster on the run", and he cultivated a criminal celebrity profile in the club. His behaviour back in Suffolk became so outrageous that the farmer on whose land the caravan was pitched insisted on a second independent mental assessment. This time the report was that Ronnie was a dangerous paranoid schizophrenic who for his own safety and everyone else's needed immediate help.

The family refused to believe it. They took the prodigal back into Vallance Road. And here, to their distress, he sank to such a point of madness that Violet was the only person he recognized as herself. Charlie and Reggie, he said, looked like Charlie and Reggie, but he knew they were really Russian spies in disguise. He really was extremely dangerously ill, displaying the identical symptoms of the Victorian fairy painter Richard Dadd who cut the throat of the kindly parent he perceived as "Satan pretending to be my father". From now on, Ronnie would need heavy medication to avoid dangerous delusions. He was, of course, dangerous when in his right mind, a cruel and brutal bully who believed in imposing his will on others by force and helping himself to their property. But a part of him was also genuinely convinced that his life was threatened by everyone he saw. He was liable to attack innocent people, including those who loved him, for no reason at all. He was at one and the same time a loathsome criminal and an unfortunate lunatic who couldn't always help himself. Just as the Krays as a whole constantly present us with the paradox of a supportive and loving family, two members of which – who were capable of a good deal of generosity and consideration – nonetheless practised sadistic cruelty when they felt their wills thwarted.

The other symptom of paranoia, delusions of grandeur, wasn't helped by Ron's chosen fantasy world. It was harmless that he promoted himself to the rank of his hero, Colonel Lawrence. It was beneficial to some that he enjoyed the role of benevolent philanthropist, giving cash to (some bad) individuals and (some good) causes, rejoicing in the newspaper coverage that followed his acts of public charity. It was disastrous for him and everybody else that he became increasingly obsessed with "living up to" the wretched standards of American Mafiosi. It would spell death for George Cornell and Jack McVitie.

Ronnie's condition was so manifestly serious that the Krays did the unthinkable. They shopped him to Scotland Yard and drugged his tea with sleeping pills to ensure his peaceful arrest. This was one of the kindest and most caring things they ever did for him – and something that itself exposes the crass stupidity of the vaunted code of the East End.

Although at first Ronnie went back to Long Grove, he had completed his six months at liberty and he was not immediately re-certified. He was again prescribed Stematol and after a few months was transferred back to prison to complete his sentence, emerging in 1959.

And with "the Colonel's" return to the driving seat, all hope of a relatively peaceful and definitely prosperous future for the club-owning Kray Bros came to an end. Ronnie downgraded the entertainment, introducing midgets or a singer who paraded through the room on a donkey. He brought in a monkey. He was showing off absurdly. He also helped himself to the takings as he felt inclined. It was his money, wasn't it? He could use it himself or give it to others if he felt like it. Bookkeeping was a boring and impossible task for the twins who were barely numerate and, it was suggested by their enemies, hardly ever gambled because they simply couldn't understand odds.

Enemies remained important to Ronnie. It was fun sitting in a club surrounded by smoke and celebrities. But it was necessary to prove oneself a leader by imposing one's will on other people. Reggie and Charlie had adroitly abandoned the defeated Jack Spot and cultivated the Clerkenwell Italians under Albert Dimes who inherited the mantles of Billy Hill and the Sabinis. With Hill's benign patronage and with his lieutenant's advice and encouragement, Charlie and Reg hoped to break into West End club ownership and protection. Indeed, with the legalization of gambling casinos in sight, there was every hope of profitably carving up London as syndicated crime had carved up America. Albert Dimes had contact with Angelo Bruno, the Philadelphia Mafia chief, and he would know all about the advantages of crooked co-operation rather than crooked competition. Charlie and Reggie negotiated diplomatically for an alliance.

"The Colonel" blew that at the first meet he attended, intemperately announcing that they didn't need a lot of cheap Italians to help them. It was hopeless for Reggie and Charlie to try and explain and patch things up. Their apologies were politely accepted, but cooperation was tacitly withdrawn. In the future, Mad Frankie Fraser would have a nice little earner in West End slot machines whenever he was out of prison for a brief spell. George Cornell would draw income from blue movies and films. The Richardsons would prepare to be a major power in Soho. But the Krays would always struggle to become a high-earning presence in the vice paradise of the West End.

Finally Ronnie wanted some real war. Another pointless fight with the Watney Streeters took place in the Hospital Tavern, across the road from Whitechapel underground station. Reggie fought alongside his brother. Both sides used bicycle chains and knuckledusters. The Watney Streeters were routed. And nothing useful had been achieved.

Nor did Ronnie achieve anything by carrying gang warfare over to Paddington. He had grandiose ideas of unifying all the London gangs by force, and bringing them under one leader (guess who!). The police were mystified by the sudden outbreak of seemingly pointless mob warfare in the summer of 1959. And Reggie, bemusedly supporting his brother in this absurdity, had to watch the good wealth-producing empire he and Charlie had started to build, start to unravel in a welter of unpaid taxes and unkept books.

Why did Reggie, seen by all observers as the more intelligent and stable of the two, allow his brother to set the pace? Gang members tended to assume that it was because Ron had the stronger personality, the more powerful ego. In fact, I think, the reverse is true. Ron had an exceptionally weak personality. If ego is interpreted as meaning the central self that gives us our identity, Ron's was almost entirely lacking. He had to substitute some sort of visible action that secured a response from other people to feel that he really existed. He had to make a lot of noise (or overawe by an intimidating silence) to be sure he was present at all. He had to impose his will on anyone and everyone, or he felt that he had shown weakness. He had none of the resilient personality's ability to absorb defeat and plan recovery. If he wasn't exercising freakish control, he felt he was losing. He couldn't yield temporarily to secure a long-term advantage. He had to feel himself on top and in command at all times. In fact, Ronald Kray's perception of himself as a leader is startlingly reminiscent of Adolf Hitler's. Both believed in the "triumph of the will", nursing the delusion that pounding down anybody who opposed their wishes represented strength of character. Both reacted to defeat with rage and disbelief and blamed other people for the devastating consequences of their own mistakes. Both confused self-centred wilfulness and complete blindness to other people's reality with admirable fixity of purpose. Both wrongly assumed everyone else was at heart as self-interested and dishonest as they. *Mein Kampf* was one of the most demanding books Ronnie ever read. Much of it understandably bored him. But he was impressed by Hitler's advocacy of propaganda, his cynical perception that most people would believe what they read and would hold a good opinion of anyone about whom they usually read good things. It came quite easily to a centreless role-player to cultivate a favourable image.

Of course Ronnie, like all the Krays, was no racist Fascist. Kenny Lynch had been a friend; Billy Bellamy had been a mentor; great black boxers from Joe Louis to Sonny Liston would become heroes he was proud to entertain. He had many Jewish friends and associates and many Irish (despite the supposed Irish ethnicity of the Watney Streeters). His aggressive remark about "cheap Italians" is the rare and uncharacteristic racist gibe made by a Kray. Ronnie acknowledged his own gypsy and possibly Jewish blood without any embarrassment. He was morally one up on Adolf there.

Reg made a serious mistake as Ron's expansionism led them to look over Paddington. In Edgware, a car dealer called Daniel Shay became a gangland hanger-on who accepted being nipped for "loans" in return for the honour of knowing the twins. And in 1959 he decided to imitate his heroes. He bought an expensive leather briefcase on credit from a shopkeeper called Murray Podro in Finchley. A few days later he came back, accused Podro of overcharging him and demanded £100, threatening to cut him up if he didn't produce the money. Podro wisely called the police as soon as Shay left his shop. And two days later the police were forewarned when Reggie came in with Shay and Georgie Osbourne and Reggie head-butted Podro in an attempt to enforce the payment.

All three crooks were bang to rights. Reggie got 18 months for demanding money with menaces. Like every Kray conviction, this has produced self-pitying whingeing from the family. It was really a gambling debt, they say. Reggie was just a good friend collecting for someone else. With four clubs at the time, £100 was chickenfeed to him. Podro accused Reggie before the magistrates of having threatened to cut him, but didn't repeat the claim in the higher court, which proved he was lying. How unfair to hang the tag "demanding money with menaces" around Reggie's neck for such a simple, kind attempt to help a friend get money from a welcher! Except that by Reggie's own account he not only menaced, he assaulted. And even if it were true that the debt was a gambling debt and not an attempt at extortion, the law does not regard gambling as incurring justifiable enforcement.

With Reggie in Wandsworth, Ronnie was able to show what rule by Kray ethics meant. Sheer bloody mayhem! He led his gangs out to fight other villains and demand extortion from all and sundry. He let the Regal and the Double R fall into lossmaking. He didn't give a toss. He could pick up all the money he needed by taking a couple of plug-uglies into a spieler or a car dealer's and demanding it. He gave West London an uncomfortable reminder of what the Merrie Englande of robber barons felt like. T. H. White had just completed his tetralogy modernizing the Arthurian legend; it would become another icon of the sixties when turned into the musical *Camelot*. Ronnie firmly cast himself as the villainous Sir Bruce Saunce Pité. But his exploits were never the subject of overwhelming police attention, because of a much viler escapade involving his friends the Nashes.

Towards the end of 1959 Selwyn Cooney, who managed the New Cabinet Club in Gerrard Street, Soho, for Billy and Aggie Hill, was in a minor car collision with "Blonde Vicki" James, a hostess and friend of Ronnie Nash. Cooney sent his bill for 54 shillings and ninepence – (£2.70p but worth, say, 50 times more at today's values) – to Vicki. She didn't pay as she wasn't insured, and when Nash and Cooney met by chance in a Notting Hill drinking club they first exchanged words and then black eyes. Two days later Cooney went into the Pen Club in Durward Street, Spitalfields, on the other side of the road from the site of Jack the Ripper's last and most terrible murder. Shortly after, Ronnie Nash's brother Jimmy or "Trunky" came into the club with boxing promoter Joey Pyle (a friend of everyone in the underworld), boxer John Read, and a hostess called Doreen Masters. Doreen pointed Cooney out to Jimmy Nash, who promptly went over and broke his nose with one blow, saying, "That'll teach you to give little girls a spanking". Cooney retaliated, saying he had done no such thing, whereupon Nash shot him twice in the head. So, at least, said Cooney's girl-friend, the New Cabinet's 19-year-old barmaid Joan Bending, and young John Simons who hit Read over the head with a bottle as outraged club members drove Nash, Pyle, Read and Doreen Masters out to their cars.

This was bad enough. What followed was the first dreadful evidence of the degree of witness intimidation and jury nobbling that the "glamorous" gangs of 1960s "faces" were willing to practice. Nash, Pyle, Read and Doreen were all charged with murder. On 16 March Johnny Simons was attacked with razors in a Paddington cafe. It took 72 stitches to repair his face. Then these gallant criminals, who assure the world that they only attack each other and never lay a finger on women, turned their attention to Johnny's girlfriend, 23-year-old Barbara Ibbotson. She was snatched off the street in Soho, bundled into a car, and given four razor slashes to the face. Three weeks later, three thugs broke into her flat and held her under the water in her bath while they inflicted further razor cuts, requiring 27 stitches. Quite a conclusion to a quarrel that started by someone objecting that sending a bill to a woman was "giving a little girl a spanking"!

It is, I suppose, possible that this unspeakable crime had nothing to do with Johnny's intention of giving evidence against Nash, Pyle and Read. It is possible that three entirely unconnected men had an entirely unconnected quarrel with Barbara that she was never willing to divulge to anyone. It is even possible that the Nashes or Joey Pyle profoundly objected to vicious action taken on their behalf but unknown to them. But without remarkably strong assurances that this was so, I shouldn't myself want Joey Pyle as a friend, or Johnny Nash as a pallbearer. I wouldn't feel that a solemn handshake over Ronnie Kray's coffin between Johnny Nash and other London gang leaders was a moving moment presaging a sacred peace. Although many of the Nashes have passed into respectable careers, the huge blot of the cruel assaults on Barbara Ibbotson remains a matter needing explanation and atonement.

Nor was this the end of the affair. With Simons and Joan Bender given police protection, the case came to court. The first trial was dismissed when evidence of jury tampering and possible jury bias was put to the judge. At the second trial a wholly new witness came forward with the claim that Simons had been drinking in another bar when the affray took place and Joan Bender had been so drunk she had to be carried out of the club. In the end nobody was found guilty of the undoubted murder of Selwyn Cooney, but Jimmy Nash drew a five-year sentence for grievous bodily harm, and Pyle went to prison for 18 months.

According to Freddie Foreman, the twins were tangentially involved in this horrible business. He and they served as honest brokers between their friends the Nashes and the Pen Club's owners, Jerry Callaghan and Billy Ambrose, who had fought on the other side during the affray. Foreman and the Krays apparently oversaw a meet at which it was agreed that the attempts to save Jimmy Nash from the gallows should not be obstructed by a vengeful gang war. Freddie Foreman has made some statements suggesting considerable gallantry on his and his associates' part. He is, for example, one of the very, very few ganglanders to have written sympathetically about Charlie Kray's wife Dolly, who left him for George Ince while he was in prison. He was happy to see a villain get his nose broken when he laid out a teenage girl during a brawl. He takes pride in having looked after the welfare of young girls drinking in his Lant Street pub. Barbara Ibbotson must wish that Freddie's gallantry ran deeper than criminal confraternity and he had been willing to see to a spanking for those colleagues who went far beyond "breaking a little girl's jaw". Fred's actual attitude? "Loads of witnesses in the club, they all had to change their statements and do the right thing, and between us we sorted it out." Since Johnny Simons didn't change his statement and had to be rebutted by the pretence that he was in another bar, somebody undertook to punish him. And he was cut again when he tried to return to England from Spain where the police sent him after the trial.

And what was this savagery really in aid of? Could it really be nothing more than a quarrel about a little fender bending and the bill for damages? A fraternal wish to avenge Ronnie Nash's black eye and his embarrassed hostess friend? Commander Bert Wickstead, who led successful gangbusting operations in London ten years later, did not think so. He was sure this was the opening salvo in wars that were intended to decide who was going to take over the vacated throne of Billy Hill or decide whether Albert Dimes, who the young men thought "couldn't fight for fuck", was to continue unchallenged in his half-acknowledged overlordship of the underworld. The Nashes were eliminating a Hill employee as a warning to Hill's former henchmen to get out of the way.

Certainly this was the first crucial instance of the forthcoming 1960s gangland rivalries and vicious criminal cruelty that the BBC mirrored in "Big Breadwinner Hogg", a somewhat sanitized dramatization of what the police were up against and which so upset Mrs Mary Whitehouse. Her National Viewers and Listeners Association primarily wanted television to pretend that sex only existed as evangelical christians preferred to see it. But perceiving that almost the entirety of the intelligentsia was more concerned about televised violence than sex, the NVALA proceeded to make a typically wrong-footed judgement, implicitly preferring the kind of old-fashioned Warner Bros gangster picture that really did glamorize villains (as played by James Cagney and Humphrey Bogart) to a series which showed speciously "glamorous" young rogues as even more vicious and dislikable than their seedy elders.

The police were sufficiently shocked by the Pen Club killing to make an all-out effort to bring the Nashes to justice, ultimately putting several of them away for possession of unlicensed weapons. The family screamed blue murder that they had been framed. But in those days, before Commissioner Sir Robert Mark made an issue of all kinds of police corruption, nobody was unduly worried if known villains were sent down for something they hadn't done. It was a small payment on account for all things they had done and got away with.

The attention on the Nashes took the heat off Ronnie and his misdeeds for the time being. And Reggie had momentarily become more involved with the sort of crime that drew down larger head-lines at the end of the 1950s, the vicious activities of cosh boys and juvenile delinquents. In 1958, 25-year-old Ronald Marwood took part in one of the regular rumbles outside Grey's Dance Academy in Seven Sisters Road. When young PC Raymond Summers inter-vened to stop the fight, Marwood pulled a knife and killed him. It was a senseless spur-of-the-moment act. One of the more lamenta-ble side effects of capital punishment was that Marwood, destined to hang, attracted more sympathy than his victim, two years younger than he. The young policeman had been acting courageously and correctly against great odds to save the public from the danger of youths scrapping with lethal weapons on the highway. Marwood was deliberately letting himself go on an adrenalin high with a reck-less contempt for life. Reggie Kray didn't see it that way. He believed he had once been something of a hero to the yobs who went to Grey's. It was there that he had once been asked whether as a Bethnal Greener he knew the Kray twins. Now he played a part in hiding Marwood out on an estate near Canon's Park, Edgware, and making him comfortable by supplying beer and hostesses. The police got to know of this, and Reggie believed this led them to pay that extra special bit of attention, which brought about his arrest for demanding money with menaces.

Now while I personally have no objection to officers of the law taking extra measures against villains who aid and abet the murderers of their young colleagues, I can see that some people might feel that Reggie was indeed being put upon when he suffered a light charge of uttering menaces. And, very possibly, the charge was brought because the police couldn't get the evidence to bring a justified one of accessory after the murder. But, happily, Reggie has gone out of his way to make sure that we don't get his messages wrong. He really was more concerned that the public should extend sympathetic understanding to vicious young bullies and killers than that they should remember their victims. For Reggie was in Wandsworth at the time 18-year-old "Flossie" Forsyth was executed there. Naturally, a topping used to upset prisoners very much and Reggie wrote an essay in which he took much pride, expressing his abhorrence of capital punishment in the light of Forsyth's plight. He made many good points. He noted that Forsyth would have no privacy at all for his last few days and that the warders' presence was not friendly support but officialdom's way of ensuring he did not take his own life. He noted that everyone's greatest concern, even the chaplain's, was that things should go smoothly with no scenes. And he noted that one life lost was enough and the second would be no deterrent to this sort of crime. Above all, Reggie showed a sensitive awareness of the fear and isolation a mere boy like Flossie must have felt. "Would one stamp on a flower if it began to wilt?" Reggie asked poetically.

Reggie said he thought of the victim, too, "and it distressed me that a young life should have been taken. To me they were all victims, there were no victors...I also thought of the parents of each side, and felt great sympathy". But that is all Reggie says about Flossie's victim, except for his account of the crime, which runs as follows: "Flossie... would ...go out with his mates each night to have some fun. It was just one of those kind of nights that led to his present predicament, this nightmare. He and his mates had gone out and met another kid on the towpath on their way to a local dancehall. Remarks were exchanged between Flossie's group and the other kid. A fight started and all joined in because the lone teenager had put up such a fight. This same boy fell to the path where he lay to die. Forsyth…is not an evil person or a killer in the true sense of the word. Fights and attacks were common in Peckham at the time. This must have weighed heavily against the accused, been a deciding factor of guilt by association to such an area."

Let's look as dispassionately as possible at the true facts of this crime. It happened in Hounslow, not Peckham, but that is of little importance. Flossie and his friends were not, however, going to any dance. 23-year-old Norman Harris was unemployed and skint. He and Forsyth both had convictions for theft, and Harris now suggested that they screw a shop while Forsyth preferred the idea of hitting a scrap-yard. 16-year-old Terence Lutt, who liked a fight, probably proposed that they mug a passer-by. And Forsyth, Harris and the fourth member of the gang, Chris Darby, agreed. They went to a place they knew in a local park where a broken streetlight left a dark patch on a path leading to a footbridge over a railway line. Local residents often used it as a way home.

Allan Jee, a 23-year-old engineer, was the boys' third possible victim. The first had been saved because a group of people came onto footbridge before he could be attacked. The second was a man whose size and strength were intimidating, even though there were four of them. Allan had just seen his fiancée Jacqueline Herbert home after a trip down the river to Richmond to celebrate their engagement the previous day. He was an ex-choirboy, a young man who had completed National Service in the RAF, and a responsible hard worker who agreed with Jacqueline that they had to save for the deposit on a house and wait two years before they got married.

No words were exchanged. Terence Lutt hit Allan in the face without saying anything as soon as he came within reach. "What do you want me for?" was Allan's only utterance. For answer, Lutt and Harris held him on the ground and Harris searched his breast pocket for a wallet. He didn't have one. He was carrying 14 shillings - about 72p in today's money. It bought a lot more then, but it seemed to his attackers totally inadequate. So Harris and Lutt went on holding him on the ground while Forsyth put the boot in. He kicked Allan Jee five times. One kick cracked his skull. One reduced his left eye and one his left ear to bleeding bruises. The pathologist was later unable to credit that a pointed-toed shoe of soft Italian leather had caused these lethal injuries. The four ran off leaving Allan lying on the towpath bleeding from the nose and ears. He died in hospital that night.

Harris and Forsyth were hanged. Darby was given a life sentence for non-capital murder. And Lutt was detained at Her Majesty's pleasure. Harris attracted little public sympathy. But Forsyth was good-looking as well as young. So the band-wagon in his favour started rolling and Reg jumped aboard.

Ignoring that his essay distorts the facts to the point of absurdity, Reggie gives us a classic example of evil sentimentality. Sentimentality is not sensitive feeling. It is not merely mawkishness. It is the misplaced indulgence or abuse of sensitivity. We should all feel some distress at the idea of an 18-year-old being held in the condemned cell to await execution. But it is an abuse to try to sustain and elevate this feeling at the expense of the equally distressing fate of Allan Jee. James Baldwin writes of "the sentimentalist's cold heart". It seems an extraordinary impossibility, until one reads Reg Kray vapouring about his equal sympathy for the two victims of the incident. His perfectly real and sympathetic feelings for Flossy Forsyth are cold-heartedly twisted into a distorting apology for vicious crime. Because, of course, it has been necessary his whole life to be a sentimental glamorizer of vicious crime to sustain that respect which some people foolishly accord the memory of the Kray twins' and their firm.

In Wandsworth, Reggie met one of his twin's great admirers for the first time. Frank Mitchell was still incarcerated, but there had been a subtle change in his status. His uncontrollable tantrums and childish mentality had led to the view that there must be a more sensible way of handling him than punishment cells, the birch, and the cat. So Frank had gone to Rampton secure hospital, from which he escaped, with another inmate who threatened people with an axe. One paper called them "the mad axemen". He had been returned, to Broadmoor, the other major asylum for criminal lunatics. And, its security being notoriously inadequate in the 1950s, he escaped from that, too, in July 1958. He broke into the house of elderly Mr and Mrs Edward Peggs and forcibly took Mr Peggs's watch, stealing also a change of clothes (blazer, shirt, trousers, shoes and socks), ninepence from Mr Peggs, ten shillings (50p) from Mrs Peggs, and the Peggs' Ford Prefect car. Now Mitchell was remembered as a "mad axeman".

When he was recaptured, this escapade was technically "robbery with violence". Of course the experience was distressing and intimidating for the couple. But it wasn't really as bad as the summary, "threatened them with an axe", suggested. Ten years later, the press universally dubbed Mitchell "the Mad Axeman". "Mad" is a nice short word that catches attention in a headline and can be applied to any inmate of Broadmoor or Rampton without fear of a libel suit. John Allen "the Mad Parson" of the 1930s wasn't even a parson, just a Broadmoor escapee who used a hospital theatrical-box dog-collar and a black shirt as a disguise. A mad axeman on the loose sounds terrifying and sells newspapers. But one of Frank's sisters received a comforting letter from Mrs Peggs when national press descriptions of their brother were at their most sensational and scurrilous. Frank had not been violent, Mrs Peggs said. He had been footsore and bleeding after his escape, she had offered to bathe his feet, and he had been grateful. Quite remarkably, this victim of "the Mad Axeman's terror" gave Frank Mitchell much the same assessment as his family and his daughter's mother. He was a gentle person, in no way violent.

But, in his time, he undoubtedly had been very violent with prison officers. And forcibly taking a watch from an elderly man's wrist in what should be the security of his own home is not a pleasant crime, especially when it is committed by a big man built like a Sherman tank. Had Mitchell prolonged his freedom for six months, his certification would have been invalidated. But he had not and, charged with repeated robbery with violence (he asked for two other offences to be taken into consideration), Mitchell, an undischarged criminal lunatic, was imprisoned for life, or at Her Majesty's Pleasure. He was in exactly the situation Ron Kray had feared.

Life sentences that don't mean life are an exasperating fraud on a public which, like it or not, still probably has a majority in favour of capital punishment. They are also a tantalizing torment to their recipients and can cause unnecessary distress to others. Myra Hindley, the object of trumped-up tabloid press moral hysteria, is constantly used as an excuse to wheel out her victims' relatives and encourage them to make extravagant statements whenever the possibility of her parole is raised. Nothing is achieved, except keeping innocent people in a state of seething turmoil over traumatic events more than 30 years in the past. The Kray twins' recommended minimum sentence of 30 years seems to hold out the hope that Reggie might be released at any moment. Yet the overarching term "life" makes him the helpless football of Home Secretaries' and their advisers' assessment of public feeling, their judgement on imponderables like "remorse", or even their fashionable whims about crime and punishment.

If the barrack-room lawyer can quickly identify injustice in a "life" sentence that is really indeterminate, the sentence itself in Mitchell's case was open to even more question. Hindley and the Krays, by any standard, deserved the maximum penalty the law prescribed. However, by the moral standards that you and I probably share with the shifty copper Alec Eist, and with the overwhelming majority of rogues and villains, Frank Mitchell was not one of the worst of men. He was not a murderer or a rapist or a child molester. True, his offence had been committed against old people, but there were immensely mitigating circumstances. He was on the run and opportunistically raiding the first house that seemed suitable. By Mrs Peggs' account, his violence had been minimal. With childlike simplicity, Frank never questioned that he had committed robbery with violence and deserved to be punished for crimes he knew he was committing (He contrasts favourably with the Krays in this). But as Reggie quite properly pointed out, if Frankie was mad, he should have been under the milder therapeutic regimen of Broadmoor or Rampton. (A former escapee obviously couldn't be risked anywhere with relatively low security like Grendon Underwood.) If he was not mad, he was entitled to know the length of his sentence. What was being done to Frank Mitchell was unjust.

An even more important criminal associate whose friendship was cemented over the cusp of the '50s and '60s was Freddie Foreman. Married to Tommy Wisbey's sister and working with him and another future Great Train Robber, Buster Edwards, Freddie was wanted for a job the three had pulled in Southampton, after which Tommy had been caught with stolen goods in a van registered to Freddie. Foreman was always a responsible family man, seeing his children through good private education and asserting that he wished he had enjoyed their advantages. It kept him generally sensible and stable compared with better-known and more reckless villains of the period, and he decided that he must disappear "on his toes" if his children were not to lose contact with him throughout vital years of their growth. A useful way of leaving a home environment and vanishing in London was simply to cross the river. Freddie put himself in the hands of the Krays and for three or four years stayed in a flat in Adelina Grove where Ronnie had hidden out during his escape from Long Grove Hospital. Freddie's spell in the East End not only confirmed his friendship with the Krays, it introduced him to a Canning Town plug-ugly who would become one of his closest associates, but who had none of the charm of the train robbers. Alf Gerard was, by Freddie's own account, an animal and a neanderthal. Freddie added that he had a heart, but it is not clear that that organ did anything more than pump blood round Gerard's fat frame. In fact Freddie seems to describe a repulsive, coarse, greedy and brutal man whose companionship can hardly have been conducive to good nature.

Ronnie cultivated a very different new associate in Leslie Payne, who had been introduced to Reggie by one of their car dealer associates just before he went to Wandsworth and who was to prove central to the Krays' more successful activities. Payne was a businessman, most of whose ventures had ended in bankruptcies and liquidation. Only another businessman could judge whether these were the result of bad luck, bad judgement, sharp practice, or a sensible assessment of the right time to wind up a business with minimum personal loss. I have no idea. But "Payne the Brain" had real business acumen, which the innumerate and not very literate Krays lacked. He would guide them in setting up "long firm" frauds, that popular confidence trick whereby a newly registered company quickly establishes a good reputation for promptly paying for small-ish quantities of goods received and then makes a huge quantity of much larger orders – and decamps, leaving an empty warehouse, an abandoned office building and a well-paid stooge as the front-man to take the heat, if the authorities traced him. Payne also helped Ronnie when he turned his "thieves' poncing" on another astute racketeer.

Peter Rachman, the Paddington slum landlord, did not become nationally notorious until after his death, when his former mistress Mandy Rice-Davis hit the headlines on the fringes of the 1963 Profumo affair. But Ronnie knew that Rachman's outfit was vul-nerable to threats if stronger-arm men than his violent "rent collec-tors" deterred them from going about their dirty work. Rachman was not himself a violent man. But he was clever enough to work out a deal that cost him nothing and got the Kray thugs off his back. He offered the twins what they dearly wanted – entree into the West End.

1960 saw serious moves started to legalize off-course gambling and permit gaming clubs. It was a long overdue reform. The 1906 Act had done nothing to stop the working classes from enjoying a flutter. It had planted bookies' runners permanently on city streets. It had ensured the chronic petty corruption of beat policemen. It was socially unjust, because the rich could always telephone their off-course bets to their "turf accountants". And the welter of squalid spielers in Soho and the East End were now being matched by the up-market "floating casinos" of the likes of John Aspinall and Robin Cook.

The Macmillan government was peculiarly innocent about the attraction legitimate gambling had for Mafiosi as a way in which illicit profits could easily be laundered. Warnings from the opposi-tion were vulnerable to the criticism that a puritanical wing of the Labour party really wanted gambling to remain legally harassed. Strait-laced Hugh Gaitskell had told his intimates how much he deplored Macmillan's premium bonds "making a casino" of his country. So inadequate safeguards about the good character of proprietors were placed in the original Act and the way would be open for the Krays to become owners of a good, posh, legitimate gaming club. Peter Rachman knew that the very best was up for grabs.

Esmeralda's Barn in Wilton Place, Knightsbridge, had seen the approaching legalization. The proprietor took swift action to secure the best manager, the best croupiers and the best clientele. On paper it was owned by a company called Hotel Investors Ltd, with some minor shareholders including the manager. But Rachman was an expert on the subject of hiding personal ownership behind a tangle of paper companies. He knew that in the end Hotel Investors Ltd was Stephen de Faye, author of a book called *Profitable Bar Management* and the real brains behind Esmeralda's Barn. And he knew that de Faye was not a man of violence or with violence at his beck and call. He was vulnerable to pressure.

Reggie was briefly out of prison awaiting the (unsuccessful) result of his appeal, when a retired naval commander called Drummond, who sometimes served as a liaison between the reputable and the disreputable, organized a meeting between de Faye, the Krays, and Payne and his business associate Freddie Gore. De Faye was shown that Payne knew the details of his business operations through and through, and offered the alternatives of selling out for £1,000 or... Well, the alternative wasn't specified, but the twins were there, looking amiably threatening. De Faye decided to sell his interest. Reggie went back to Wandsworth knowing that when he completed his sentence he would be part-owner of a really upmarket gaming club. Its frontage might be relatively dingy. American money had not yet shown how to give the air of glitz in the Playboy or Colony Clubs. But the address was Wilton Place and the Wilton thoroughfares led on into Belgravia. Vastly superior to Soho. The clientele for Esmeralda's Barn's legitimate gambling would include titled heads, up to and including the Duke of Kent. The little crooks from Bethnal Green had made it to the social big time.

From now on the business and bookkeeping side of the firm would have its own important and near-separate existence. Leslie Payne and Freddie Gore were the men with the briefcases. They made the deals, formed the companies and brought in the big money. They did not go out and do the hands-on work of collecting and negotiating pay-offs. A small red-haired man called Tommy Cowley oversaw that, an unthreatening figure who was often to be seen with the more violent mobsters in their favourite pubs where they menaced their enemies and sometimes started brawls. Cowley was a competent arithmetician who could be trusted to collect "pensions", a term the firm used for regular payments from victimized clubs, pubs, shops and dealers, as well as for the regular payments made out to the handful of full-time Kray criminal employees. Some of those paying pensions had been blackmailed into this extortion. Johnny Hutton, the car dealer who had introduced Leslie Payne to the twins, subsequently threatened to get out of line. As he had a record of having once gone to the police when in trouble, serious frighteners were put on him. He was tied to a chair and four of the firm's strong-arm men in balaclavas walked threateningly around him. Now the heavies knew his face but he didn't know theirs. So he'd never know where an attack came from if he did what the twins called "naughties". The victims paying pensions were always so intimidated or agreeable that there was never any risk of their offering violent resistance. Tommy Cowley and ex-boxer Billy Exley, too infirm to fight, could be used to pick up the cash.

Some victims were expected to cough up out of gratitude to the twins. The old villain Franny Daniels, survivor of the battle of Heathrow with the Flying Squad, paid regularly for the Mount Club in Mayfair. When a later employee, Fat Wally Garelick, acquired a mini-cab firm and eased himself away towards greater independence from the twins, he paid them £20 a week for the privilege. When the crunch came, this gratitude would prove less than skin-deep. The "friendly" contributors of weekly pensions were quick to sidestep the East End code.

Some club-owners actually invited the racketeers in as minders or providers of "security". It is this last group which has led protection racketeers, from that day to this, to pretend that their business is not, or at least not necessarily, illegal, and that it provides a useful service. George Mizel who ran the tiny Green Dragon Club in Green

Dragon Yard, Whitechapel, personally asked for permanent strong-arm minders after Kray employee Big Albert Donoghue tossed an irritating drunk out of the place. George had known Albert a long time. Albert and his thieving pals of the early days had done a few days at the races for him when he was a bookmaker working under Albert Dimes' aegis and with the support of the Krays had persuaded Dimes to stop enforcing his own collection for the "aways" being imposed on them at the racetrack. A private piece of work carried out for one of Mizel's Jewish friends, was casually assaulting and seriously injuring individual members of Mosley's British Union Party. An old Kray associate called Billy Maguire took a regular fee per Fascist hospitalized. Mizel later tried to have the work handed over to Albert Donoghue when he joined the firm after Maguire left. But Donoghue thought it was infra dig. He took the first payment and did nothing. This was a practice the twins favoured, taking payment for criminal work and then not delivering. Who was going to be in a position to complain?

Since some of the extorted pensions were based on a percentage of fluctuating weekly take, it was necessary for the collectors to multiply and divide in their heads. Mental arithmetic was not a skill that was widely shared among firm members. Cowley could do it. Billy Exley collected £50 weekly from the New Casanova Club, and another packet from the Starlight Club off Oxford Street. (In this instance the twins were, in the end, extorting money from a club they themselves part-owned. But their financial simplicity always reckoned tax-free wads of notes in the hand were a more real income than that generated by Payne and Gore and coming through detailed accounting procedures.)

After 1964 when he joined the firm, Donoghue provided support for Cowley and Exley in the hands-on financial work, and paid out the firm's wage packets. He reckoned that the little pensions he picked up here and there on his "milk run" of pubs and clubs brought in about £3,000 a week. Albert was primarily muscle, responsible to Reggie Kray, whereas Cowley was seen as Charlie's man. For Charlie, the third part-owner of Esmeralda's Barn, was on the business side of the firm, too. Provided, of course, he didn't know anything was illegal. Albert Donoghue makes no bones about the bite being put on the New Casanova Club, whose owner, Pauline Wallace, finally secured herself peace for the future by paying down a big lump sum in settlement of her protection before emigrating to a new life in America. But Charlie tells an elaborate tale of the twins' having employed Pauline to oversee their croupiers when she was down on her luck and Ronnie's lending her £800 without expecting any repayment when she was about to be evicted from her flat. This lovely lady, in Charlie's version, won the family's affection by sending Violet some beautiful flowers, and then insisted, over Ronnie's protests, that she would repay her debt in small weekly instalments. Hidden inside that story, however, is the fact that Ronnie really was spontaneously and recklessly generous. He would give large sums and extend massive credit to people without calculating the return. His instant charitability contributed to the failure of Kray Bros.

1960–1962 saw the decisive establishment of the firm on the footing by which it would be remembered. The Double R had been going downhill as the twins paid more attention to other ventures and it received its final comeuppance when the police prevented the renewal of its licence. Undeterred, the Krays started a new East End club, the Kentucky in Stepney. It was given a grand gala opening in 1962, with Barbara Windsor (starring in *Sparrers Can't Sing* in the West End at the time), as guest of honour. And it became the great stopping place for celebs out slumming in the East End.

The police were paying some peculiar attention to the Krays at this point, possibly hoping to nip in the bud what they saw as a potentially dangerous criminal family. Reggie had not been out of gaol more than a few weeks before he was picked up and charged with housebreaking. An elderly woman called Mrs Hertzberg identified him. To most of the underworld this seemed absurd. It was notorious that the Krays didn't go in for thieving. They ponced off thieves and dismissively wrote off habitual robbers as "jailbirds". The case was ultimately dismissed with costs to Reggie after Mrs Hertzberg withdrew her story in court. One would feel that justice was done in this case, were it not for the fact that Charlie Kray boasts that Mrs Hertzberg and her husband were offered a £500 contribution toward their emigration to Australia, provided her testimony changed and Reggie was acquitted. The corrupting bribe that was never paid once the satisfactory "result" had come through.

Still odder was the case when Ronnie and Charlie were pulled under the old "suss" laws and charged with loitering with intent. The notion of this pair of executive-class villains trying car door handles, as was alleged, really does seem absurd. One wouldn't often want to take the Krays' word against an observant detective constable's, but this time it seems one should. This was, after all, the period when Sir Joseph Simpson, the first Metropolitan Commissioner to have worked his way up from the beat, was proving his street-smarts by starting new crime-busting squads (drugs, vehicle theft, fraud, obscene publications, art and antiques) and strengthening the Flying Squad under its legendary commander Tommy Butler. Simpson's was one of the strongest voices in favour of legitimizing off-course betting and minimizing victimless crimes on the statute book. But as a corollary, he was not especially concerned about "noble cause" corruption, if it put villains behind bars. The famous phrase, "You can't touch me without the poppy," was allegedly used by Charlie Wilson, implying that he held part of the Great Train Robbery proceeds. It uses a slang term ("poppy" for money) apparently unknown to the underworld, but recurrent in confessional statements produced by Butler's interviewing. It is still felt by some in Scotland Yard that Butler was not above the "noble cause" corruption of "putting the verbals" on a suspect, always provided that it was absolutely certain he was the perpetrator.

At the bottom end of the scale, petty but quite serious and ignoble corruption went on. Many retired officers from the period remember with some distress their inability to deter colleagues from the "Marples marble" con trick, in which a policeman would stop a vehicle whose driver he didn't like the look of and politely suggest that his engine didn't seem to be running well. From under the bonnet the constable would then produce an oily ball-bearing and, telling the grateful driver that this had worked loose, sent him direct to the nearest garage to avoid writing off his motor. The still more grateful garage owner would carry out a completely imaginary "repair" and split the proceeds. The con was named for Macmillan's popular Minister of Transport, Ernie Marples. And it could not be eradicated for some time, because to some extent the police shared the code of the East End and were under immense peer pressure never to shop a colleague and so dent the solidarity that helped them survive their high-stress occupation.

D. C. Bartlett's evidence, that he saw the Kray brothers trying door handles while their friend Jimmy Kensit kept a lookout and hooted his car horn when the Law approached, may have been given because it seemed a good opportunity to rid the streets of two evil men (as the twins, though not Charlie, were increasingly being described). He may genuinely have mistaken what he saw. Or Ronnie and Charlie may have been up to something devious – though it would hardly have been stealing from cars.

Ronnie hired Nemone Lethbridge, at that time one of the highest-profile barristers in the country since she was blessed with youth, beauty and brains. A private detective rounded up eight witnesses to give the Krays an alibi and to testify that Kensit's car horn didn't work. Having got the charges dismissed, Miss Lethbridge was quietly complimenting herself when she realized that the witnesses had been fixed. However, she went for a congratulatory cup of tea at Vallance Road, but was shocked when Ronnie tried to stuff £500 into her pocket. He in turn was shocked when he took her outside, apologized very graciously for trying to pay her off in front of other people, and found that she still refused the back-hander.

It didn't stop him from briefing her again when he needed another important case handled, Frank Mitchel's trial for the attempted murder of the fellow convict he thought had grassed him up in Wandsworth. Ronnie paid for Frank to be fitted with a new suit for the trial and won the everlasting gratitude of "the Mad Axeman" for his acquittal. From now on, Mitchell believed that Ronnie Kray was his truest friend in the world and could fix absolutely anything.

With Esmeralda's Barn a sure-fire big money-spinner and cash from the long firms set up by Leslie Payne, the Krays were rich and living high on the hog. At this period, humorist Lee Gibbs wrote his Keeping Up With the Joneses books. It wasn't altogether clear whether they satirized the trendies of the late '50s and early '60s, or identified the "in" things that wannabe trendies needed to know. But they certainly offer a useful socio-cultural guide to the birth throes of the swinging sixties. Gibbs included "Jones types", like "Intellectual Jones", a Colin Wilson lookalike with hopes and pretensions rather than Colin's achievements. But "Criminal Jones" was something new. The likes of Darby Sabini had never tried to infiltrate society. Jack Spot and Billy Hill lived surprisingly modest family lives and kept their heads down, until their self-destructive competition for publicity in the sensational press at the ends of their careers. Brash "Criminal Jones", well-dressed, with gold rings and cuff-links, a big cigar and a confident charming manner, combined Frank Norman's success in marketing his crooked past to the serious press through books and plays, with the Krays' (and Nashes' and Richardsons') capacity to see and be seen in the clubs and watering-holes where the fashionable and rich gathered to prove that they were fashionable and rich.

The Krays fitted this world of new celebrity to perfection. They desperately wanted to be seen mingling with the best. A seemingly endless portrait gallery of photographs shows them in company with visiting celebs. Their need to be known gave Sammy Lederman a central place in their entourage. He is referred to so often in lists of the gang members surrounding the twins at pubs and clubs that it might be assumed he was another East End heavy. In fact he was a little old man only about 5ft 2ins tall, who would hardly have put the fear of God into anyone. His importance was that he was a former theatrical agent and road manager. Lita Roza had been one of his clients and the queen of the dancehalls of their adolescence was a celebrity the twins wanted to meet. The Clarke brothers, American tap dancers who had a studio in Tottenham Court Road – where Reg suggests he polished up his terpsichorean skills – were also introduced by Sammy. He constantly brought round the American singer Billy Daniels, whose hit with Old Black Magic lay in the past and whose repeated appearance in photos of Kray gatherings are marked by his evident wish to draw the camera's attention to himself. Which leads one to suspect Albert Donoghue was probably right to characterize him as a bit of a pain in the neck, whose devoted attendance at the Krays' parties whenever he was in London ultimately grew wearisome.

Dickie Morgan, the twins' first criminal friend from their army days, was their other great representative "up West". He was a trusted confidant, listed as one of the inner circle of the firm. But bringing important guests into the twins' orbit was one of his major functions. Contact with West End crime was important for an admirer of the US Mafia like Ronnie Kray, for Albert Dimes was still a powerful figure and "The King of the Points", who had inherited the old control of bookies at point-to-point meetings, also had the connections with Angelo Bruno that came down from the Sabini days. Ronnie Kray was a somewhat undiscriminating celebhunter. He would later have himself photographed with Johnny Nash entertaining Christine Keeler at the height of her notoriety. The presence of an Italian-American heavy called Eddie Pucci at the Krays' restaurant table was recorded for posterity simply because he came to London as Frank Sinatra's son's minder.

With his bobbing neck and high-pitched titter, Dickie Morgan would encourage the great and famous, or the minor but headlined, to come down to the Kentucky Club. Older American women stars were especially prone to enjoying the well-mannered twins' company quite genuinely. Sophie Tucker visited whenever she was in London. Judy Garland, entering the home straight of her long and losing struggle against drink and pills, became a valued friend. Was she indulging the Hollywood appetite for "gangster glamour"? If so, she showed considerable wisdom in attaching herself to the English rather than the American version. American mobsters regarded all women as broads. Sam Giancana crassly imagined he proved himself a great stud rather than a sexual cripple when he once raped Marilyn Monroe while she was drunk and incapacitated. The Kray firm might privately dismiss many of their women associates as slags, and distribute "hostesses" like candy to villains in hiding "on their toes". But they were mildly critical when Albert Donoghue exploited his romantic "gangster" status to his sexual advantage.

They were definitely not into raping guests and would have administered the severest of "spankings" had anyone taken such a liberty under cover of their good name.

It must be remembered that, taken in small doses at least, the twins had charisma. The word "charismatic" was, at that time, just moving away from its strict theological meaning of "freely bestowed by the grace of God without any necessary desert on the part of the recipient". Theology hardly ever used "charisma" as a noun. But it was now used voguishly to describe an indefinable impressive quality, akin to theatrical "presence". Ronnie's combination of Stematol and alcohol was making him increasingly heavy and sluggish, but he could still have charisma, just like Reggie. The twins' good manners, stylish dress sense and confidence, together with their flashes of sinister threat, made their presence instantly felt when they came into a room. Especially to those who knew they were "leading gangsters".

In fairness to their picture gallery of celebrity acquaintances, however, it should be observed that they were genuinely part of the boxing world. Former boxers themselves, they contributed generously to East End sports organizations offering training to youngsters. Their benevolence was lavishly recorded in the local press and justifies those local councillors who supported and accompanied the Bethnal Green philanthropic "businessmen". Local boxers – the retired Ted "Kid" Lewis, Terry Spinks, Terry Downes – had valid reasons for associating with them. A raft of past and present American champions, Joe Louis, Archie Moore, Sonny Liston, had every right to accept their hospitality and were certainly mingling with nobody whose criminality outweighed that in the background of American boxing. But Henry Cooper disdained further association with the Krays after having opened the gymnasium above the Double R Club, just as American singer Tony Bennett was not impressed when he was inveigled into their company.

For the very serious downside of London's '60s gangland was apparent in the Krays' conduct by 1962. In that year a petty crook called Lenny Hamilton offended the twins. Ronnie took fearsome revenge. He branded Lenny's face using a butcher's steel like a red hot poker, almost putting his eye out in the process. When Lenny's friend Albert Donoghue saw him he demanded to know who had done it, saying he would kill anyone who did the like to him. When he found it was the twins, he went and bearded them in their den at Vallance Road, taking a gun. The meeting passed off peacefully. It was quite apparent that Donoghue was ready for a shoot-out, but the twins were careful not to give him the excuse or opportunity to start one. Their casual attitude, "It's no use crying over spilt milk," was, astonishingly, shared by Hamilton, who subsequently went to work for them. Donoghue went to prison for a couple of years shortly afterwards, and there the matter might have rested had not someone reported back to the twins that he had said he would kill the people who brutalized Hamilton. Seven weeks after his release he heard that Limehouse Willey had been leaving messages all over the place that "the Other Two" (as gangland usually referred discreetly to the twins) wanted to see him. So he dropped in at the Crown and Anchor, a pub near the top end of Vallance Road where the twins often drank and made cash gifts to "aways" who had emerged from prison without the immediate means to set up in business again. His excuse would be that he hoped for a cash "loan". All the Kray henchmen moved away from him as he came in and while he was facing the bar, Reggie shot him in the leg. Turning round, Donoghue saw that the incompetent gunman was fiddling unnecessarily with the slide of a self-loading pistol, apparently thinking he was cocking it to shoot a second time. Albert advanced on Reggie, only to be seized from behind and hustled out of the pub by Ronnie. Colin "Dukey" Osbourne, the gang "armourer" who supplied and looked after guns for the firm (and who later liked it to be thought that he had deliberately supplied his flaky bosses with weapons that wouldn't work) was deputed with a man called "Bob the Painter" to take Donoghue to hospital. Donoghue insisted that he would look after himself, hoping that the bullet had gone right through and he could avoid having treatment. It was, however, still lodged in his ankle and he was forced to have it removed and his leg cased in plaster. And in that condition he visited the twins again, after another of their gofers, Bill Ackerman, had brought flowers to his hospital bed and taken money to his wife. And this time the twins, impressed by his "staunchness" in accepting the "spilt milk", offered him a job on the firm. He would get a regular pension and avoid the perpetual risk of imprisonment that went with his occupation of thieving. Donoghue accepted. He was being offered good remuneration and, as they said, far less risk of arrest and conviction. There was status in the underworld attached to being one of the Kray firm. So he swallowed his pride, concealed his resentment of the assault he had suffered and became Reggie's right-hand man, a collector of "pensions" from victimized club owners and one of the most valued and trusted members of the gang.

He was not alone in the extraordinary position of working for the twins after they had physically abused him. His own brother-in-law was in the same position, having had a broken glass ground in his face during a fight with the Krays in the Coach and Horses. Lennie Hamilton was another, as we have seen. A minor gang member, Charles "Nobby" Clarke, was shot in the leg in 1967, two years after he made offensive remarks about Reggie's wife that festered in Reggie's mind until he went round to Nobby's house in Newington Green, watched it all night, and then shot him in the morning. The twins apparently nursed the delusion that these men had been shown who was master and would now prove themselves faithful dogs. Time would prove that many of the dogs were only waiting for a chance to bite the savage hands that fed them.

One victim who did not accept employment from the Krays after enduring their violence was "Buller" Ward, who offended Reggie and had his face slashed in return. Ward plotted to throw a hand grenade through Reggie's ground-floor flat window when he lived in Stoke Newington, and he missed an opportunity to run him over in Green Dragon Yard. Donoghue had also contemplated the hand grenade through the window, but at the time when he was injured the twins' address was still Vallance Road and he decided against risking injury to their parents. Had he done so, the certainty was that his own parents and family would all have had to leave London in a hurry.

The violence was sometimes offered at the informal "parties" the twins would suddenly extemporize while drinking at pubs or clubs. The parties might be intended primarily to administer a salutary "spanking" to some unsuspecting invitee found guilty of "naughties". Jack "the Hat" McVitie was only the most extreme and best known victim of such condign punishment. Or the violence might suddenly erupt as something lit Ronnie's notoriously short (or Reggie's only slightly longer) fuse. The occasion when Ronnie found his overcoat on the floor and striped the man who had let it fall there to secure a place on the coat-rack has been well documented. The intensity of the fraternal "twin thing" could seem equally startling to the unprepared. One of the young men brought along to ornament the social scene never forgot an incident in which Reggie got into a fight at a party and was not acquitting himself successfully. Whereupon Ronnie, reverting to the "raging bull", weighed in, and had to be dragged off Reggie's assailant before he maimed or killed him. His apologetic response to those who restrained him was memorable. "But he's my brother," he pleaded, with sincere tears standing in his eyes.

While Reggie was in prison, Ronnie had moved from Vallance Road to a flat in Chelsea and become part of the incipient King's Road "scene". When Reggie emerged, it transpired that he had fallen passionately in love with beautiful 16-year-old Frances Shea from Hoxton. Ronnie did not approve. Love broke things up. Domesticity was bad for mateyness, let alone fraternally twinned mutual identity. The two quarrelled fiercely. Ronnie gave up his Chelsea flat, and after spending a few weeks living in a caravan, bought the flat in Cedra Court, Cazenove Road. This handsome block of Bauhaus style "mansion flats" has been variously located by different writers, one putting it as far adrift as Walthamstow. The difficulty is that it lies where three former boroughs almost abut. Cazenove Road runs between Upper Clapton Road (at the end where the Krays lived) and the point where Stoke Newington High Street becomes Stamford Hill. So it is liable to be described as being in Stoke Newington, Stamford Hill or Clapton.

It was a good address; after his marriage Reggie took another flat in the same block. One of the best known photographs of the twins shows them striding out of Cedra Court, their long narrow lapels and low buttons making their fashionable suit jackets look just a little short by the standards of the next couple of decades. Fort Vallance continued to be the firm's business headquarters, where the twins met every morning and received reports from grateful former "aways" about which thieves in their areas were worth poncing off; sent out collectors to pick up the "pensions"; and held court to decide who had been guilty of "naughties". The clubs and pubs they owned or controlled or dominated were locations for the start of the evening's entertainment. And from drinking in the West End or at the Kentucky Club or the Regency in Stoke Newington, the party would move on to Cedra Court.

Many of Ronnie's parties there were rumoured to be, or to lead to, homosexual orgies. Allowing for exaggeration, it is probably better to describe them as "encounters", where some of the pretty boys Ron loved to have around him might have made closer acquaintance with some of the more respectable upmarket gay acquaintances he also liked to entertain. One mixed result of the criminalization of homosexuality was that it brought together people from all walks of life, who would not otherwise have met. For the most part it was a wholly good thing. It was beneficial in the broad sense that somebody as influential as E. M. Forster should have close personal knowledge of the life of a London bobby on the beat, at a time when most of the educated classes saw a policeman as a piece of street furniture that might become a nuisance to motorists. It is probable that homosexual men still have the advantage of a wider and more socially varied circle of friendship than their heterosexual confreres. (Lesbians, by contrast, are more prone to restrict themselves to the social circles of their birth, education and occupation.)

But illegality had its serious downside. For Oscar Wilde, the term "rent boy" was synonymous with "blackmailer". Nobody would dare to blackmail Ronnie Kray. But his criminality made him an inappropriate associate for the members of the business world and the upper echelons of the criminal justice system who were compelled by the absurdity of that system to conduct their sex lives out-side the law. We are not aware of any policemen or judges who put their reputations at risk in Ronnie's hands. But through the freema-sonry of homosexuality he did become intimate with two well-known and thoroughly irresponsible legislators.

Tom Driberg was one of the most preposterous figures of his gen-eration. A champagne socialist par excellence, he was a journalist who started by writing gossip columns for Lord Beaverbrook. Once in Parliament he abused his position and his professed beliefs by becoming a double agent for the British and Russian secret services. It is impossible to say where he felt his final loyalties lay, but he exploited the position lavishly for his personal ends. One of the most enthusiastic "cottaging" homosexuals of his time, he was con-stantly in danger of being arrested in public lavatories. If he could-n't overawe a patrolling officer with his membership of the House of Commons, he would produce identification and claim to be engaged on a secret service operation. His malarkey let down every-one who held the serious ideals he professed and made ridiculous. Left-wing MPs of unimpeachable reputation like Fenner Brockway and Leslie Hale suffered the suspicions of Special Branch because the malign figure of Driberg purported to share their wish to see the Cold War ended by the establishment of friendlier relations with the Soviet Union. Naive and honourable Labour party chiefs who were by no means fellow travellers – notably Barbara Castle and Michael Foot – looked foolish when they cited Tom Driberg as a courageous example of a man whose sexual orientation had put him in constant and unnecessary danger because of the illiberality of the law. Actually it was Driberg who put himself in danger and made himself completely unemployable in any government by reckless misbehaviour that would have contravened public decency under any circumstances. And while people like me who write books about villains may be seen to deserve what we get told, John Pearson might have been forgiven for expecting something a little better than barefaced lies about being an innocent MP for Barking – with a remote constituency responsibility for the Krays – when he wanted to know why Tom Driberg was at Reggie Kray's wedding and other such disreputable Kray-infested social functions.

The other legislator swept into the twins' toils was from the other side of the political fence. Bob Boothby was one of the buccaneering bounders who enliven Tory politics from time to time. A charmer and a fine orator, he had once been seen as a future leader of the party and probable Prime Minister, until a financial scandal clouded his reputation and Churchill was compelled to halt the rising career of this young and promising supporter.

Relegated to the back benches as a "knight of the shires", Sir Robert Boothby retained public popularity as one of the regular broadcasters on BBC Radio's "Brains Trust". His rich and resonant voice was perfect for radio. He had a gift for the popular soundbite before the term was invented. He was an influential public figure. By the time he drifted into the Krays' ken he had been kicked upstairs to the House of Lords. As the long-term lover of Harold Macmillan's wife, Lady Dorothy, he had no hope of being acceptable to the party leadership. Indeed, in the moral climate of the times, that relationship alone would have ruined him in the eyes of the public had it become known. He was not a man who could afford a scandal. Whereas Driberg ultimately told all (or as much of it as could be passed off as harmless mischief) in his autobiography, Boothby misled his official biographer Robert Rhodes James into believing that he was profoundly (if very promiscuously) heterosexual, and any rumours to the contrary were bosh.

In fact he was bisexual. The pleasure he took in Ronnie Kray's company was a shared interest in good-looking young men. And he didn't let the infra dig quality of the Krays as companions, or the dangers of scandal, stand in his way. And so he came to play the major part in bringing the twins to national attention.

They were at the height of their power in the mid-1960s. This was the period when Lord Howard of Effingham (later the Earl of Effingham) graced their headed notepaper as a member of the directorial board of Esmeralda's Barn. Ronnie lent money to the impecunious peer, addressed him as "Mowbray" (his forename), and denied having made the simple joke, "Let Effie make the effing tea". Although it is sometimes suggested that the twins enjoyed 14 years of criminal success before the police could do anything about them, this places their position of power too early in time. Prior to their ownership of Esmeralda's Barn they were petty protection racketeers with control of or interests in some grubby downmarket spielers. From the acquisition of Esmeralda's Barn to their downfall was just seven years. And it was rocky at the top.

Boothby first gave Ronnie national prominence in 1964. He let Ronnie bring round a photographer to his flat to snap a set of those "me and a celeb" pictures that gave the twins such satisfaction. The photographer took a reel of film showing Boothby and Ronnie standing and talking, or sitting on a settee, sometimes accompanied by young Leslie Holt, who looked more like one of Ronnie's chosen pretty boy companions than the young business-man he was described as. In July the photographer suddenly offered these photographs to the *Mirror*. The interest of the story, of course, was Boothby. A headline, RONNY KRAY ON SETTEE WITH FAMOUS PEER, would have evoked the response "Ronnie Who?" everywhere except Bow and Bethnal Green. But the Mirror played its cards very cautiously and didn't name anyone at all. The photographer had changed his mind the day after delivering the pictures and tried to reclaim them. Then he tried to have an injunction brought against the *Mirror*'s publishing them. The paper's crime correspondent, Norman Lucas, had excellent sources of information about the twins and their doings. The paper published a teasing article about the picture they "dared not publish" which showed a well-known peer and a gangster on a sofa together. Many people misread between the lines that this was a compromising snapshot of homosexual lovers. And, sending their barely existent "dossier" to Scotland Yard, the *Mirror* announced that Sir Joseph Simpson the Metropolitan Commissioner was investigating the questionable links between the two unnamed men.

Agitation spread in several directions. Sir Joseph denied that he was authorizing a witch-hunt against titled homosexuals – something that had been unhappily attempted ten years earlier under Sir John Nott-Bower, probably at the instigation of the Director of

Public Prosecutions. He did say he was having the gangster's doings investigated.

Colonel Marcus Lipton, MP for Brixton, placed one of the news-making parliamentary questions that always made his presence on the back benches interesting. Was the Home Secretary, he wondered, aware of the alarming increase of "protection racketeering" in London?

Boothby quickly got in touch with Arnold Goodman who was Harold Wilson's solicitor and the outstanding establishment "Mr Fixit" of the day. The *Mirror's* piece had been carefully written and no immediately obvious libel suit lay. But London society had little doubt who was intended. Boothby had been confronted by three MPs and a fellow peer, all warning him that the town was seething with stories of the "Mayfair parties" at which he had supposedly been seen with the "King of the Underworld" and other men of dubious sexual orientation including a couple of clergymen. *Der Spiegel* in West Germany, undeterred by British libel law, had published Boothby's name, as "Lord Bobby".

With the help of Goodman and the Labour Lord Chancellor, Gerald Gardiner, Boothby grasped the nettle. He and Ronnie authorized the *Daily Express* to publish one of the innocuous pictures that did not include Holt. Boothby signed a carefully drafted letter to *The Times* stating that he was the peer in question and he had met the person in question, accompanied by two other men, in the same way that he met a lot of other people. They were discussing a business proposition that seemed to him important. He had acceded to the request that photographs be taken. He had only later learned that the man had a criminal record. He had met the so-called "King of the Underworld" no more than two or at most three times. He was not a homosexual. He hadn't been to a party in Mayfair for years.

And the denial worked. The *Mirror* agreed to pay Boothby £40,000 in compensation for his embarrassment and he gave £5,000 of it to King Edward VII Hospital. The general public impression was that Boothby had been naive, but it was all a storm in a teacup (And, indeed, the general impression was correct). If

Ronnie Kray had any sense, he would have been thankful that his name had not been mentioned. Ronnie was not sensible. He tried to see whether he could extract some compensation from the *Mirror*. He failed. He received a public apology, but unlike Boothby's it was not signed personally by Cecil Harmsworth King, the chairman of *Mirror* Group Newspapers. And it was not accompanied by cash.

Publicity inevitably stirred Scotland Yard into action. Area Detective Superintendent Fred Gerrard ordered Detective Inspector Leonard "Nipper" Read to form a team around Commercial Street Police Station and get the Krays. Many of the young "aides to detectives" on the team (uniformed officers given a probationary start in the CID) had never heard the name Kray. Ronnie was not, whatever he fondly imagined, a new Darby Sabini.

Gerrard and Read were a contrasting pair, Gerrard an enthusiastic optimist who expected to come through all his cases with flying colours, Read a more cautious and dogged worker who learned from every setback. Read, too, was prepared to use a minimal version of old-fashioned disguise when "keeping obbo". His nickname "Nipper" is usually ascribed to his "nippiness" in the ring when he was a young boxer. It may equally have related to his small, slight stature. He was allowed into the Met by a sympathetic sergeant who noted that he was below the required minimum height (5ft 8ins) but who accepted his optimistic claim to be "still growing". It was a prescient and valuable piece of rule-bending. Detectives on the short side have always been suitable candidates for disguised surveillance and observation. And Read got to know his enemy by putting on a flat cap and shabby raincoat, buying an evening paper with the racing results, and reading it over a pint of half-consumed beer in the empty Grave Maurice. And so he witnessed Reggie's flamboyant entry. First "Duke" Osborne came into the pub, his hand holding what seemed to be a gun in his pocket. He checked the place out, then signalled for two minders to shepherd Ronnie from his car across the broad pavement and to his commanding banquette. Ronnie's immensely long overcoat suggested conscious imitation of Capone. Drinks were brought for him and the minders withdrew discreetly to adjacent banquettes, leaving him to conduct private business with whomsoever he chose. Read did not see two other details that would later become distinctive features of the Krays' pub gatherings: the pint mug on the bar into which all those who were reasonably flush of cash would stuff ten pound notes, so that no drinker ever had to pay for his order and those who were skint were not embarrassed; and the occasional presence of local off-duty policemen, who would slip in and were always welcome to pick up a free drink. Their presence was useful to the twins because they reinforced the legend that they had the police in their pockets and were untouchable. Gerrard and Read were well aware of this and believed that the twins made great play with forged "witness statements" on stolen or forged Scotland Yard headed paper to persuade their followers that they had access to confidential police documents and would always know if anyone grassed. Intelligent and well-informed gang members like Albert Donoghue thought the twins were not deceiving their followers: they really did have contacts with access to confidential records. But Donoghue was also aware that nothing ever came of nothing and man did not live by bread alone. Money on its own would not keep bent coppers sweet, they had to have "bodies" as well. The wholesale corruption of the Obscene Publications Squad meant that unwanted rivals of Frank Mifsud and Bernie Silver were arrested and convicted. Alec Eist's career was studded with the successful arrests of all those who did not pay him off and were shopped by those who did. Donoghue had no doubt that any association between the twins and the police entailed a two-way exchange of information.

Gerrard and Read made inroads into a number of the long firms that were supplying much of the Krays' income at the time. But the twins and Leslie Payne were well distanced from these activities by dummy companies and cut-outs. The only hope of catching the twins as extortionists rested on a complaint received from Hew Cargill McCowan.

This upper-class homosexual was well known to Marylebone police to whom he often brought complaints about rent boys who stole things from his flat off Oxford Street when he took them home. Now he had reported that the Krays were threatening him.

A young man called Sidney Thomas Vaughan had been employed to manage the Hideaway Club in Gerrard Street, Soho, whose owners included Albert Dimes and Mad Frankie Fraser. In the autumn of 1964 they lost interest, and the club closed temporarily. At Vaughan's twenty-first birthday party in October, McCowan met a Kray associate called Johnny Francis and it was agreed that McCowan would finance the club's redecoration and re-opening, paying a regular retainer to Francis's company and installing Vaughan as manager. Pretty quickly he was recommended to accept the Krays' protection as "security". When he declined, Mad Teddy Smith turned up drunk and caused a bit of a disturbance, smashing a few things in the club. And very swiftly the twins invited McCowan to a meet at the Grave Maurice and pointed out that they could have prevented such an occurrence. They wanted 20% of takings, rising to 30%, rising to 50%. Indeed, they really wanted the entire 50% as soon as possible.

McCowan and Vaughan made statements that clearly convicted the twins of extortion. Read had them arrested in the Glenrae Hotel in Seven Sisters Road, an establishment they had taken over as a Kray firm centre, installing Billy Exley and Sammy Lederman in its basement club as barmen and "Tommy the Bear" as bouncer. On being arrested, Ronnie said, "It's taken you long enough. This is all down to the *Mirror*. It was the same with Spotty, he was framed". So the twins had been anticipating serious police attention ever since Boothby lifted the stone under which they crawled. And despite Ronnie's later claim that they always intended to dethrone Jack Spot, they still saw him as a significant role model (unaware that Read now visited the ex-ganglord for information).

Mrs Phoebe Wood, landlady of the Glenrae, was almost hysterical with gratitude that the twins had been taken off her back and she could return to running a clean, straight hotel for non-criminal guests. Read thought her too distraught to give a statement then and there, and received his first object lesson in the firm's ability to intimidate witnesses. When she turned up the following day she was completely composed and declined to say anything incriminating about the villains who had taken over her business. Nobody, of course, thought the twins would kill her. They weren't into killing people yet. But nobody forgot what had happened to Barbara Ibbotson at the hands of men who purported to protect weak and helpless women.

Before the case was heard, Lord Boothby behaved as Lord Booby. The twins started a prolonged action to win themselves bail. This wound its way through the courts, ending with a long and complex judgement from the Lord Chancellor which said, in effect, that while the courts were sitting, habeas corpus did not mean defendants could shop around from one judge to another trying to get themselves out of custodial remand. Regina vs Kray, Kray and Smith remains the textbook case on this point of law. By today's standard, when it normally takes more than a year for a serious case to reach court, the twins had suffered very little inconvenience. But things moved faster in the 1960s and on 13 February Boothby raised their case in the House of Lords, asking how long the government intended them to be kept without trial. The moment their lordships realized that old Bob was using his position to try and intervene on the Krays' behalf, the most extraordinary uproar broke out. The House of Lords normally prides itself on the calm and deliberative quality of its debate, unlike the House of Commons where members plume themselves on behaving like unruly schoolboys. But Boothby was now literally shouted down. Most of his speech was unheard and reporters were unable to get it down. It was quite clear that their lordships thought that Boothby was making a shameless and disreputable attempt to use them on behalf of the underworld, and they were simply not having it. Boothby looked corrupt rather than naive now. For the Home Office, Lord Stonham explained the obvious: the arrest of the Krays was no business of government's and the legislature had no power to intervene in a matter before the courts while it was sub judice. And the Leader of the House, Lord Longford, delivered a stinging rebuke, concluding, "I think the noble lord will regret that intervention when he comes to read it in cold blood".

Boothby's political judgement was pretty wonky that year. His contribution to Lord Arran's homosexual law reform proposal in the summer amounted to an admission that a young policeman had once recognized him and warned him against going cottaging in a public urinal where plain clothes officers were waiting. But it was a short speech and passed unnoticed on a day when Field Marshal Lord Montgomery's tirade against "perversion" dominated the news.

Manny Frede, clerk to the solicitors Sampson and Co, now made his first prominent appearance, acting on behalf of "the firm". As a clerk, he could not be struck off and so could sail closer to the wind than an articled solicitor. He received, from an ex-policeman, a useful statement that would win the twins' acquittal. The former officer had observed "Tommy the Bear" shepherding Sidney Vaughan into Fort Vallance. He and the new priest of St Matthew's church, Mr Foster, had quickly followed and in their presence Vaughan made a statement that effectively retracted the information he had given the police and claimed that he was afraid of forfeiting the £40 a week that McCowan paid him if he told "the truth" about the twins' innocence. When the case was heard, the twins enjoyed the apparently unimpeachable testimony of a priest and a former police officer, both suggesting that McCowan was bribing Vaughan to frame them. McCowan was made to look dodgy by the revelation of his homosexual past and the fact that he had brought four blackmail charges against rent boys. The jury could not agree and a second trial followed.

This time the judge stopped the hearing. Vaughan's original statement was not allowed in evidence and McCowan's word alone did not constitute a safe case against the Krays and Smith (Francis had fled abroad). But the judge was clearly not convinced of their innocence. Prosecuting counsel had wondered pertinently why the information the ex-police officer supplied to the defence had not been given to the police at the same time. The judge refused the twins their legal costs, pointing to the hung jury at the first trial. McCowan and the landlord, Gilbert Francis, sold the club to the twins that afternoon and the renamed El Morocco became their toehold in Soho.

This was their moment of triumph, when they returned to a flamboyant welcome in Vallance Road and distinguished themselves by their modest acceptance of congratulations. The local press exulted in the "sporting brothers" who had been cleared of the distressing allegations and the famous picture of Ronnie, Reggie and Charlie making their threefold crossed handshake was taken. The old villain Arthur Harding came out of retirement to have himself photographed with the new generation. Reggie went on to marry Frances Shea, their white wedding a great East End occasion at which fashionable photographer David Bailey took the pictures. If they really did have good inside contacts in Scotland Yard, they would have known that Gerrard's superior, the powerful Commander Ernie Millen, had been opposed to the protracted pursuit of their firm, which he may have felt caused uncomfortable stirrings among his own network of informants. Read was promoted and shifted to West End Central with a new brief. Now the twins felt they were untouchable.

Actually, this was almost the worst thing that could have happened to them. Their raised standing gave them false confidence at a time when a business failure and a highly publicised murder might have warned them that their house was built on shifting sands.

The business failure was that venture over which Boothby claimed Ronnie approached him. It had been put before them by Ernest Shinwell, son of the MP Emmanuel. Manny Shinwell's was just the sort of big name the twins loved. Unpopular as Attlee's Minister of Fuel and Power during the disastrously hard winter of 1947–48, he was well on his way to great popularity as the nonagenarian Father of the House of Commons and sole survivor of the glory days when Labour declared, "It's our turn now!" and created the Welfare State. His son Ernest has been described by Nipper Read as a confidence trickster and the project he put to the twins as a scam.

Scam or risky venture, it appealed to Leslie Payne. Ernest Shinwell offered an introduction to members of the Nigerian government who wanted to erect a housing project outside the city of Enugu. Whoever put up the capital for this could expect to reap a couple of million pounds. Payne the Brain liked it, though he ought to have calculated that this was a risky long-term venture and the twins had already shown themselves too impatient for cash to let his profitable long firms grow to full fruition. Ronnie met Manny Shinwell at the House of Commons and with his blessing went out to Nigeria where he saw the Minister of Health and was given red carpet treatment by the government. He came home convinced that he was set to become a great man in West Africa and sent Payne, Gore, Charlie and a Canadian associate, Gordon Anderson, to further the business.

Which promptly went pear-shaped. Payne and Gore had accepted £5,000 from a Nigerian contractor who now wanted his money returned. They hadn't got it (The twins had withdrawn half the £10,000 from the GAS – Great African Safari – bank account set up to finance the business). Payne and Gore were arrested and thrown into prison. Ronnie had to wire £5,000 to Charlie to secure their release. The Great African Safarists realized they had been Ernest Shinwell's last hope in an undertaking that had been turned down flat by everyone else he had approached. And the twins lost confidence in Leslie Payne.

That might not have mattered if, as Ronnie boasted, they really were as brainy themselves. But they weren't. They still needed financial advisers and business associates who could bring them introductions. And they started their fateful association with the Americans Allan Bruce Cooper, "Mr ABC", and Joe Kaufman.

The murder that now took place was nothing to do with them. But it stirred up a hornets' nest of police interest in East London crime that outweighed the interest in them, but ultimately ensnared the firm.

Nobody who read, watched or listened to the news in early 1965 could have doubted that something very serious had happened to Thomas "Ginger" Marks. The police broadcast repeated appeals for information about the whereabouts of this East London "car dealer", accompanied on television by photographs. It was transparently obvious that Mr Marks dealt in something more than used cars and that the police feared he had come to an untimely end. But the true story did not become public until 1975 and was not given first-hand confirmation until 1997.

On 2 January 1965, the police were told that Ginger Marks' wife had received an anonymous telephone tip-off that Ginger had been shot in Cheshire Street. A visit to the street proved that there had certainly been a shooting. There were bloodstains in the road and on the pavement, a recent bullet pock in a wall, and spent bullets and a cartridge case. People in the Carpenters Arms pub had heard shots. A visit to Ginger's wife suggested that she had received more than a telephone tip-off, since the missing man's spectacles were at his house and he would not have gone out without them.

The immediate police fear was that this heralded the start of a gang war. There had not been one in London since the days of Hubby Distleman and Babe Mancini (The threatened war between Jack Spot and Billy Hill had never proceeded further than the battle of Frith Street and the cutting of Spot). But it was known that some seriously dangerous men were now organized into territorial gangs Above all things the police did not want the streets of London to become the scenes of internecine shootouts. So there was heavy pressure on the underworld.

After intensive questioning, something akin to the truth began to emerge. Ginger had been overseeing the burglary of a jeweller's in nearby Bethnal Green Road with his friend George "Jimmy" Evans. While other members of the gang did the actual break-in, George and Ginger were on their own round the corner, either watching television or keeping a lookout. When they started to walk along St Matthews Road towards Cheshire Street, a parked car pulled out and followed them. When they turned into Cheshire Street, someone in the car called out, "Come here, Ginger. I want you." Ginger turned back and was shot dead. Evans hid under a lorry and saw the men in the car throw the body in the back and drive away east. He recovered Ginger's hat and glasses and took them to Mrs Marks with the sad news.

The police thought this account was wrong. They believed the voice had not said, "Come here Ginger" but "Come here, Jimmy", Ginger had misheard and gone back to his death.

The incident was not the outcome of criminal competition. It was a curious kind of domestic revenge. Jimmy Evans' wife had been having an affair with Freddie Foreman's brother George. By normal underworld ethics, Jimmy was entitled to exact savage revenge. Ginger Marks had accompanied him to George Foreman's home and, giving a false name, knocked on the door to establish that he was out. The two removed the landing light-bulb, waited for Foreman in the dark, and when he came home, Evans shot him in the groin at point-blank range with a sawn-off double-barrelled shotgun. Though he nearly killed George, Evans' basic intention (which almost succeeded) was to emasculate him. George, respecting the code of the East End, would not admit to the police that he recognized his assailant. But he told his brother Freddie.

Many villains would have said that George Foreman got what he deserved. But Freddie notes in justification of his brother that the love between George and Mrs Evans proved genuine and resulted in a 30-year marriage. And Freddie is consistent. As we have said, he has not joined the chorus of abuse heaped on Dolly Kray for falling in love with George Ince and leaving Charlie.

Evans came under suspicion of Ginger Marks' murder. He was arrested for a second attempt to rob the jeweller's shop, but got off. He was charged with the attempted murder of George Foreman, but also got off. He wrote an article for the *News of the World* denying his involvement in either crime and saying he did not know who Ginger's murderers were. Then, in 1975, he found himself in Parkhurst serving seven years for manslaughter, where Alf Gerard was also imprisoned. You will remember that Freddie Foreman characterized this associate as "an animal". It is, perhaps, unsurprising that Evans feared for his life when he heard that Alfie was still interested in completing the unfinished business in Cheshire Street. He promptly told the truth about Ginger's murder and Foreman and Gerard, who had fired the shots, went on trial along with Jerry Callaghan and Ronnie Everett, who were said by Evans to have been in the car.

Everett was quickly dismissed from the case, as Evans' belief that he had seen him refuelling at a garage that night was upset by evidence that the garage was closed at the stated time. And the judge stopped the trial when it became clear that Evans' testimony was the only evidence against the men. It would be legally unsafe to rely on the word of a man who had been saying for ten years that he did not recognize the killers in the car. Not that the judge disbelieved his new story. He pointedly said that the police were quite right to bring the case, which he would have allowed to go forward had the Scottish verdict "Not Proven" been an option for the jury to consider.

When Freddie confirmed the truth of Evans story in 1997 (at least insofar as he and the dead Alf Gerard were concerned), he made it clear that the police had made only one mistake. He had not, as they thought, said, "Come here, Jimmy." He had summoned Ginger, whom he had every intention of killing as well as Evans. His only regret was that he had not succeeded in killing Evans at the same time.

Now the Krays, friendly with both Evans and Foreman, refused to be drawn into this quarrel when Evans came to them. But they noted Foreman's skill in disposing of the body and the numerous rumours that raced around London as to its whereabouts. (In Hackney Marshes...in the concrete of Chiswick Flyover...burned in an incinerator...). Freddie was their friend and would ultimately be called upon to dispose of two bodies that were surplus to their requirements.

The police, meanwhile, had Foreman marked down as one of the most dangerous men in London. When the twins' flamboyance gave the law a chance to have Freddie on a major charge, they jumped at the opportunity.

Over the next couple of years Reggie's love and marriage seriously upset the profound but tempestuous "twin thing". No individual can be blamed for the tragedy that struck the Krays and the Sheas. God created sexual attraction that can be a completely overwhelming and irrational passion. God allowed women to feel sexual attraction to power and wealth. God created homosexuals with a mistrust of heterosexual love. These three things destroyed the happiness of several people.

Reggie had fallen helplessly in love with 16-year-old Frances Shea when he came out of prison. She was outstandingly pretty in the style of the times, her hair slightly bouffant, her eyes heavily made up in the post-Cleopatra fashion. If only then or later she had been able to see that ten years' or more difference in their ages made Reggie too old for her, or that he was too fixed in ways she would never grow into, a lot of suffering would have been avoided.

But Frances was only self-aware enough to say she was too young to marry just yet. She was dazzled by the courtship of the successful local "businessman" whose picture was always in the papers, who drove to her house in big new cars and gave her expensive presents, whose manners toward her parents were always perfect. Those beautiful manners Violet and Charles had instilled in their boys helped Reggie in winning him the Shea parents' approval, at first. He wasn't a cradle-snatcher, he was willing to wait. But by the time Frances hazily grasped that this was a mistake, it was too late. She was seen as Reggie Kray's girl and no local boy was prepared to cross that line.

Ronnie was deeply upset by his twin's now deep and exclusive relationship. He took every opportunity to slag off Frances behind her back, though when he finally met her he was gracious and courteous to her face. The mismatch stumbled towards what, with hindsight, seems its inevitable conclusion. The big wedding when Frances was 18 was followed by a jet-setting honeymoon on which she expressed her delight in the Grand Tour sights of antiquity and the visit to La Scala in Milan to see *Madame Butterfly*, though neither she nor Reggie really enjoyed Athens. Conjugal life back at home began in a rented flat off Lancaster Gate, then in a Cedra Court flat below Ronnie's. Frances learned that a top gangster's wife was expected to look beautiful and be happy on a pedestal, sitting at home doing nothing. She was prohibited from working – that would suggest Reggie could not keep her. She did not much enjoy evenings out in the pubs and clubs. Of the firm's regular members, only Mad Teddy Smith could make conversation she enjoyed. She did not like the noise of Ronnie's parties floating down from upstairs. And she found Ronnie sinister and frightening as he gave her his reptilian smile through gold-rimmed spectacles and asked with condescending courtesy how she was. After eight weeks

Frances went back to her parents.

For the next two years the marriage was a half-on, half-off affair. Reggie was reduced to standing outside the Shea house and talking to Frances through her bedroom window. Attempts to revive marital life in Cedra Court failed. Frances made an unsuccessful suicide attempt. And then a successful one, with an overdose of sleeping pills in 1967. The Sheas bitterly blamed the Krays for making her unhappy. Reggie bitterly blamed the Sheas for putting her in a "tug-of-love". They were unfair to each other. Nobody had ever wished Frances anything but good. But nobody knew how to disentangle Reggie from his intense passion. Nobody could be sure that his temper would not rebound lethally on anyone who helped Frances get right away from him. And where could she go in any case? Hoxton was her home and Hoxton was Kray territory. She was in no way equipped to start a new life anywhere else.

Fellow ganglanders saw the tragedy approaching but were helpless. Albert Donoghue observed Frances' dismay at the presence of a host of broken-nosed scar-faced villains among her wedding guests. She told him that she had been unhappy on her honeymoon. What could he do? Reggie wouldn't have listened to him. And not even womanizing Albert would have the temerity to cuckold the heterosexual twin, even had not the code of the East End generally proscribed messing about with a fellow crook's wife.

Albert was also asked by Reggie for advice on satisfying lovemaking. He concluded that Reggie, like Tristram Shandy's Uncle Toby, didn't "know the right end from the wrong end of a woman". He was obviously wrong. Reggie contracted a dose of urethritis at one point (obviously not from Frances) and on his final arrest was in bed with a young hostess he had picked up at a club. Albert was really hearing the very sad anxieties of a man who was desperately in love, yet whose unhappy wife was quite unresponsive to his physical advances and gave her mother the impression that she was still a virgin.

These stresses and strains did nothing to encourage easy running of the firm. Reggie was unable to control or even keep an adequate eye on Ronnie. "The Colonel's" freehanded generosity started to damage their flagship club, Esmeralda's Barn. Ronnie felt free to pick up large wads of cash from the takings whenever he felt inclined, or to extend unlimited credit to gamblers whose bouncing cheques eroded the profits. These practices started making a hugely profitable enterprise into a loss-making one. Tony Mancini, the manager, decided to cut his losses, abandoned his investment and started a new club elsewhere. The bulk of the good class, high-rolling gamblers went with him, encouraged by the twins' propensity to start inappropriate additional ventures on the premises, like a lesbian-flavoured disco in the basement. With unpaid taxes piling up, the club finally went into liquidation. The twins were stupidly sure this didn't matter. They believed they had secured their position in the lucrative world of West End gambling and imagined they were recognized associates of American syndicated crime.

This delusion was occasioned by the opening of "George Raft's" Colony Club. Meyer Lansky saw the rich opportunities in London gambling and with Raft as a front man set up the Colony Club to milk suckers and launder money. The twins felt that as native representatives of organized crime they were the right people to supply security (or protection) to this first important entry of syndicated American crime on British shores. The idea of Reggie and Ronny shaking down Lansky is hilarious. This was the Jewish gang leader who joined Lucky Luciano in the 1920s to override the ethnic exclusivism of New York's "Mustache Petes", assassinate the old and powerful "bosses of all bosses" and build up the massive empire of cose nostre (each single cosa nostra actually being one of the interconnected crime "families"). This was the man who controlled the finances of the largest criminal enterprise in the world, the man who had bankrolled Bugsy Siegel to start Las Vegas and authorized his old friend's murder when he failed to deliver on the dream in the desert. Had the corrupt President Batista not been overthrown by Fidel Castro in 1959, Havana would have been Lansky's personal fiefdom. Lansky, who was able to persuade the Israeli government that he was a desirable resident for the ending of his days, would never have blinked at London's little bullies, whose reckless claim that they could put 200 armed men on the streets was never tested.

Yet the Colony Club agreed to pay the Krays £3,000 a year. Why? Albert Donoghue, who collected it for them in quarterly tranches, was sure he knew. The Colony Club intended to be the smoothest and most stylish casino in Mayfair. The sort of roughnecks and riffraff who appeared with the Kray entourage would frighten off the serious punters as they had frightened them away from Esmeralda's Barn. The Krays were being paid to keep their and their friends' ugly faces out of the Colony Club!

They swallowed the insult, which the suavely tactful George Raft allowed them to describe as an alliance with the big American syndicated criminals if they wished. Raft, once a reasonably popular dancer and film star, had reverted to being a gangsters' hanger-on as he had been in his New York adolescence. He had fronted for the mobs in Cuba where journalists had been delighted by his increasingly desolate post-revolutionary appearance, touting for trade outside his virtually abandoned casino before Castro got round to kicking him out. After three years in England, he would be equally ignominiously despatched back across the Atlantic, as the Labour government tightened the inadequate controls over casinos and indicated that Raft and "his" manager Dino Cellini were personae non gratae. Raft made a whingeing appearance on British television, wondering what on earth the Brits had against Lansky, Bruno and the other top mobsters. "It's not like these guys are Communists," he offered, blithely unaware that many of his audience would know at least one present or former card-carrying member of the Communist Party of Great Britain whom they liked or admired.

Raft may have been a fading has-been, but he had the grace, charm and style of an experienced actor and hoofer. He was delighted to be another of the Krays' "celebrity friends". He knew just how to flatter the English. Asked by Freddie Foreman who had been the real criminal mastermind during Prohibition in New York, he named "Owney" (Owen) Madden. Since the Liverpool-born rum-runner was the only Englishman in the upper echelons of the New York mobs, this was interesting information indeed. Especially as Owney had been in jail when the Jewish "Bug and Meyer" mob and Lucky Luciano formed the new system of collaborating criminal gangs, with Lucky as unostentatious head and Meyer as the financial wizard behind the throne. It also cast a glamorous light on Raft himself who, when still a tea-dancer and gigolo in 1920s New York, once rode shotgun with one of Owney's trucks, learning in the process that he didn't have the nerve to be a hands-on hoodlum.

Before the convenient "arrangement" with the Colony Club had been reached, the Kray brothers and Leslie Payne made two apparently useful contacts there. Joe Kaufman and Allan Bruce Cooper claimed to have important transatlantic criminal contacts. (They claimed a lot of things in due course.) They certainly did have contact with people trying to dispose of a quantity of stolen bearer bonds acquired by organized crime in Canada, the resale of which at face value was virtually impossible in America where the numbers were recorded and circulated. European brokers would be less suspicious, and there was a cut offered to any knowledgeable distributor.

As emerged at the subsequent trials, it was not obvious why the Krays were needed as part of this deal. They contributed nothing. They simply took a cut. The transatlantic bond owners would rather they had not been present. Payne the Brain and Fred Gore were quite capable of selling the bonds without the assistance of the brothers. Reggie might carry a briefcase in imitation of Leslie Payne, and Charlie might accompany him on business journeys. But that did not mean the twins were now competent financial executives. They were greedily inclined to take big sums of money out of the long firms Payne set up while the businesses needed funds and solvency to establish their reputations. And such money was all too likely to be thrown away. A racehorse for their mother? Nip £1,000 from one of the firms. The nag proves useless? Raffle it and let the somnolent cockney actor Ronald Fraser wake up to find he's won a horse he doesn't want. Need a few grand? Payne and Gore have got £10,000 in a special account for their Nigerian project and £5,000 will be enough for that.

And the twins' irrational violence was increasing. Charles "Nobby" Clarke took a bullet in the leg for agreeing with Ronnie's criticism of Frances. A man called Fields was shot in the leg in a Highbury club when he refused to give Reggie £1,000. A man called Joe was given a taste of Ronnie's branding steel for beating up "Buller" Ward's son. Then Buller himself was striped when his friendship with the Krays came to an end. George Dixon, a former friend, got up Ronnie's nose and was shot in the head at point blank range. Or would have been, if the gun had gone off. Its misfiring produced one of the most extravagant examples of Ronnie's unpredictably mercurial temperament. He calmed down, gave Dixon the bullet that should have killed him, and told him to wear it on a chain as a memento.

During this period the firm expanded, and personnel whose names would become infamous alongside the Krays were recruited. According to John Dickson's memoirs, he and "Ian" (John) Barrie were a pair of innocent young Scotsmen who found civilian life boring after National Service and gave up honest work on the trawlers or the oil rigs to come down to London and seek their fortunes in 1964. And in London, after taking legitimate occupations, they just happened to be invited to a Brick Lane spieler run by the twins' Uncle Alfie, who just happened to take a shine to them and introduce them to the twins, who just happened to offer them work. This is the sort of economy with the truth that allows Dickson's enemies to brand him a liar. As he admitted in court, he and Barrie shared an eight-month sentence in Ireland for safe blowing before they moved to London. The twins may have been pretty daft, but they weren't so goofy as to hire a pair of hard men who hadn't been engaged in any villainy or even violence since their days in the army. "Scotch Jack" and "Scotch Ian" became Ronnie's personal minders, Dickson driving for him and Barrie, whose face was marked by a sinister burn scar, as the threatening muscle, younger and fitter than the faithful old heavies "Tommy the Bear" and "Big Pat" Connolly.

In 1966 a young distant cousin of the twins', Ronnie Hart, was on the run from prison. Naturally the firm sheltered him. And he joined Big Albert Donaghue in Reggie's back-up group, Hart driving and Donaghue providing the muscle.

Ronnie's dreams of expanding the criminal empire seemed to be coming good. He established contacts with the Glasgow underworld, whence Barrie and Dickson came. The intention was to provide out-of-town hit men (or at least grievous bodily harmers and aggravated assailants) for each other, as American hard men had done since the Long Strike of 1870. Information from grateful "aways" gave the Krays insight into the activities of protection racketeers in the North and Midlands. A man called Eric Mason was enjoying considerable success with clubs in Manchester and his power was reinforced by the suggestion that he had links with the notorious Krays. The twins didn't mind, provided they took a cut. A former London teddy boy of Greek descent called Christopher Lambrianou found that he had great success with the protection racket in Birmingham and Leicester, and he was happy to add the weight of the firm to his name. He and his brother Tony fraternized with the twins when they were in London and Tony took especial pride in being associated with the first firm to have national tentacles and the best-known name since the Sabinis.

Hangers-on and ground-level near-members accumulated in London, too. Cornelius ("Connie") Whitehead, who was once jointly acquitted of GBH with George Dixon, survivor of the shooting in the Green Dragon. Ronnie Bender, who was doing some house decorating for Whitehead when Reggie Kray called one day and gave him a job as a fetch-and-carry driver, picking up his suits from the cleaners and cleaning his shoes. The promise of higher things was dangled before Bender, as it was before the 22-stone 28-year-old Wally Garelick, who looked after the Green Dragon Club for Mizel. These men, like other names seen around the pubs and clubs – "Harry Jew Boy", Harry Cope – all felt they were not part of the firm proper – that was confined to the twins, Dickie Morgan, Scotch Ian and Scotch Jack, Albert Donoghue and Ronnie Hart. Sometimes a drunken, pill-popping tearaway called Jack McVitie was included, as he could be used to put the frighteners on recalcitrant club owners. But such assessments overrate the importance of the "hard men" at the expense of Tommy Cowley, a competent business brain who was trusted with a good deal of hands-on fixing and who frightened some people who were not themselves hard men.

But all these men were unfortunate in joining a firm that had peaked. It was great to be at the thoretical top of the crime world for a year or two. But by 1967, inner-firm members were calling the twins "Gert and Daisy" after the comic cockney women in Ethel and Doris Waters' music-hall act. And they longed for Ron and Reg to retire, go and live in the country and get out of the way of the businesses they were ruining with their silly pipe dreams of gangster glory.

Beyond the active criminals there were the scores of spies and former "aways" who kept the twins posted about villains worth nipping, and sometimes about capers that had been left unattempted and so lay vacant for Freddie Foreman's crew. There were people who could be cajoled or intimidated into supplying the "safe houses" that were increasingly needed as the twins' actions grew more reckless. There were a lot of white-collar fraudsters and "stooges" involved with what remained of Payne's and Gore's ventures.

And Ronnie's dreams of transatlantic connections were growing, fed by the encouragement of Cooper and Kaufman. Before the Labour government got rid of them, the visiting Americans had plans to fly jet-loads of high-rollers over to London to gamble in their clubs. To this end, Angelo Bruno re-established connections with Albert Dimes. Ronnie assumed that the firm would be on a nice little earner, collecting money for the "protection" of keeping out of their way. He could not, he feared, visit America himself, as his criminal record would deny him a visa. "Mr ABC" knew his way round that. He took Ronnie to Paris, where the consulate issued a visa without demur. If you wanted, you could believe that Allan Cooper had contacts. If you didn't, you could assume that the American consul in Paris in 1968 was not kept supplied with a list of English undesirables.

In New York, Joe Kaufman was to provide the introductions to leading gangsters. Only the ones Ronnie met weren't leading. Angelo Bruno melted away out of town, apparently aware that this was "a little pissant hood" and not a great ganglord whom he needed to meet. Ronnie was taken around and feted by the lesser and the has-beens and apparently never suspected that he was being fobbed off. When it looked as if he was under police surveillance, he took this as a compliment rather than evidence that he had been blown. When he came home, laden with presents for the family, he had tales to tell of the sights he had been shown. And one feels a little sorry for this outwardly impressive but stupid man as he lost prestige instantly in the eyes of such gang members as had any knowledge about crime history, by boasting of having been shown the original garage where the St Valentine's Day Massacre took place. Didn't he know that that building (in the unlikely event that it still stood) was in Chicago, not New York?

But the American obsession had a still worse impact on the childish side of Ronnie Kray. He now felt it incumbent on him to kill somebody. Ronnie wanted his "button". The great canary Joe Valachi, who got J. Edgar Hoover off the hook of denying the existence of a Mafia by offering him the alternative phrase "cosa nostra", had given an insight into the weird practices and locutions of Sicilian-American gangsters. Sensible people thought their elaborate rituals and silly prestige points showed the ineluctable stupidity of most organized criminals. But Ronnie was deeply impressed. The fully-fledged Mafioso, it seemed, was a "button man", or "made man". He won his button by killing for the organization. Ronnie hadn't killed anybody yet.

He started compiling his "hit list". People went on it and came off it with the inconsistency of his changing moods. But legend insisted that it was easy to get on and almost impossible to get off. Ronnie gloated over his list of people who were going to get theirs. People against whom he had old or new scores to settle. Gangland rivals. People who took liberties.

When the time came, George Cornell seemed to fit each and every one of these categories.

5

MURDER

In 1960 the twins had joined with Freddie Foreman to prevent the outbreak of gang warfare following the Pen Club shooting. Everybody was sane enough to see that their interests would be damaged, and Johnny Simons and Barbara Ibbotson accordingly lost blood to ensure that the up-and-coming young villains didn't suffer any hindrance to their growing prosperity. But six years later, Ronnie's bedazzlement with American gangster glamour led him to want a war. It would be exciting to go "on the mattress". Strategies worthy of "the Colonel" could be planned. Those 200 armed men he had once boasted he could bring on the streets ... Well, at least the best-known hard men on the firm could be tooled up.

And there was an appropriate enemy. The Richardson brothers of South London seemed, at least in Ronnie's paranoid mind, to threaten the successful balance of power negotiated between the Krays, the Nashes, Freddie Foreman's team, and the Mifsud-Silver commercial-sex-peddling outfits in Soho.

The truth was that a pretty good balance existed. The Krays were drawing "pensions" from clubs and spielers in the East End and as far east as Walthamstow; from scrap merchants in Poplar and Hackney; from a casino in Stoke Newington and a club in Chris Lambrianou's Leicester. They effectively commandeered the Cambridge Rooms on the Kingston bypass as a base for entertaining visiting celebrities. The Krays and Nashes left each other's East and North London territories undisputed. The Nashes gave the Krays a cut of their takings from the Olympic in Camden Town, the Bagatelle off Regent Street and that 1960s faces' favourite gathering place, the Astor. What the Krays gave the Nashes as quid pro quo has never been made public, but it is safe to suggest that it included useful information from their spy network of grateful ex-"aways". Freddie Foreman was receiving such information. In 1963 the Krays tipped him off about delivery times and movements that gave him the Sharps Pixley bullion robbery from the City of London. That little caper netted half a ton of gold to dispose of – something Freddie insists kept him too prosperous and busy to accept an invitation to join the Great Train Robbery that August. The Krays got a grateful cut of the gold proceeds. Freddie, meanwhile, was putting some of his ill-gotten gains into clubs (opened in the names of relatives and associates of good enough public character to gain licences). And being one of the most important, if sensibly low-profile, villains of the day, he shared in a pay-out to keep trouble away from other people's clubs, although he was primarily a thief and not a protection racketeer. The Colony Club, the Casanova and Bernie Silver's Soho clubs paid out cash that was split three ways between the Krays, the Nashes and Foreman. The twins chose to believe that this was because they provided "security" – the happy hypocrites' mask for protection. Freddie Foreman accepted George Raft's tactful indication that what was really required was for the faces and their flat-nosed razor-scarred friends to stay away. Provided they kept off his territory, Raft was quite happy to try to upgrade the image of the gangsters' joints with his presence. So he made a personal appearance for Foreman at the formal opening of the 211 Club in Balham.

In their right minds, the Krays knew that gang warfare put all this co-operative income at risk. A theoretical code of accelerating and increasingly violent revenge for gang members assaulted by other gangs could have led to the deaths of half the underworld. So when Mad Frankie Fraser went for Eric Mason with an axe and put him in hospital, the twins heard Eric's complaint sympathetically, gave him some money and quietly let his associate membership of their firm lapse. Hence his position in Manchester, justifiably claiming an association with the Krays, but more dubiously letting it be supposed that he was their man in the North.

Ronnie's right mind, unfortunately, was not a guaranteed commodity. Frankie Fraser amusingly suggests that he might have suddenly felt like killing a glass for shining in the light. Albert Donoghue points out how quickly he could change his mind and forgive without forgetting. With Reggie under stress over his collapsed marriage, nothing could hinder the Colonel from putting the gang on a war footing and issuing orders to eliminate the Richardsons.

If there was no sense in the Krays going to war, there was less sense in the Richardsons' even being criminals. Both Eddie and

Charlie had competent business sense and were quite capable of earning good livings as the "company directors" they called themselves. Unlike Frankie Fraser or the old villain Arthur Harding, they had not been born into the sort of grinding poverty that made juvenile theft a useful contribution to a below-subsistence family budget. Unlike Fraser and Chris Lambrianou, they had not watched the system grind down very hard-working, very honest fathers into very great poverty. Charlie Richardson's chain of scrap-metal businesses didn't need to be crooked to support his Park Lane office. Eddie Richardson's wholesale chemist's warehouse enabled him to live independently of his brother when he wanted. So why didn't they stay on the right side of the law (even if sailing a little close to the wind) and keep out of grave trouble?

The answer seems to be that they shared the Krays' attraction to gangster glamour. Ronnie and Reggie's loving childhood home had not left them deprived by local standards. They had not joined with other "rough kids" and stolen the envied toys of better-off neighbours' children as Frank Mitchell and Albert Donoghue had done. Both the Charlie Krays were not adverse to dealing in a little stolen property, but they would have preferred the twins to become good professional boxers than traditional East End villains. But many of their district's heroes were villains, and the twins were invited to be impressed by Dodger Mullins and Wassle Newman. The Richardsons likewise came from a district that had a long reputation for nurturing criminals. The Sultan Street area of Camberwell was a "shy" neighbourhood as early as Dickens' day, when chiseller Jemmy Greenacre murdered and dismembered his equally chiselling fiancée there on learning that she had been trying to cheat him. If a neighbourhood gains a reputation as a nest of villains, some children born there will see criminals as local heroes and start trying to emulate them. Some will graduate as full-time professional rogues, like the Krays. Some will abandon their childhood "adventures" and become honest citizens. The Richardsons straddled the fence. They were good boxers (Charlie pro, Eddie amateur), and earned local criminal "respect" by preferring to settle arguments with "straighteners" (one-to-one fistfights). But they never experienced the solid terms of early imprisonment that constitute the university of crime. Charlie in particular seemed to Frankie Fraser to be a poor judge of criminal character and rather naively unaware of just how "the boys" expected people to behave. In later life Charlie certainly got up John McVicar's nose, and left him with the impression that he would willingly throw spoilers into other people's best-laid criminal plans if he wasn't allowed to profit by them.

The Richardsons had begun with "jump-ups", the lucrative thefts from lorries at which the Krays had proved less than adept when on the run from the army. They then settled into establishing the scrap-metal business that would provide the basis of their empire. Of course scrap metal offers a fine cover for dealing in stolen goods and turning hot cars into marketable materials. Charlie Richardson was never content to be an entirely honest businessman. He would always incline to the belief that he was not cheating, just trying to win. In 1959 this brought him a short prison sentence for stealing bacon. A year later he slipped out of the country to Canada rather than face charges of receiving stolen metal. Thereafter, witness intimidation would be the Richardsons' preferred way of avoiding the legal penalties for their malfeasance.

Eddie Richardson's presence in the curious photograph of the "Soho Rangers Football Club" is symptomatic of his more central criminal standing. If this photograph had been published at the time it was taken, the only figure known to the public would have been actor Stanley Baker, standing to one side like the team manager, dapperly dressed in a smart little trilby hat, camel waistcoat and overcoat, narrow trousers and gleaming elastic-sided boots. He grins broadly, as was so often the case when Baker was pictured with gangland friends. Behind the team, for all the world like their trainer, stands Albert Dimes. The players include Frankie Fraser, George Wisbey, Eddie Richardson, and the Richardson associate Billy Stayton, who would play his part in the growing Kray-Richardson tension. These are not mobsters as small boys, being encouraged by the benign, football-loving Baker and Dimes. These are grown men with places or relatives on the south London crime scene, enjoying a little organised relaxation. Eddie is among friends.

A glance at those friends' friends builds a pattern looking back to the past and forward to the future. Frankie Fraser, older than many of his partners in crime, worked as a sponge boy for Darby Sabini when he was little. Anyone who knew George Wisbey had access to one of the central figures in the world of top-class thieving, his brother Tommy, who became best known as leader of one of the two major gangs involved in the Great Train Robbery. He was also Freddie Foreman's partner and brother-in-law and would much later become Frankie Fraser's father-in-law, too. Start looking beyond his friends in a recreational game of football to the friends of the friends of the friends, and Eddie Richardson had tenuous links well across the major criminal world.

Look closely at Frankie Fraser. Thief and hard man, he first "went away" when he was 13 and was mostly in jail for 32 of the next 40 years. He was 39 in 1962, when he emerged from his seven-year sentence for cutting Jack Spot at Albert Dimes' behest and started one of the longest periods at liberty since his childhood. It was to prove an important three years in the history of crime, marked by the Great Train Robbery, the Mr Smith's Club affray and its immediate sequel, the murder of George Cornell.

On his release, Dimes and Billy Hill gave a party for Fraser at the Pigalle Club in Piccadilly, with Shirley Bassey and Winifred Atwill the ragtime pianist as guests. Hill opened a bank account with £5,000 to set Mad Frank up again in some business. The Kray twins also gave a party for him at the Regency, and a whip-round provided another £300 or £400. Fraser started running slot machines in spielers for Dimes. His usefulness in this particular business was to ensure that clubs accepted Dimes' one-arm bandits in preference to anybody else's, and to see that nobody skimmed off money claimed by the proprietors. Frankie Fraser's memoirs frequently refer to giving somebody "a few clumps" for getting out of line. If it is true, as he claims, that the Great Train Robbers invited him to Letherslade Farm the following year to consider recruiting him, this casts an extraordinary light on their much-touted claim to intend minimal violence. Mad Frankie Fraser had been a competent thief in his day. But in this climax to his career he was certainly far better known as a game fighter whose violent determination outweighed his relatively short stature.

The following year Fraser's slight acquaintance with the Richardsons deepened. He felt indebted to them for having given a beating to Jack Rosa, an erstwhile friend with whom he had attacked Jack Spot. While Fraser was (as usual) in prison, Rosa had beaten up a young relative of his wife's and Fraser was grateful to the Richardsons for administering punishment. It was the start of a friendship and partnership with Eddie Richardson. The two formed the Atlantic Machines Company with an office in Windmill Street off Tottenham Court Road, putting one-armed bandits in clubs and pubs. To look good on their headed paper, they incorporated the knighted, little known and clapped-out parliamentarian, Sir Noel Dryden, among the directors. In employing a non-celebrity they showed more sense than the twins. While Effingham could do Ron and Reg no harm, Boothby's newsworthiness had proved him to be an undesirable public supporter. And only the fact that Tom Driberg was himself a working journalist gave him the protection of the journalists' code that dog doesn't eat dog and kept his preposterous antics out of the scandal-sheets.

Charlie Richardson expanded his businesses in all directions. His personal downfall would come from South Africa, where his interest in smuggling stolen diamonds hidden in wet fish rapidly developed into an interest in directly investing in his own diamond mine. He formed a partnership with a geologist called Thomas Waldeck, who believed there were real possibilities in diamond mining in Namaqualand, but they eventually quarrelled, each man suspecting the other of cheating him. Shortly after, Waldeck was shot dead on his porch.

Meanwhile, back in England, the shadier Richardson enterprises were expanding and being orchestrated with violence. The Richardsons had Mad Frank as an enforcer and could offer clubs their services as providers of security. 1964 was a busy and important year for them. When Frank and Eddie ran a broken glass into the face of the gaming manager of the Horseshoe Club in Southport, the witnesses who were to support his charge of grievous bodily harm were frightened into silence. When a Heathrow Airport car-park attendant declined to hand over half the £1,000 a week he was taking from a major fiddle with the time clocks, he was stripped naked and beaten with a wet towel. When a man called Taggart was held responsible for delaying repayment of a loan that was intended for investment in the Namaqualand diamond project, he was given a serious beating. And quite outrageous punishments were dished out to refractory associates and uncooperative victims. Those villains who had an eye on the growth of the Richardson mob felt that Fraser was its mainspring. But then, villains were always likely to be more impressed by sheer savagery than by intelligence. Frank had no hesitation in admitting that the Richardsons' business skills provided the basis from which his violence could be turned into a useful money earner.

Only the Richardsons did not confine themselves to sensible "enforcement". Just as their infamous "torture" punishment paralleled the Krays' increasing delight in chastizing those of their firm who "did the naughties", so the Richardsons seemed willing to play silly gangster games with the Krays, like kids playing cops and robbers and teaming up against each other. The sort of Montagues and Capulets behaviour which had marked the nascent criminal conduct of the adolescents in the dancehalls of the early 1950s was now carried on by adults who glared at each other in the West End clubs of the mid-1960s. The Richardsons tried to move in on the Starlight Club off Oxford Street. The owners asked the Krays for protection and the twins and Freddie Foreman became part proprietors. The Richardsons got the hump. The Krays wanted a share in the London Airport car-park racket. The Richardsons refused. The Krays got the hump. George Myers, now calling himself George Cornell, married a south London girl and moved over the river to team up with Frankie Fraser and the Richardsons. He felt the twins had interfered with a long firm he was running in the East End and this gave him the hump. The Krays approached him to repeat a demand they had already made, that Billy Stayton's blue film racket in Soho be brought under their protection. They had already been told that the Richardsons couldn't help them. It was a short-term venture under their protection and had a mere three months' "licence" granted by a corrupt police officer. Cornell was definitely annoyed to be approached again by the Krays in the Stork Club and he was not polite. It has been repeatedly stated, and sometimes denied, that he called Ronnie "a fat poof". The Krays' claim that Ronnie would have wreaked instant revenge if it had been said to his face seems likely enough. An old friend called Johnny Dew was seriously cut merely for making a lighthearted remark to the effect that Ronnie was carrying too much weight. But it is typical of the Krays' carelessness about truth that Ronnie has also claimed that it really was just this insult that signed Cornell's death warrant.

It is certainly possible that the Krays believed that Cornell's snide remarks at another joint meeting endangered the American Mafia's interest in the venture to bring punters over by jet and shake them down at the Colony Club and Esmeralda's Barn. And when a big meet was arranged at Astor's to agree the territorial division of London, the Krays were furious that the Richardsons treated the whole idea with contempt. They were doing very nicely, thank you, and they weren't going to ask the Krays for permission to run long firms in Southend or the east of London, and they certainly weren't going to divvy up any nice little earners they got going in Soho.

And so the Krays ordered the gang war that the police had long feared. The firm's members were given access to firearms, but ordered not to go around tooled up all the time, which could have led to arrests and trouble. And, teamed in pairs, the firm was given Richardson gangsters to assassinate. Ronnie and Nobby Clarke were to kill Charlie Richardson. Reggie would take out Eddie. Scotch Jack and Scotch Ian were to kill Frankie Fraser. And Albert Donoghue and Connie Whitehead were to rub out Brian Mottram, who had annoyed the twins by starting a long firm on their turf in Hackney. Billy Stayton, who had started a long firm in Southend in addition to the blue film racket, was also identified as a possible future victim. The "Soho Rangers" football team photograph was passed around the Kray firm so that the Kray soldiers could know and identify their enemies.

The enemies were willing to play. Frankie Fraser had once visited the Grave Maurice as a friend to receive a valuable tip-off about a grass from the twins, which came to them via their spy system. Now when he ventured on Kray territory, he had a car full of fellow Richardson gangsters parked at a little distance as back-up. Somebody fired some desultory shots at The Lion in Tapp Street. Somebody ran a car onto the pavement in Vallance Road in an apparent attempt to mow down Ronnie Kray, mistaking a mini-cab owner who looked rather like him.

While Charlie was abroad, Eddie and Frankie Fraser decided to improve the shining hour by taking over the protection of a recently opened club in Catford called Mr Smith and the Witch Doctor. The owners had previously owned the Horseshoe in Southport, which probably led Fraser and Richardson to think they had been softened up and intimidated. The protection security was being handled at the start by Billy and Harry Hayward, relative newcomers to the business of villainy. The Richardsons were no more willing to see new talent springing up on their manor than the Krays were to allow others to operate in the East End. The managers of Mr Smith's became unhappy with the Haywards after they started to use the club as an unofficial headquarters and receive telephone messages there. The situation was highly inflammable when Fraser and Eddie Richardson dropped in at the club with a few friends on 7 March 1965. The Haywards believed they were still in charge of protection. Fraser and Richardson felt they had been invited to take over.

There is as much agreement as to just what happened as there is mystification as to why such violence and mayhem was deemed necessary. After 3am, the two gang leaders, Eddie Richardson and Billy Hayward, snarled at each other over which of them was entitled to decree that the bar should or should not continue to serve. And as the insults and obscenities mounted, Eddie started fighting with the Haywards' man, Pete Hennessy. According to Frankie Fraser this was an honest "straightener" between the two men. If they had been left alone, the best man would have won and everybody would have accepted it. It seems a little unlikely, however, that Mad Frank would have agreed that the Haywards should be left in undisputed control of the club if his side's man took a beating. Other observers see the scrap between Richardson and Hennessy as the start of a general brawl.

Everybody agrees that the Hayward "soldier" Dickie Hart was the first to draw a gun and fire it. Such a unanimous story is easily agreed when, as in this case, a protagonist dies, so that any amount of blame cast on him is not "grassing him up".

Shooting having started, it continued. Other people pulled guns and various light injuries were sustained. Eddie Richardson was shot in the thigh and the backside. Harry Rawlins was shot in the arm and would have bled to death from a severed artery had not Jimmy Moody and Ronnie Jeffrey put a handkerchief on him as a tourniquet and carried him outside. Jeffrey, a Richardson man, realized that the noise was rousing the neighbourhood and the police would be along soon. He shouted, "Turn it up" at his warring colleagues, but nobody was listening.

Hart ran outside, followed by Frankie Fraser. Exactly what happened next cannot be ascertained. Fraser says he hit Hart in the face and tried to take his gun, but as he did so it went off. Fraser's thighbone was shattered. At some point the Haywards' man Henry Botton saw Fraser savagely kicking the fallen Hart and shouted, "You're fucking mad, Frank".

When the police arrived, they found Hart almost dead under a lilac tree in a garden. He had been shot in the face, which was smashed in. Frankie Fraser was immobilized with his broken leg, in a privet hedge. They were both taken to Dulwich hospital, where Eddie Richardson was also being treated and Henry Rawlins had been left draped over a cot in the casualty department. Hart died that night and the police had the hard centre of the Richardson gang bang to rights for affray. Frankie Fraser was charged with Hart's murder, though he was later acquitted.

Now that should have been the end of the Kray twins' intended gang war. The enemy had mostly been mopped up. And Charlie Richardson had too much on his plate in South Africa to come personally looking for revenge. A former mercenary soldier called Johnny Bradbury had come forward to say he had killed Thomas

Waldeck, but the instigator and beneficiary of the murder was Charles Richardson. Charlie was also worried by another matter. A number of men who had suffered the Richardsons' serious "punishments" had taken their complaints to the chief Constable of Hertfordshire, Gerald McArthur. If the Met had been investigating the Richardson gang's tortures, someone in the Flying Squad could have been relied on to leak information. But McArthur, who had left the Met when he felt his part in solving the Great Train Robbery was undervalued, wasn't the kind of copper who ran a leaky ship. The following year, Charlie would be convicted, with Frankie Fraser and others, at the notorious "Torture Trial". The evidence that Richardson and his henchmen broke victims' toes, pulled out their teeth with pliers and attached an electrical generating machine to their genitals horrified the public. The evidence that Charlie Richardson liked to carry out these "punishments" after mock "trials" in which he played the part of a formal judge, exposed his childish need for some more dignified identity than birth and education had granted him. Charlie and Frankie hardly came across as glamorous gangland heroes when they were sent down for those particular pieces of vicious and infantile vileness. They weren't left with much dignity in the eyes of the adult public. Small wonder that the pair subsequently took the opportunity to minimize and deny much that was testified about them. In any event, they were hardly a serious threat to the thieves' ponces across the river as they awaited trial on these numerous damaging charges.

But the Colonel had psyched himself up into a mood for serious violence. His own childish admiration for American Mafiosi encouraged him to feel that he could and should become a "button man". And, notoriously, his opportunity came two days after the affray at Mr Smith and the Witch Doctor. Again, the details of what happened are generally agreed; the explanation is far more puzzling. The twins and several members of the firm were drinking in The Lion in Tapp Street, when one of Ronnie's spies came in to say that George Cornell was drinking in The Blind Beggar. Ronnie immediately spoke to Reggie, gathered his team of John Dickson and Ian Barrie, and left. Dickson's great difficulty in telling an exact and full story leaves an uncertainty over the two-minute drive from Tapp Street to Whitechapel Road. Giving evidence three years later, he first said he hired a car, next that he used a friend's. And he said the journey took 20 minutes. Which seems impossible. When he came to write his book in later years, he added a visit to Vallance Road en route, which might account for some of the apparently extra time. But all the huffing and puffing by the Krays and their followers about "John Dickson's lies in the witness box" are a smokescreen. Dickson didn't see the shooting and never suggested that he did. He provided evidence that Ronnie and Ian Barrie went into the pub, came out again pretty sharpish, and had him drive them back to The Lion. On the way, Ronnie said either, "I hope the bastard's dead ", or "I got the fucking bastard". In this case, Dickson's apparently differing stories to the police in his first statement and thereafter in court are by no means evidence that he was lying. Ronnie might have said both. Dickson could easily have been confused as to exactly what he heard, given the stress of the situation. There seems little reason to doubt that he heard something that might be interpreted as a confession. Some of the interruptions the defendants made at the Krays' trial when Dickson gave evidence against them were very ill-judged, as they apparently aimed at incriminating him by showing that he knew exactly what Ronnie intended to do before they left The Lion. But although this would have made him accessory before the fact, it would have proved quite conclusively that Ronnie went with the clear and premeditated intention of committing murder. Nothing, it seems, will prevent villains from thinking that they've won a vital point if they can only make stick the accusation, "You're another!".

Inside the pub, George Cornell was sitting at the end of the bar talking to a colleague, Albie Woods, and a young man, Johnny Dale. He had just been to the London Hospital across the road, to see his friend Jimmy Andrews who had been shot in the leg in the course of a domestic dispute. The barmaid, who still prefers to be referred to as Mrs X, was replaying her favourite record of the time, the Walker Brothers singing The Sun Ain't Gonna Shine Any More. She knew Cornell as a fairly frequent drinker in The Beggar's and was telling him that she would be playing the same number a few more times. An Irishman was drinking on his own at the centre of the bar. A couple sat at a table. And an old man called Thomas Slarke, known to the bar staff as "Pop", was sitting near the door. The publican, Patsy Quill, was upstairs in the private quarters. His brother Jimmy was out (The Quill family of brothers ran a number of East End pubs). The barman, Ivor Richards, had gone home for a quick meal. Mrs X was in charge on her own. The time was about 8.15.

Ronnie and Ian Barrie strode in with drawn pistols. Cornell looked up and said, "Well, look who's here. Let's get a drink." As he put his hand into his pocket for money, Barrie fired two shots in the ceiling. And Ronnie put a bullet straight between Cornell's eyes.

The couple at the table hit the floor. The man from the centre of the bar raced into the ladies' lavatory and locked himself in. Woods and Dale slid off their barstools and Dale bolted out the door. Mrs X dived for the cellar stairs, hurting her back sliding down them into the darkness. Pop Slarke didn't, apparently, notice anything.

Ronnie and Barrie strode out and went straight across the wide Whitechapel Road to where John Dickson waited in the car as he had been instructed. And they drove back to The Lion. When Patsy Quill had checked that his children were all right and come down to the bar, it was virtually empty except for the body on the floor. Mrs X told him what had happened and the two tried to make Cornell as comfortable as possible before Quill called an ambulance. George Cornell was taken to Mile End Hospital, and then on to Maida Vale, where he died that night.

Back in The Lion there was confusion. Ronnie's young companion for the evening, a boy called Buckley, was terrified, and left at once. Other lesser members of the firm who had expected a party, melted away. Reggie sent for two brothers, Alfred and David Teal, whose criminal record made them as vulnerable as their family home at Walthamstow made them useful. Nobby Clarke was given two guns to dispose of in the canal. Billy Exley was sent to Fort Vallance to get some clean clothes for Ronnie. Reggie ordered everyone "off the manor" and the central figures in the firm piled into cars and drove to Walthamstow. At the Chequers, Ronnie washed his hands and was sick. On they went to the Teals' house, where Ronnie washed again, with Vim, to get the gunpowder stains off his hands, and was given a clean suit that didn't fit him.

He was to stay five nights at the Teals'. Reggie and Ian Barrie stayed one night at a safe flat in Lea Bridge Road and then Ian returned to his girlfriend's flat in north London, an address known only to Scotch Jack. Gang members were told to take it in turns to stay at Fort Vallance in case any of the Richardson mob turned up looking for revenge. They didn't. They were all either locked up or preoccupied with the increasing police interest in their doings. Only Cornell's wife Olive came round, screaming abuse, quarrelling with Violet on the doorstep and throwing a brick through a window. She was fined £1 at the magistrates' court, and was regarded by much of the East End as an extraordinarily brave woman. But Ronnie insisted that under the circumstances the "liberty" of damaging Fort Vallance was not something they could properly avenge. It gave him yet another opportunity to say that the Krays never hurt women, something Mrs X for one did not believe.

The police investigation got nowhere. Mrs X knew Ronnie Kray by sight, but was certainly not going to say so after seeing him cold-bloodedly kill someone in front of her eyes. She claimed to have ducked behind the bar and been unable to recognize the men who came in (and it was true she did not know Ian Barrie, though his scar should have made him very memorable).

Albie Woods and Johnny Dale didn't need to be told about the code of the East End. They were not going to say what they had seen. Michael Flannery denied recognizing anyone. Pop Slarke was too old, infirm and uncertain in his mind to make a witness to anything. Freddie Foreman says that he undertook to see these various witnesses and make sure their stories were all appropriately uninformative. Tommy Butler, fresh from his fame as the man who had caught nearly all the Great Train Robbers, came and took charge of the case. He had the barmaid's flat kept under observation and made a very good impression on her. But not good enough for her to be willing to identify the murderer.

When the initial panic had died down, the twins left town for a brief holiday in a hotel in Wisbech. Ronnie was unpleasantly changed by the experience. He dwelt on it in his mind, and he loved going over and over it. He gloated at the fear he remembered, or imagined he remembered, in Cornell's eyes as he knew he was really going to be shot. He felt he was indeed a "made man" and many of the firm heard him boasting to Reggie, "I've done mine. When are you going to do yours?"

There was every reason for the twins to feel untouchable. Ronnie had killed openly, in a public place, in front of witnesses – and witnesses of good character. Such senseless recklessness, he wrongly believed, was favoured by the hit men of American organized crime. The police knew perfectly well what he had done. So did the whole of the East End. But since the witnesses dared not say what they had seen, he couldn't be arrested and charged. Literally, Ronnie Kray had got away with murder. Stealth no longer mattered.

And why was this atrocious and unprovoked murder committed? Ronnie offered different excuses at different times. He referred to the alleged "fat poof" insult, which he placed at a meeting with American Mafiosi, where it humiliated him. He told Billy Exley it was because Cornell had told the brother of one of his young friends that he only took him to Newcastle in order to go to bed with him. He claimed that Dickie Hart, a distant cousin, was actually a member of the Kray firm, and it therefore behoved the Krays to take out "one of theirs" for the "one of ours" the Richardsons had killed. Twice he told the world the blatant lie that it was revenge for Ginger Marks who, he pretended, had been killed by Cornell. This, he claimed, had been confessed by Cornell to a prison cellmate. Ronnie was stealing a very shabby leaf from a very disreputable police notebook in offering the alleged confession to a cellmate as evidence. Despite the importance of Susan Atkins' confession to a cellmate that she was one of Sharon Tate's killers, alleged cellmate confessions have been responsible for many dubious convictions. It is obviously easy to taint a convict witness with offers of reduced sentences. Not that I suggest Ronnie corrupted anybody for his story of Cornell's murdering Marks. I have no doubt he knew perfectly well who had done the killing and made the entire story up. He was dim enough to have imagined it would be helpful to his friend Freddy Foreman to have such a falsehood muddying the waters.

Freddie asserted that George was killed because he was "running around with, as [Ronnie] looked at it…the enemy, who were looking to take over their territory. And he was from the East End; he was a local feller; he should have been with them rather than with a south London firm… So naturally he had to show his authority".

Friends of the Krays have claimed that Cornell deserved to die because he was a wickedly brutal man, deeply involved in the tortures practised by the Richardsons. They tell horror stories of his driving golf balls at the open mouth of a victim tied in a chair across the room. They expect, fairly enough, that all right-minded people will be horrified and disgusted. They must hope that such right-minded people are unaware that the Krays brokered the "satisfactory" handling of the Pen Club affray investigation that led to equally loathsome treatment of Barbara Ibbotson. They also expect that the world will necessarily believe their description of George Cornell. They don't, unfortunately, have a particularly good record for truthfulness.

Billy Webb, as we have seen, suggested that the murder was revenge for Cornnell's winning one of those early scraps with the Watney Streeters, in the days when he was still George Myers. Albert Donoghue and other gang members believed that Ronnie simply lost his irrational and uncontrollable temper because, at that particular moment, it seemed to him a "liberty" that George should come back to his own home territory for a drink. They note, further, that Ronnie was so unstable that on any other day Cornell's movements might have seemed to him perfectly harmless.

This last view seems closest to the truth. The murder really seems to have been the outcome of Ronnie's paranoia and his childish belief that killing would make him into a great gangster. Reggie was instantly critical, as well as instantly efficient in cleaning up the mess. Ronnie's capacity to be physically sick after killing Cornell does him more credit than he would ever have imagined at the time. It is a further example of the Krays' peculiar and improbable streak of sensitivity, which did not fit them for their chosen role of gangsters.

After it was all over, the twins went for a holiday in Tangier with Billy Hill. He had been useful to them, they thought. His contacts with Ernie Millen had been exercised on their behalf, they hoped. In "defeating" Tommy Butler they appeared to have vanquished the best Scotland Yard could throw against them. And Ronnie in particular now felt that they were the true "Kings of Gangland". The extent to which they urgently needed the help of the younger and wiser Freddie Foreman would become apparent the following year.

6

TWELVE DAYS IN GANGLAND

The end of 1966 saw the twins' highest-profile, nationally reported, front-page, headline-grabbing exploit. On Monday 12 December they sprang the Mad Axeman.

By this time they rather needed some good publicity with both the public and their criminal confreres. The torture trials in the middle of the year had not been good for the reputation of gangland. The Great Train Robbers of 1963 had been popular villains. Good-natured and pally with each other in the dock, cheeky with the police and generally adventurous, their violence strictly kept to a minimum, they won a great deal of public sympathy. Their 30-year sentences suggested that the judiciary cared more about property than about physical injuries. Few people were convinced by the somewhat strained attempts of the police and prosecution lawyers to justify the severe penalties by maximizing the seriousness of the blow to driver Mills' head. Anybody with the slightest spirit of adventure could easily imagine himself up there in the darkness with the robbers on Bridego Bridge, enjoying the thrill of handing sacks of money down the human chain. The escapes of several Train Robbers were, by and large, greeted with public satisfaction. Altogether the Great Train Robbery was good publicity for the criminal world, suggesting that major theft was an ingenious caper carried out by likable rogues.

The same could not be said for the activities of the Richardson gang. The vicious battle at Mr Smith and the Witch Doctor was far from enticing. The mock courts and actual physical torture of associates and employees seemed sick. Nobody sane imagined themselves enjoying such activities and the torturers were viewed with contempt and disgust. London's criminal gangs needed a bit more jolly adventure if the press and public were not to demand a fierce police crackdown.

The criminal world was not happy to write off George Cornell under the "we only kill each other" justification. There were those who liked George. The fact that Frankie Fraser thought him likable and brave might not cut much ice in a year when people remembered just what Frankie had been convicted of doing to Bennie Coulston. The fact that Big Albert Donoghue had nothing against

Cornell, and regarded him as "one of us" should have been taken more seriously by the twins. But Albert was something of a strong silent man, keeping his mouth shut most of the time. Like everybody else with a criminal background, he fully understood Cornell's brother Eddie going around saying he was going to get the twins. That was a fair enough response to having someone in the family murdered. Freddie Foreman was generally forgiven for the fearsome revenge he had taken on Ginger Marks for the injury to his brother George. But Albert thought Ronnie was daft when he handed out axes to Ronnie Hart, Connie Whitehead and Donoghue, with the general instruction to kill Eddie Myers without any further shooting. The three hard men rather publicly told people they were looking for Eddie, and left it at that. Eddie would hear about them and lie low. Ronnie would hear about them and accept that they'd tried to carry out his orders.

It was also serious for the twins that Freddie Foreman regarded Cornell as a friend. And although he would not think of going to war in his memory, Freddie felt that Ronnie had been completely out of order in shooting a man publicly in a bar. It was like making a deliberate mess in Jimmy and Patsy Quills' front room. As a publican himself, running the Prince of Wales in Lant Street, Southwark (with his wife as licensee), Freddie was well aware that the immediate effect of such a violent incident would be a severe drop in trade. The Quills had always been friendly and straight with the mobsters who used their taverns. The Krays had taken an unjustifiable liberty in carrying out an open murder on their premises.

So the twins needed to do something striking and adventurous to restore the good name of metropolitan gangs with the general public and themselves with their fellow crims. It may well have been Mad Teddy Smith who came up with the embroidery to justify their original mad idea of adding the strength of Frank Mitchell to the team warring with the Richardsons.

Frank Mitchell had always been a favoured figure among the "aways". He was famous right across the prison system as the man who would fearlessly take on the screws if he were crossed. There was prestige accruing to the firm that supplied Big Frank Mitchell with regular visitors and looked after his needs as far as possible. There would be still more prestige for a firm that employed him.

By 1966 Mitchell had been in Dartmoor for four years. The old prison, built for French prisoners-of-war in the Napoleonic period, was regarded as something of an outdated, damp and freezing hell-hole, situated well behind God's back. Escapes were fairly frequent, because Dartmoor prisoners spent a good deal of time working on the moor and it was not too difficult to abscond from work parties. The escapes, however, were generally very short-lived. The moors are beautiful but inhospitable. Even in the summer, when crowds of schoolchildren undertake the adventurous "ten tors" hiking and camping weekend, a vast contingency of army and emergency service personnel has to be deployed to guard against their loss of life through exposure and fatigue. The runaway convict who struck out east across the moorland was most unlikely to reach its edge unscathed. The convict who made straight for the nearest roadway, on the other hand, was likely to be captured by roadblocks on the A30, the A38 or the A382. There wasn't any other feasible route away from Devonshire to London or the Midlands. A return west to Cornwall would bring the runaway to an even more easily sealed off peninsular.

Frank Mitchell had not really contemplated escape from Dartmoor. His behaviour had been good on arrival. He seemed to have out-grown the need to show off by attacking warders and the governor, Mr Denis Malone, felt that he should be given a date to be considered for parole. Indeed, he said he would recommend it, if Frank behaved well for five years. This was a most unfortunate piece of well-intentioned liberalism. The governor might recommend the allocation of a parole date; he had not the power to enforce it. That lay with the Home Office. And the Civil Service did not regard such recommendations as matters to be given urgent priority.

For big Frank, on the other hand, this was a tantalizing prospect. A glimpse of freedom where there had been only endless prison stretching ahead. His simple mind took the offer as a "release date". And he looked forward to it passionately, imagining liberty in a life that had been nearly all captivity so far and promised nothing more for the future.

His hope of taking lasting pleasure in liberty, however, was sadly misjudged. After years under lock and key, Frank was thoroughly institutionalized. He accepted the daily routine, adding to it his own regimen of sit-ups and press-ups and constant fitness training. He slept well and was accustomed to regular hours. And the complete freedom from responsibility that went with captivity was well suited to his limited intellect. It is hardly possible to imagine him looking after himself in the cold, competitive outside world.

What's more, he was by now enjoying easier prison terms than he had known since he began his long career of incarceration. Mr Malone had decided that Frank was sufficiently settled to constitute no serious escape or riot risk. He raised his status to blue band: a "trusty" prisoner with relatively pleasant duties and responsibilities, and increased privileges. Frank had extra association hours with other prisoners and could spend his weekends in the gym, in the television and social rooms, or in his cell, as he chose. It interested sympathetic screws to see that he no longer trusted everyone as he had once done. He chose his friends very carefully and spent a great deal of his free time on his own in his cell, working at the miniature model-making and clock-repairing that gave him so much satisfaction. He was becoming aware that his great strength had been exploited by other prisoners who wanted his "leadership" in troublemaking. Now he wanted a release date. So he set troublemaking aside and enjoyed his trusted status.

But the great and important privilege he was granted was allocation to the "honour party". These little groups of two to five, constituting 1% of the prison population, enjoyed vastly freer working conditions than any of the other inmates. As trusted prisoners, who gave their word of honour they would not try to escape, they went out on the moors a considerable distance from the prison and spent the day out there, cooking their own meals, in the company of just one guard, who could easily have been overpowered. Officer Derek Brisco, who led the honour party from which Mitchell ultimately absconded, has given the following account of their working day:

The location was about 12 miles from the prison. It was on the edge of the moor. We used to get driven there in a van and arrive there about 7.30 to 7.40 in the morning. Then we'd walk maybe a third of a mile, and we had a little hut which had a coke fire. We would take water and some provisions with us, but somebody had to walk a couple of miles or a mile to carry the coke up to the site. And the actual work was constructing a barbed wire fence with metal stakes on top of a dry stone wall which fenced in an army firing range. It was to keep sheep out, because once they got into the area – it was about four square miles – it was so big that they had great difficulty getting the sheep out. So it was a long job, and it was – the weather conditions at that time of year, end of summer, early winter – were quite appalling from time to time. So we spent a lot of time in the hut...

The first job in the morning was always to make breakfast because they didn't eat before they left the prison, and I used to stop in a little shop and sometimes buy eggs and a bit of bacon out of the subsistence I got, and we'd have a little fry-up or make an omelette. And we'd have a couple of newspapers so they could read the newspapers. If the weather was bad we would sometimes stay in there for hours on end, play cards, chat, whatever...

Once, when we were on the honour party, and it was a clear nice day and we had been working in the morning, we came down for some lunch about half past one, two o'clock, and there was a helicopter buzzing around. And [for] the prisoners, [helicopters] were a bit novel in those days in the middle of Dartmoor, and I think a couple of them waved to the helicopter. And it landed. And it was an army helicopter, and the pilot was an NCO or a warrant officer and actually got out and had a cup of tea with us in the hut. Frank Mitchell thought that was brilliant. I mean, for weeks he couldn't talk about anything else. This was a real wonderful experience in the middle of an otherwise dour prison life. He really took it to heart, and that was a bit of life – he touched a bit of life – outside the prison system.

For Brisco, the honour party allowed a few men to lead a pretty normal working day on Bagga Tor, and the warder accompanying them was a human companion and group leader more than a guard. Conversation, inevitably, revolved around prison. The closed society turns in on itself in fascinated navel-gazing. But Brisco encouraged some more outward-looking and self-improving possibilities. He used the time in the hut to try and help Frank master reading. Near-illiteracy was an embarrassment to a convict as much as it would be to anyone else. Brisco would propose five new words a day for Frank to learn.

They talked, too, about families and family matters. Frank showed every sign of deep attachment to his younger sister. But he also showed himself acutely aware that he did not live with a family of his own and had no experience of being married or living in a domestic relationship. Frank really wanted to know what father-hood would feel like, it seemed. He had no inkling that he had a daughter back in Poplar.

The real freedom of the honour party came outside the hut. The men were not required to work together or be under the guard's eye at all times. Individuals might be given tasks away from the main party and out of his sight, for example when coke was needed for the shed, which had to be fetched from a mile away. And men could occasionally wander off a mile or more from the main group, enjoy-ing the scenery or petting the wild ponies. And provided they were not misbehaving and arrived back at the hut in time for the midday meal, or the van pick-up at the end of the afternoon, nobody minded. What, after all, were they going to do with themselves? The moor itself constituted an enormous secure area. Prisoners were not allowed money, so it would be impossible to escape by taxi or bus. Nobody, as far as was known, had ever abused the system.

It was known that Big Frank particularly enjoyed the chance for solitude on the moors. It was thought that this was because he had a certain rather simple love of nature; he greatly enjoyed petting and feeding the Dartmoor ponies (as, indeed, do so many people that they have become an absolute pest to anyone trying to picnic on the moor!) It was quite unknown that he was enjoying other recreations, supplied, courtesy of the firm and left at agreed drops. Money. Booze. Female company.

From March 1966, Frank's visits from the firm were connected with Ronnie's decision to rescue him. If the firm could bring goodies for him when he was out on the moors, they could bring a motor-bike and arrange a safe house. Ronnie was reacting to the complaints Frank made to him. Mr Malone retired in 1966 to be replaced by Mr Cresswell Jones, who didn't seem interested in Frank's promised release date. Were there any advance rumours about the replacement of Mr Jones, which would take place the following year? Had anyone heard that the next governor would be a Major Golding? And did the cons suspect that the military title foreboded more discipline than release dates? In any case, Frank had behaved himself for four years and felt badly let down. Ronnie's promise to get him out was just the sort of brilliant benevolence Frank had come to expect from his hero.

Ronnie's promises didn't always mean anything. But the circumstances suggest that his initial reason was his characteristic spontaneous generosity. Ronnie liked to be liked for doing things for people. He liked Frank. It was already a feather in his cap that he headed the unofficial Frank Mitchell Comforts Fund. It would gratify Frank and greatly impress the underworld if the Krays freed a man who had been locked up for 12 years. And Mad Teddy Smith had the mad creative idea that might make sense of the escape.

It wasn't that Frank was needed any longer as muscle for the war with the Richardsons. That was over. The Richardsons' most notorious fighting soldier, Frankie Fraser, was well out of harm's way, slowly repairing a shattered thigh in prison hospitals. Big Frank was hardly needed if the most important remaining Richardson associate on Ronnie's "list" was Billy Stayton. No, Big Frank's escape would just be a wonderful present for him and a wonderful piece of underworld publicity for the twins. It could be justified by an appeal to the famously liberal-minded Home Secretary, Roy Jenkins. Frank should make it public that he intended no villainy. Under no circumstances would he be violent. In fact, his purpose was to behave as well for six months on the run as he had behaved for the last four years. Then everyone would know he was no longer dangerous. He could be offered a release date, would immediately give himself up, and go meekly back to prison.

With hindsight the idea may be written off as utter foolishness. The firm, accustomed to saying what it wanted and enforcing its wishes, imagined it could lay down the law to the Law. Ronnie may have had a hazy recollection of the laws on certification, which made his own six months as an absconder so important in 1956. There shouldn't have been a hope of their achieving their ends for Frank Mitchell, running away from a civil prison and not an asylum. But this is to overlook the genuine fair-mindedness of Roy Jenkins. Frank Mitchell really was getting a raw deal. Of all the gang, Mad Teddy Smith, author of the short radio play "The Top Bunk", was the one most likely to be aware of the possibility of winning a hearing from Jenkins that no Tory Home Secretary would have considered for a moment.

As for the escape plan, that really was virtually certain of success. For Big Frank enjoyed privileges going well beyond even the normal ones enjoyed by a trusty who was also a member of the honour party.

When Derek Brisco came to Dartmoor in 1964, he received a briefing about Frank Mitchell that surprised him:

When Mr Peckett, the former Chief Officer, interviewed me before I joined the "honour party", he told me that when Mitchell had worked on no.12 party, he had information that he was going to escape with Wilkinson and Turley, who had recently escaped. He said that Mitchell had changed his mind at the last minute and had put in for the "honour party" in order to get out from being involved. I said to Chief Officer Peckett, "If this is the case, this man should not be out on any working party". He said that they had had Mitchell in but he had denied this, but he said that they were trying to treat him leniently to get him a date. I asked what would happen if the bloke ran away whilst on the "honour party", and he more or less said that if this was what the powers that be wanted they must take the responsibility."

At its best, as Brisco understood it, the management's policy with Mitchell was "a firm control but with a light hand". Equally, he knew other officers who had found Mitchell troublesome and threatening, but whose complaints to higher authority had been rebuffed. This meant that when they were out on the moor, and Mitchell made mildly extraordinary, but not obviously objectionable requests, they were likely to be granted. For, as Brisco put it, with a nice touch of litotes, "being so far from the prison and knowing what he was capable of, I did not feel inclined to argue with him".

Fellow prisoner Fred Benson declared that there was an "unwritten law" in the prison that Frank Mitchell was free to do what he liked. And he meant a law that was respected by the screws, not imposed personally on the cons by Mitchell himself. It was an extreme and ad hominem example of the common sense of warders guarding long-term prisoners. Since screws and cons are locked in together most of the time, and will be so for many years, it is as well to make the relationship as frictionless as reasonable discipline permits. The room for disagreement lies in the interpretation of "reasonable discipline". Niggling and nagging enforcement of every little rule and regulation seems unreasonable to most people. But so, unfortunately, was the degree of licence granted to Frank Mitchell.

Mitchell's commonest unusual request to his honour-patrol guard was to be allowed to stay in the hut and "help" James Whelan, who was regularly deputed to cook the midday meal while the other prisoners worked. This meant that Mitchell and Whelan would be completely unsupervised for about two hours. On especially fine days, when it was possible to get more work done, Brisco and the working party would stay at the dry wall for an extra hour and a half, arriving back for lunch at 2pm. This was particularly necessary that December, as they wanted to finish the fencing job before winter made work impossible, so if a day was especially fine, Frank Mitchell could count on something like four hours' freedom to roam where he pleased. He and Whelan only once alarmed Brisco by their absence, and then they arrived back explaining that they had been fetching water. This came from a cottage three-quarters of a mile off, in the opposite direction from the work site. There was rarely enough water in the shed for the whole of the day's culinary needs and Brisco did not question this excuse.

But it wasn't water that Frank and Whelan went off for when the weather permitted. It was alcohol. If they had three to four hours at their disposal, they could get to and from the village of Peter Tavy and the Peter Tavy Inn. Still closer, by a telephone box at the hamlet of Horndon, stood the Elephant's Nest pub. Brisco, a relative newcomer to Dartmoor, did not know of its existence and thought Peter Tavy was too far for men to walk. And in any case, prisoners had no money. So it never occurred to him that he was leaving two convicts with access to a few swift lunchtime pints. Or more.

According to other convicts there was quite a bit of money available in the prison that evaded the spot cell searches the prison staff carried out. And Frank Mitchell had plenty, brought down by the firm members who came visiting him. (They brought tobacco, too. He didn't smoke, but it was the great internal prison currency). The landlord of the Peter Tavy could be quite definite about Frank Mitchell's money. He had plenty of cash and stocked up with bottles of vodka and brandy when he came in.

Frank became quite a familiar figure in the pubs. The publicans reckoned they remembered seeing him on 28 and 29 November, and 2 December. Certainly these were days when the honour party worked through midday and did not return for lunch until 2pm. Frank introduced himself in the bars as a contractor from Hertfordshire overseeing trench digging. This seemed reasonable. When the landlord of the Peter Tavy asked why he didn't let his men come in for a quick one, Mitchell explained airily that he left them to work on their own to show them how much he trusted them. His mind was evidently shaped by prison experience rather than the commercial world of personnel management. But the explanation passed muster.

On occasion, members of the firm joined Frank in his chosen pubs. Big fat Londoners were easily remembered. A small man with heavy glasses sounds like Sammy Lederman, though goodness knows why he should have gone down to Devon and nobody ever testified that he did. Three times a young club hostess, Clare I-, came with Wally Garelick and made a definite impression on the Devonian licensees.

If it was not possible to meet Frank in the pubs, money could be left for him at Standon's Farm, the empty building where the coke for heating the honour party's shed was kept. A mile away from the shed in the opposite direction from the work site, it was somewhere Frank visited legitimately to pick up the coke, but somewhere he could drink some vodka in lieu of lunch, enjoy a private frolic with a girl from London – should one be brought for his entertainment – or, it is said, with a local schoolteacher he met in the pubs. And it was somewhere he could keep a stash of money safe from the screws.

His longest and most celebrated absence from Bagga Tor was a taxi journey into Okehampton to buy a budgerigar for Fred Benson, who was one of the best-esteemed breeders in the prison.

Mitchell had ten visits from firm members between March and December. Alf Willey and his missus from Limehouse had been going regularly under their own names for a long time. Fat Wally Garelick went down for the first time in March, accompanied by Big Pat Connolly and 18-year-old Clare I-, who had been general-ly spronced up to look fetching for Frank. Connolly gave his own name to the prison officials. Garelick routinely used a false name: Walker or Jacobs. On their next visit Garelick and Clare were accompanied by Alfie Teal. On this occasion Clare did not go into the prison to see Mitchell in the visiting room. But she did spend some time with Garelick and Teal as they drove around country lanes, timing distances with a stopwatch. In May Clare went down again with Garelick on his own. Her visits to the pubs on these trips were remembered by the publicans, who evidently found the London hostess too well-dressed and sharp-faced for their bucolic tastes. Clare would later tell the courts she had been Garelick's girl-friend, but fell out with him after the trips to Devon.

In October Billy Exley and Charlie Kray went to Dartmoor. The name Kray was not one to flaunt at the prison officials and Charlie discreetly used a nom-de-guerre. The men discussed the possibility of providing something less uncomfortable and hazardous than a motorcycle for Frank's escape. In October Ronnie paid a personal visit, supported by Albert Donoghue and Teddy Smith. Naturally Ronnie gave a false name, as did the other two.

Thereafter, Smith, Garelick and Connolly liaised with Frank, picked up maps of the Bagga Tor and Peter Tavy district, and made the final local plans. They went down to Devon on 4 December, a visit made memorable because Garelick's car skidded on black ice at Two Bridges and struck a passing woman motorist in an Austin. Fortunately she and her car were unhurt, and despite some damage to Garelick's door, the villains discreetly declined to exchange insurance details.

On 9 December Billy Exley was ordered to hire a car for the great escape. On Sunday 11 December, Garelick, Connolly and Smith made their final briefing visit to the prison. As usually happened, Connolly gave his true name and address, Garelick and Smith called themselves Mr Walker and Mr Bishop. The following day, after their return to London, Mad Teddy Smith made another run straight back down, driving Big Albert to Bagga Tor for the great event in the hired Humber.

When details of some of these visits came out after Mitchell's escape, and the publicans confirmed seeing him as an occasional customer, sometimes with up-country "business" friends and what they clearly saw as a tarty-looking woman from London, there was a public outcry. How could it have happened? How could prison officers admit that they dared not control a big villain because they were left alone without back-up on the moors, and they thought their superiors would rather they calmed him with improper favours than let him start a ruckus? What was a notorious criminal like Ronnie Kray doing, being let in to visit Dartmoor prison? Was Frank Mitchell being allowed the services of imported hookers from London? Lord Stonham was either naive or disingenuous when he stonewalled the flurry of furious opposition questions in the House of Lords. Ronnie Kray couldn't possibly have gone to Dartmoor. All visitors had to sign their names and Ronnie's didn't appear. It was out of the question that Frank Mitchell could have enjoyed an active sex life in prison. All his visits took place in the presence of warders in the visiting room. Frank had only ever been visited by two unaccompanied women, and one of them was decent old Mrs Willey from Limehouse. (Lord Stonham seems to have thought that Limehouse Willey, the Kray firm representative, was an old family friend.) All these shocking stories were exaggerated in the press, Lord Stonham intimated.

Back in Scotland Yard, "the Grey Ghost", "Mr Flying Squad", wrote his own thoughtful comments as an addendum to a report on the case. Tommy Butler was a workaholic who played his cards very close to his chest. Often his men didn't know where they were going or why, until he had them at the exact site of a raid. And everybody knew that he stayed in the office, tapping away mysteriously on his typewriter for hours after the rest of the squad had gone home. What was he doing? No memoirs ever came from this famous detective. He was, in fact, putting the final gloss of his own experience on reports from his juniors. Up to the Deputy Commander went Butler's wise and world-weary observations on Detective Chief Inspector E.G.Harris's report on the Mitchell escape, a sad tale of incompetence and folly in the prison service:

When one first reads the statements of the two prison officers, local licensees and others, the general situation at Dartmoor prison seems to be a mixture of appalling mismanagement of prisoners and sheer comic opera. However, this would be a completely unfair criticism. The woeful situation that has come to light as a result of this escape is born of two ingredients, (a) over-population of the prison, and (b) chronic staff shortage. When viewed in this context, much of the contents of the statements become understandable – even logical.

To change a simple routine like the Visiting Order system would prove extremely difficult. Short of taking fingerprints at the prison gate and comparing them with readily available specimens, no change could be effected with the guarantee that it could end exploitation by criminals so minded. The ever-ready critics of the prison system would pounce upon any restriction as another example of hard-hearted bureaucracy.

Butler was not recommending shutting the stable door once the horse had bolted. But we need to examine that bolt.

The final planning took place in November. At a morning meet in Vallance Road, after his own trip to the prison, Ronnie declared that springing Frank Mitchell was definitely on, and asked for volunteers to play various parts. Albert Donoghue said incautiously that he'd been evacuated to the Dartmoor area during the war, in Ashburton. This is the other side of the moor from Princetown and Bagga Tor, but nobody cared about that. Albert was enthusiastically co-opted to go down as head of the rescue team.

A driver was wanted. Mad Teddy Smith put up his hand. A safe house to hide Frank in London would be needed. Nobby Clarke volunteered his parents' home in Priscilla Road, Bow. Everybody was quite jaunty about letting their names go forward. These sorts of things had been proposed before, and rarely came off. Springing Frank Mitchell had been under discussion for some time. It wasn't really going to happen.

Only it was. The car hired by Billy Exley made it definite. Smith, Connolly and Garelick confirmed that they knew the exact location of the Elephant's Nest and the telephone box, and fixed the time they should be there.

Monday 12 December was the first of the 12 days in gangland when the whereabouts of Frank Mitchell, the Mad Axeman, became a great national mystery. It was a perfectly foul morning. Mist and rain cut visibility down to about 30 yards. It was cold. And from breakfast around 8am until about 11, the honour party just sat in the shed and read the newspapers. Frank Mitchell must have been on tenterhooks for work to begin.

At 11 the sky cleared a little and Derek Brisco decided to take the men up to the fence. It was about two miles distant and he didn't expect to be back before 1pm for lunch. In fact, 30 years later, his recollection is that he spent a little extra time at the fence and didn't get back till two. But this was not something he would necessarily want to report at the time.

His formal report described coming back with all the men and having lunch, then playing cards as the weather had turned nasty again until they made a cup of tea at 3.30. At that point, Frank Mitchell asked if he could go and feed the horses down at the gate across the lane leading to Bagga Tor, where Mr Finch's minibus from Princetown would pick the party up. Frank had done this before and Brisco was perfectly amenable. Nor was he concerned that Frank didn't come back for his tea. He had stayed at the gate with the horses in the past. He would be there when they joined up with Mr Finch at 4.20.

Only he wasn't. Well, then, he would be 200 yards down the road where the horses were kept. Only he wasn't. The van had to drive to Peter Tavy where the nearest telephone box was. Derek Brisco called the prison to say that he'd lost Big Frank Mitchell.

So, with 50 minutes to an hour's start, Frank Mitchell was off and away. Which made it a little hard to explain why Albert Donoghue later recollected that they heard the first report that he had escaped from a prison work party as they passed through Fulham at 4.30pm. To drive from Peter Tavy to Fulham in 50 minutes would defeat the most determined racing driver in the fastest car.

Thirty years later, Derek Brisco explains. It was not, in fact, 3.30pm when he last saw Frank Mitchell, it was 11am. As the main body of the honour party set off for the distant fence, Mitchell was going in the other direction to deserted Standons Farm to fetch coke. He had done this before. There was no reason to suppose he would abuse the freedom. It could be expected to take him an hour and a half, so there was no instant need to be worried when he was not back in the hut for lunch. After all, he genuinely did like to dawdle around feeding the ponies.

But as time went on and it became increasingly clear that Frank was not going to stride in with a big guffawing laugh, Derek Brisco's worries increased. There were no such things as personal radios or mobile phones for issue to prison officers. He was alone on the moors, responsible for half-a-dozen men, with no means of communication that he knew of nearer than Peter Tavy. Frank might have suffered an accident. He might have been kicked and trampled by the unpredictable ponies he loved to feed. But this was no terrain for the inexperienced to mount a search in poor visibility. There was absolutely nothing Brisco could do but sit tight and wait for Finch's minibus to take him to the telephone.

And so at half past four the news was broadcast. Frank Mitchell had escaped from Dartmoor. But not with an hour's start on pursuit. With five and a half hours!

The Great Escape had been quite easy. Teddy Smith and Albert Donoghue set off for Devon before dawn. They found the telephone box near the Elephant's Nest, parked the car, and Teddy pretended to use the phone to make it look as if there was a reason for the hired Humber to be stopped below Bagga Tor. When Big Frank came tramping round the corner in his prison work clothes and a nylon mask he had made for himself, he rushed at the man in telephone box, not recognizing him. Albert shouted, "Hey, Frank, get in the car. It's all right! He's with us!" And the escape was on.

It was uneventful. They had brought civilian clothes for Frank, borrowed from "Tommy the Bear" Welsh, the only gang member who seemed roughly Frank's size. As Frank changed, a whacking great knife made from a bit of bedstead came out of his pocket. Albert and Teddy had to persuade him to jettison it. What if they were stopped? What would become of the claim that Frank was determined on a life of non-violence? Regretfully Frank agreed to throw away the tool in which he took such pride. At least they let him keep the beret and mask he had fashioned and which he apparently hoped would help him make the reputation he had never really acquired as a serious criminal, outside prison. It was characteristic of Frank's immature and confused mind that he hoped to establish himself as a good and quiet man who didn't threaten society as far as the Home Secretary and the parole boards were concerned, and at the same time to win recognition in the underworld as a great bank robbing "pavement artist".

Not that Albert and Teddy were that much brighter. They simply bundled up the giveaway clothes and the incriminating knife and heaved them behind a hedge near Bittaford, about 20 miles from the prison. By the time they were found the following day, the clue that Frank had escaped along the A38 was useless. But DCI Harris's report on the case a month later showed how completely the knife scuppered the gang's project of presenting Frank as a harmless feller who had lived down his criminal past. "Found with the clothing," he wrote, "was a large sheath knife, which does not augur well for Mitchell's later claims... that he does not intend any violence to anyone. I can personally conceive no reason why Mitchell should consider it necessary to carry such a weapon when escaping, except to use on any person who impeded him. It was certainly not permitted by the prison officers nor did he need it for his duties with the working party outside Dartmoor prison."

Frank had also brought his transistor radio with him. All the way to London he listened to it, waiting for the news that his escape had been reported. By the time the car reached Andover, 150 miles away from Princetown, and there was no word of pursuit, they were sure they were safe. When the escape finally reached the airwaves they were already in London and there was no hope for the authorities.

Frank was childishly excited to recognize places he knew. When they reached the East End and passed Old Ford Road, Smith and Donoghue got their first warning of problems ahead. Frank's mother and father lived there. He wanted to stop and let them know he was free. This was out of the question. Frank's family were not villains and would not necessarily respect the East End code. They didn't approve of the Krays in any case and didn't think Frank's prison friendship with them boded well for his future. And the gang's first and most important job was to get him under cover in the safe house promised by Nobby Clarke. The car rolled on through the gloom to Priscilla Road.

There they found Clarke in a great state of agitation. He had never given serious thought to the dangers of letting an escaped convict stay with his parents, had got seriously cold feet when he found that it was really likely to happen, and earlier in the day had told Charlie Kray it was out of the question as his father was unwell. Charlie had immediately arranged alternative accommodation. An acquaintance of the gang with a bookstall on the Whitechapel Road Street market was Lennie "Books" Dunn. Lennie liked to drink with them and cultivate their company. He was, in fact, ensnared by gangster glamour. So he was quite willing to help the gang out for once, and gave them the keys to his flat. Nobby now handed them over to Albert and gave him the address.

The gang, nearly all central Londoners, assumed Frank's hiding place was in Barking, something which has been repeatedly stated. In fact in was in nearby East Ham, at 206A Barking Road, a wide main thoroughfare running from the Blackwall Tunnel through Plaistow and Newham. Frank was very pleased with himself for recognizing that they would have to go to the Blackwall Tunnel. He was less pleased when he arrived at Lennie Books' flat. It was small, with a kitchen looking over the main road, a sitting room containing a leather settee and an old upright piano, a bathroom with a fanlight over the door, and two small bedrooms. And there was nobody to greet the arrivals except Lennie Books and a minder.

A conflict in testimony immediately occurs. Albert Donoghue's recollection was that Scotch Jack Dickson was waiting at Priscilla Road and came on with the escape party to Barking Road to take up his position as minder. Dickson says that Teddy Smith came back to collect him from Whitechapel underground station after the team's return from Devon, and although he remarks that police were buzzing around as though they had heard of Mitchell's escape, which hadn't yet been reported, he also seems to say that this was three days after the escape, when he started to share minding duties with Billy Exley who had been in the flat from the start. Exley said that he first saw Frank Mitchell in Barking Road "about 14 days" before his murder. It has been reported that Dickson and Exley served together as minders, taking turn and turn about with Smith and Donoghue, but this claim is certainly wrong. The sleeping arrangements in the flat were so restricted that Lennie Books had to sleep on his settee, giving up his bed to Mitchell and his small spare room to the minder on duty.

Exley's "about 14 days" erroneously expands the 12 days that Frank Mitchell had to live. Donoghue's memory is demonstrably shaky on points of no real importance. He thought the Elephant's Nest was called the "Monkey's Fist", for example. And he recollected Frank as enjoying nearly two weeks' impassioned bonking with the hostess brought in for his delectation, when it is perfectly certain that she was only present for the last four nights and days in the Barking Road flat.

Scotch Jack could have a motive for reducing his knowledge of the escape. He would ultimately plead guilty to harbouring an escaped convict. But if he really knew nothing about the escape until Mitchell was safely in Lennie Books' flat, then he could not be accused of conspiring to bring about the escape. If he accepted the duty of seeing that the transfer from Priscilla Road to Barking Road went smoothly, then he was probably a participant.

Frank, for his part, was instantly disappointed with his reception. He had anticipated a big welcome such as Albert Dimes and Billy Hill had laid on for Frankie Fraser. He wanted a celebration party with booze and girls. He wanted Ronnie, his mentor, to welcome him out and introduce him as a hero to all the fresh faces in the underworld since he went away. Instead he got thin, grey-haired Lennie Dunn, in his mid-fifties, a gangland hanger-on, and either the infirm and essentially retired Billy Exley, who preferred living as a barman and didn't like being kept away from his wife and children, or the flaccid and pasty Scotch Jack Dickson, who was quietly starting to wonder whether signing on with the Kray firm hadn't been a serious mistake.

The gang members explained to Frank that Ronnie was not there to greet him because he was "on his toes" again. The story the twins gave John Pearson linked this to his association with a "senior policeman", though they only cited his rank as inspector (two grades above constable). According to them, the officer in question had offered Ronnie free and unhindered use of an East End pub for £20 a week. Exactly what immunity was on offer, one wonders, over and above that already enjoyed by the twins in The Lion, where the police regularly drank in one bar and the firm in the other, or the Grave Maurice, where the police were welcome to pop in for one on the house when the Krays were standing permanent drinks all round? It seems more likely that we are in the murky world of police informants, which has been a fruitful area for accusations and suspicions of police corruption ever since Dickens expressed his mistrust of the Bow Street Runners' association with little crooks to get the goods on bigger villains. In any event,

Ronnie hired a private detective and had himself wired up when he went to a meeting with Detective Sergeant Townsend from Hackney station. And he passed the tapes on with a formal complaint against the police. The Director of Public Prosecutions followed this up. Charges were brought against DS Townsend. And Ronnie Kray was subpoenaed to give evidence against him.

Now here was a dilemma. According to the twins, the mighty code of the East End came into play at once. Not even against a blackmailing police officer would Ronald Kray go into a witness box and grass. His honour demanded that he go into hiding.

It's not difficult to see this story playing to another scenario, however. If DS Townsend was using Ronnie as an informant, and Ronnie felt he was not getting enough in return for his information, he might easily have set up a situation in which his handler made remarks that appeared compromising. Ronnie may not have realized that, even before Sir Robert Mark's great cleanup, the police were compelled to investigate any complaint they formally received. Something he intended as a mere nuisance to put pressure on Townsend could have rebounded into a full-scale enquiry. And faced with cross-examination Ronnie might not have looked quite the perfect East End code-follower he claimed.

We shall never know. Faced with Ronnie's resolute disappearance, even after a bench warrant was issued for his arrest, the case against Townsend was inevitably dropped, resulting in his automatic acquittal. Ronnie would at least enjoy the satisfaction of knowing he had thrown a black mark onto the record of a man he evidently regarded as an enemy.

For this piece of foolishness, Ronnie was now in hiding in a safe flat in Finchley. Scotch Jack Dickson, one of the few trusted gang members who knew the address and visited him there, felt he was depressed and wanted to be out. Scotch Jack disliked the Puccini records that Ronnie played, and he was increasingly alarmed by Ronnie's wild plans for expanding the firm's business which involved more and more names of enemies going on to his "list". Those who were close to Ronnie recognized a danger signal when he changed his records from Puccini to Churchill's wartime speeches, which meant he was psyching himself up to face the host of enemies his paranoia imagined. This occurred from time to time during his self-incarceration in Finchley. But looking at the pattern of his life, the hiding itself may well be seen as a response to general paranoia. Ronnie felt safe and great when only the chosen few knew where he was and were carrying away his orders for the running of gang-land, without his being actively involved.

As his escape became a main bulletin on the evening television news, Frank Mitchell rejoiced in his new fame, and tucked into the hearty fry-up provided by Lennie Dunn (Steak and chips by one account; sausage, egg and bacon by another). His fame had suddenly become great indeed. Not really because of the seriousness of his crimes or the actual danger his freedom represented to the public. But because he was described as "the Mad Axeman". Derek Brisco, meeting him for the first time two years previously, had never heard the nickname. Frank's family were shocked by the description that flew across the media. This was the week when Mrs Peggs wrote to them to say that Frank had not been so mad, bad or dangerous as the newspapers were suggesting. But it was an irresistible title. And as too often happens when an irresponsible newspaper campaign puts pressure on the Home Office, the authorities felt compelled to take extravagant and unnecessary measures.

The following day the army started a sweep search of Dartmoor. Helicopters flew overhead to scan the wilderness for a lone fleeing figure. Frank sat in the Barking flat and chortled over his national notoriety. His fantasies started to include becoming Ronnie's right-hand man, rubbing out Billy Stayton for him, and being the feared leading henchman of the King of the Underworld. His minders were quietly perturbed by the unreality of his hopes and ambitions. They dared not say anything. Under the circumstances, like Derek Brisco, they weren't going to argue.

For a day or two the intense publicity kept Frank happy. He had mixed feelings about a Giles cartoon depicting three uniformed searchers tramping over a Dartmoor bridge under which a simian figure cowered. It was flattering to be the subject for one of the nation's most popular cartoonists. But Frank rightly suspected that the extravagantly long arms hinted at his severe mental limitations. He did not live to see the *Private Eye* cover that parodied the old newspaper stunt of sending an unobtrusive reporter around seaside resorts as "Lobby Lud", to award cash vouchers to anyone who recognized and challenged him. "You are the Mad Axeman and I claim the News Chronicle prize", squeaked one tiny figure to another in an aerial view of wild countryside.

Lennie Books Dunn shopped for the household, and for a time took pride in his role as "the victualling officer". Frank Mitchell ate unbelievable quantities of food. Dickson estimated his steaks weighed fully a pound. But then, Frank worked off the calories almost as quickly as he ingested them. He followed his prison regimen, rising at dawn and starting his day with 50 press-ups. He broke off playing cards or chatting for more exercise whenever he felt like it. He used the doorframe to pull himself up. He lifted his minders by their belts to show off his strength. Once, at the end of his time in Barking Road, he put his arms around the piano and lifted it off the floor by main force. He fretted about missing his daily prison "exercise" of tramping round the open-air yard in circles. Whenever he wanted to go outside or visit his mother and father he had to be crossed and talked out of it.

He was obsessively clean. He brushed his teeth anything up to 12 times a day and would get up in the night to brush them again. He was vain, and would sit staring at his reflection in a mirror (He was, of course, good looking, with widely spaced open features).

There were regular, maybe almost daily visits from Donoghue and Smith. Albert was reporting back to the twins. He had found, rather to his surprise, that he had become something of a hero in the firm for bringing Frank up from Dartmoor. It was, after all, only baby-sitting as far as he was concerned.

Teddy Smith's job was to coach Frank in writing the letters to the press that were supposed to persuade the authorities to give him a release date. By every account this was a long and difficult business. The minders seem to remember Teddy coming in and starting work on the first full day in Barking Road (Tuesday 13 December). They report that it took at least 20 attempts for Frank to get it right. But Dickson's suggestion that they didn't actually take more than a night and a day to complete accords with the equally badly spelled and punctuated, but perfectly comprehensible letters Frank habitually wrote, unaided, to his family. It is easy to believe Dickson's recollection that Lennie Books had to go out and buy extra writing pads. But it is not clear just when the first letter was written. For it was not until Monday 19 December that the first pair of letters (addressed to the *Daily Mirror* and *The Times*) went into the post from Barking. That foolish use of the giveaway postmark, Barking and Ilford, suggests some haste. A postscript, which has not been published before, may explain the reason.

Each letter was on a single sheet of paper in Frank's handwriting, with his vast square thumbprint, looking more like a big toe, in the top right hand corner. The wording of the letters was identical, give or take some variety in the spelling and punctuation – mistakes Teddy Smith had to allow through. The one to the *Daily Mirror* was as follows:

19/12/66
To The EditoR
The DAILY MIRROR

Sir,
The reason for my absence from Dartmoor was to bring to the notice of my unhappy plight. to be truthful I am asking for a possible Date of release. from the age of 9 I have not been completely free, always under some act or other.
sir, I ask you where is the fairness of this, I am not a murderer or sex maniac nor do I think I am a danger to the Public. I think that I have been more than punished for the wrongs I have done. I am ready to give myself up if I can have something to look forward to I do not intend to use any violence at any time should I be found, that is why I left a knife behind with my Prison things

Yours Sincerly

Frank Mitchell

P.S
I have not been in touch with the News of the World nor with Mr Danny Darling.

The final sentence may explain why it was now felt adequate – or at any rate essential to send it – come hell or high water. Because the *News of the World* published a curious story on Sunday 18th, which surfaced and died immediately, leaving a minor mystery for Kray researchers. The paper had been approached over the telephone by a man who claimed to know how to contact the Mad Axeman. He also claimed that he himself had been requested over the telephone by someone who only identified himself as "Ronnie", to establish contact with all the newspapers on Mitchell's behalf. This looked dangerously like a "spoiler", which would handicap the plan to win Frank's release date, unless the real Frank Mitchell made himself known very quickly. And this was in fact done so quickly that the minders carelessly gave away his whereabouts with the postmark. A second, slightly longer pair of letters, laboriously written by Mitchell, went again to *The Times* and the *Daily Mirror* the following day. Again they were identically worded, though slightly differently spaced so that they looked different on the two sheets of paper each used. The haste of their composition showed in the higher proportion of wilder spelling mistakes. There are some transparent attempts to curry favour with liberals in the criminal justice system. But the real point of these letters is surely the first sentence. They were postmarked from Birmingham, the crude attempt to misdirect the police suggesting that Teddy Smith was as stupid and unconvincing a liar as the twins themselves. Perhaps Scotch Jack annoyed the firm so much more than any of the other "treacherous" witnesses against them because he was so much better than they at slanting facts plausibly in his favour.

The new letter to *The Times* read:

20/12/66
1
To THE EditoR
of the Times

Sir,
It is obvious I have moved since posting my last letters. I am

sorry that my absence has caused certain people to think badly of men like Mr Roy Jenkins. Who I am sure is trying to use modern methods of dealine with Prisoners. What Mr Jenkins has said is true... treat People like Animals and they will re--act like Animals. But treat them like human beings and they will act like human beings.

When I was in Prison I recieved some kindnes from some memmbers of the staff.

I would like to thank those officers who Offered to bring me back to Dartmoor. When Mr Malone was Governor of Dartmoor I had hope to carry on Despite the hardship of <u>life</u> in Prison. because I felt sure I would some day get a Date of release.

I have read with interest what has been written since I sent my last letters.

I can only repeat my appeall to the humane

[here Mitchell's original begins a second page]

<u>2</u>

thinking people of this country, If I must be buried alive, give me some reason to hope.

Trusting in the goodness of others

Yours sincerly

Frank Mitchell

If Smith was absurdly blatant in his attempt to relocate Mitchell well away from Ilford and Barking, the police were too clever by half when they spotted the ploy. They carried it back to the first pair of letters as well as the second. And they preferred to believe a Flying Squad informant who was giving them some intelligence that was either garbled or deliberately misleading. "The postmarks are known to have been a red herring," DCI Harris recorded later. "Mitchell at that stage was being housed somewhere in the Home Counties. The informant is quite definite about this. He avers the location was within a five-mile radius of Guildford."

They may have been the more convinced because of their very efficient follow-up of the *News of the World* letter. They traced the newspaper's informant, and found that he had also tried to sell the possibility of Mitchell's appearing on the "David Frost Show" on television. He had even persuaded another wanted man to speak to Frost programme researchers over the telephone in a gruff London voice, pretending to be Mitchell and promising to appear. They traced this second man (whose offence was only an infringement of traffic laws while under the influence of drugs) and took a statement from him. They found his story persuasive. He knew, for example, the correct telephone number for a direct line to the Frost production team. But they did not believe this trail would lead them to Mitchell, because they did not think Mitchell would under any circumstances be so silly as to put himself in front of the cameras. They did not approach the Frost programme directly because they feared that television programme-makers would give too high a priority to making capital out of the approach from Mitchell. They were quite sure their own discreet surveillance would enable them to arrest the Axeman should he actually approach the television people.

But their work was made harder by the fact that the *News of the World*'s original informant would only speak to them when he was drunk. It would have been tempting to write him off as completely unreliable, had he not made that tantalizing reference to taking instructions over the telephone from an unidentified "Ronnie". One thing the police had known from 13 December was that the Kray twins lay behind the escape.

They knew this because of those very obvious trips to Devon made by Wally Garelick in his own car. He had parked it at the prison when he, Connolly and Smith visited Dartmoor to brief Frank the day before the escape. Garelick thought the number was noticed because he left it in a space intended for the prison officers. In fact, his slightly misremembered number had been observed in various places, as very few honest Devonians much liked the look of the three visiting Londoners: two big and fat, the third tall and slim. In their smart suits, with their questions and confabs, they looked highly suspicious. And the police heard from various sources about the brown Rover numbered UMP 533, or something like it.

They broadcast an appeal for the vehicle the day after the escape. And Garelick realized it was so close to his actual number, UPM 533, that he would inevitably be traced in due course. So, sensibly anticipating events, he went to the police and confirmed his visit to Dartmoor, and that his companions were Big Pat and Mad Teddy. He also confirmed that he and Teddy had given false names at the prison.

Fat Wally made a long statement to DCI Harris in which he admitted a lot of visits to Mitchell. He claimed that Pat Connolly had introduced him to the Axeman in March, and that his own reason for going to Dartmoor in the first place was because he didn't want to refuse to lend Big Pat his car, but he didn't trust Big Pat to drive it. He made no mention of taking Clare I- on any of the trips. No mention of jaunts around the countryside and to pubs, either, no mention of buying maps or test-driving routes. The visits seemed to have been very simple and straightforward. Into the prison visitors' room. A wait for Frank if he was out on a working party. Sometimes outside for lunch. Back again for a second visiting period in the afternoon. The police had no doubt this was a concocted story covering up his actual visits with messages or instructions from the Krays.

Fat Wally was quite a useful person to take the heat of the initial inquiry. He had no previous form. Little as they may have liked it, the police reports had to describe him as a man "of unblemished character". Nobody imagined that this 22-stone vague-affiliate of gangland would have had the ability or desire to spring Mitchell on his own account. He had not worked long or centrally for the Krays. Managing the Green Dragon Club still left George Mizel as a cut-off between him and the twins. The police might be perfectly certain he was lying or covering up. But they couldn't prove it. And they couldn't bring any effective pressure to bear on him. Charging him with silly, pernickety little offences, like giving a false name to the prison officers and driving a car with no road tax disc, was no counter to the sort of threats the twins could make. Everybody knew what had happened to George Cornell.

But Fat Wally's admitted companions linked the case back to the twins, all right. Pat Connolly was one of their oldest associates and figured, large as life, in the foreground of pictures of Ron and Reg modestly greeting neighbours after their acquittal in the Hideaway Club trial. Teddy Smith had stood in the dock with them at that trial and enjoyed the same acquittal. And Pat and Teddy were clearly covering something up. Pat grouchily saw the police and replied, "No comment" to every question. Teddy anticipated them with a letter from Messrs Sampson & Co, the tried and tested Kray firm solicitors. This said that Mr Smith would only agree to be interviewed by the police in the presence of his solicitor. And everybody knew what that would mean. He would, on legal advice, decline to answer anything. You and I and DCI Harris might all feel that this amounted to an admission of guilt or of guilty knowledge. But in those days the prosecution could not comment on it in court and the judge was bound to tell the jury that a prisoner who exercised his right to silence must not have that interpreted to his detriment. The seasoned villains knew their rights and weren't going to be trapped.

Nor could the police bring identification evidence against them. None of the Devonians who were shown a very good likeness of Pat Connolly could confirm that he was one of the men they had seen. There were no acceptable pictures of Smith and Garelick available. And Devon Constabulary was not prepared to haul them in and mount an identification parade on such a poor basis.

In fact, it was another East End open secret. Everyone knew the Kray twins were behind the springing of the Mad Axeman. Nobody could report the fact in the press, thanks to Britain's preposterous libel laws. The police couldn't act on it because they couldn't bring evidence that would survive in court. But nobody knew just where the Mad Axeman was or what he was doing. The only thing everybody in the know might have said for certain was that the press hullabaloo was quite ridiculous. Frank Mitchell was not dangerous to John Citizen minding his own business. Everybody was sleeping just as safely in their beds as they had been before the commandos and the helicopters started sweeping over Dartmoor.

Three people, however, were not sleeping peacefully any longer. John Dickson, Billy Exley and Leslie Dunn spent uncomfortable nights. Their secret guest might wake up and clean his teeth or do a few more press-ups at any time. If anything went wrong and the secret got out, they would be the ones in trouble. And Mitchell would be more than they could cope with if, as sometimes seemed possible, he lost patience with the whole business of hiding and waiting, and tried to break out. It was a possibility that had never occurred to Ronnie Kray, who looked back on his own six months "on the trot" in 1956, allowing his certification to lapse, as one of his finest hours.

It is not possible to be precise in detailing the events of 13–18 December. John Pearson's informants suggested that Reggie visited 206A Barking Road three times: once the day after Mitchell arrived, when the two arm-wrestled; once on 19 December when he and Tommy Cowley brought the woman "Liza Prescott" to the flat; and once after that when Reggie gave Mitchell instructions about leaving to go to the country. John Dickson describes the last visit only, dating it to Thursday 22 December, the day before Mitchell left. Albert Donoghue says categorically that Reggie made only one visit to the flat and it was before Liza came on 19 December. Albert is undoubtedly right. Liza's very precise testimony confirms his statement that he alone took her to Barking Road, and by omission confirms that there was no subsequent visit to the flat by Reggie. From 19–23 December we can rely on her account for accuracy. But of those who could describe the earlier days, Ronnie and Reggie cannot be trusted at all. They have always lied brazenly whenever it suited them. Albert Donoghue's memory is at best shaky. John Dickson's is at worst flaky. Billy Exley and Lennie Dunn are dead and their testimony was made when they were older and more infirm, and probably more easily confused, than Donoghue and Dickson. Nobody has seen Teddy Smith for over 20 years.

So we can discard the improbabilities from Dickson's account, filled as it is with amateurish reconstructions of conversations he can't possibly have remembered verbatim for ten years. We can say that the first day or two (Tuesday 13 and Wednesday 14 December) were probably happy enough, with Lennie Dunn taking some pride in having involved himself seriously in the Krays' world. He was learning harmless criminal skills. Reggie had given him some money for provisions, but warned him not to shop in his own locale. It could arouse suspicion if shopkeepers noticed that he was buying four times as much food as usual. There may even have been a small thrill in sleeping on the sofa at first and it did have a strategic reason. He was nearest to the front door, ensuring that some unexpected caller would not find the Mad Axeman beaming at them from the hallway, or some unfamiliar and dodgy-looking East End gangster asking what they wanted.

Teddy Smith probably spent some time coaching Frank in writing his letters. And at some point there was an explosion when the runaway giant realized that the firm really did intend him to give himself up peacefully once all the arrangements for his release date had been made. The man who was "free at last" wanted to stay that way. One night Dickson woke up to find Mitchell standing over his bed with a knife in his hand. And at some point Mitchell demanded that Ronnie should come and see him and tell him personally that he really had got to go back to prison sooner or later.

His other demand, causing his minders some anxiety, was for a woman. He told Scotch Jack that it was over a year since he last had sex. That had been out on the moor, with someone (presumably the rumoured schoolteacher) he had met in a pub. If Dickson's recollection is correct and Mitchell's story was true, this rather discounts the oft-repeated allegation that the firm supplied him with a London hooker or hookers to enliven his breaks from the outside work party. It also indicates that Mitchell was able to get away from work parties (by his account to "feed the horses") even before he was assigned to the honour party.

According to Dickson, he reported Mitchell's demand to Ronnie. And, after mulling it over, Ronnie decided to let Reggie arrange something. According to Donoghue, he brought Reggie on his sole visit to the flat, when the question of the woman arose, and the letters needed to be discussed. This may well have been Sunday 18 December, when the *News of the World*'s mysterious item appeared, or the day before, if it was anticipated. On Monday night (or, to be precise, in the small hours of Tuesday morning) the promised woman was delivered.

Reggie's visit was rather an uncomfortable occasion. Big Frank's puppyish hope that this meant Ronnie would be coming soon was not very flattering. Reggie barely pretended to be interested in the Axeman and stayed as short a time as possible. Only the definite decision that Frank should be supplied with the woman he wanted made for peace.

According to John Dickson, Frank spent Monday 19 December in a state of excited anticipation. He was looking forward to the promised woman and was thrilled when a telephone call in the evening confirmed that she would be arriving around 2am. He apparently expressed the enthusiastic hope that she would be a blonde, and confided that he had never slept with a blonde. Also, though Dickson doesn't mention it, Monday was the day when the letters to the papers went off to the press and Frank may have hoped that his epistolary labours were at an end.

To find Mitchell the appropriate lady, the firm turned to Tommy Cowley. Although Albert Donaghue was their notorious womanizer, Cowley was felt to have a classier approach and a better knowledge of the available hostesses. His recommendation was a woman who worked under the professional name Liza Prescott. A northerner, aged about 30, who had previously been a hostess at Churchill's Club, she was now irregularly employed three days a week at Winston's. She described the work as "entertaining men at the club and afterwards. I am paid for entertaining them afterwards". Under hostile cross-examination three years later she would admit that (at least as far as she was concerned) "nightclub hostess" was a polite term for prostitute. But she angrily denied that she would sleep with any man for money. She only slept with men she liked.

It wasn't clear that she very much liked Tommy Cowley. He came into the club two or three times a week and she had drinks and chatted with him from time to time. But she was afraid of him. Not because he was violent, but because he boasted of his power and influence with Winston's and all the other major West End clubs. And he threatened to have her put out of work if she didn't do what he wanted. What he wanted on 19 December 1966 was for her to entertain a friend of his after the club. Liza agreed without demur, thinking that it would be easy for her to slip away without Cowley noticing. But she was prevented by a fight that broke out in the club. The doors were closed and she had to wait until it cleared, at which point Cowley and his two companions, Reggie Kray and Albert Donaghue, collected her coat, collected her, and ushered her into a taxi. Reggie told her she would receive "the respect of everybody in the East End". According to John Pearson's information, she responded that respect was all very well, but she was interested in money. She was, in any case, promised £100. Liza still had no idea what made this entertainment of Tommy Cowley's friend so important. But she felt a little frightened of the men, and she didn't question it.

The taxi took them to Vallance Road – a dark narrow road of terraced houses unknown to Liza – where Reggie and Tommy Cowley got out. She gathered that Tommy would collect her when she had attended to his friend. Albert went on his own with her to 206A Barking Road. They arrived at about 3am and went into the flat where, in the sitting room, she met Lennie Dunn and John Dickson. And then, out from the bedroom came the face that had been plastered across the papers the previous week. Albert knew there was no point in attempting deception. He made the introduction with a quiet flourish. The friend he wanted her to meet, he said, was "The Mad Axeman".

Albert stayed for a cup of tea, and then left. Frank Mitchell was obviously delighted with Liza. She was blonde. She was well-built. She had a lively manner. And, as Nipper Read later observed, she was obviously a good hostess, who could make a man feel he was the only person in the room who mattered to her. At about four Frank took her into the bedroom, which contained a bed and a dressing table, and was lit only by the glow of an electric fire. They talked for some time before making love. Liza told him she had a baby and would have to get home to relieve the sitter. It wasn't true, but she thought it would ensure that she was taken home in the morning. Frank's response, however, was to encourage her to bring the baby to stay with them at Barking Road, because he loved children.

John Pearson was informed that she refused to sleep with Frank until she had been given her money and Dickson accordingly drove to Vallance Road and collected £100 in used notes in a brown paper bag. Pearson sees this as very professional of her. If it is true, it was also extremely brave. But Dickson says that Liza was not paid until the following Friday after they left the flat, when the money was to be given to her by someone else, at a party in a pub which he deliberately missed. Liza says that Dickson gave her the paper bag of used notes in the flat just before they left, and Reggie asked her at the party whether she had received it.

By Liza's account, she and Frank stayed in the bedroom most of the next day, because she had no clothes except the black cocktail dress she had been wearing in the club. This may have been what Dickson took for a black negligee when, by his account, she came out of the bedroom with Frank at half past one and said, "Christ! He's like a stallion! He hasn't stopped all night", and added, as the men laughed, "I wouldn't want too many nights like that". Before long she had endeared herself to the typical criminal male chauvinists with her cooking skills; they were happy to let her preferred Spanish food take over from Lenny Dunn's recurrent fry-ups.

Teddy Smith came in during the afternoon to get the second pair of letters to *The Times* and the *Daily Mirror* written. Liza helped with the spelling, though many more mistakes than had been in the first pair ("dealine", "memmbers",) got through. Frank told her that Teddy was the one who had got him away from Dartmoor, and Teddy announced that this was the last time he would be coming to Barking Road, now the letters were complete. He or someone else must have driven like the clappers or caught a perfectly timed train to get those letters into the last post from Birmingham that night.

Billy Exley took over as minder during the evening, and he oversaw Liza's writing a note to her flatmate, saying that she would be away for a few days and would not be able to keep their engagement to visit her parents on Christmas Eve. This was the first evidence Liza had that she was not going to be collected by Tommy Cowley and taken home as she had expected. At about half past nine, after her flatmate had gone to work as a hostess in the Savoy nightclub, Billy drove Liza back to her flat to get some clothes. He watched her closely all the time she was there to see that she did not leave any additional messages and he searched the bathroom carefully after she had changed in it. Liza realized that she was a prisoner, and from time to time she wondered fearfully whether she would be allowed to leave alive, knowing as she did the secret of the Mad Axeman's hiding-place.

During the night she tried to escape. But she tripped over the flex of the electric fire and woke Frank, who put her across his knee and spanked her. It didn't amount to anything that the gangsters would have called "a spanking" if punishing each other, and it may well have been done as much for his own mildly kinky erotic pleasure as for the satisfaction of his childish sense of discipline. But it was severe enough to constitute a warning. Still more of a warning was his saying, with obviously genuine concern, that she mustn't try to get away, because then he wouldn't be able to protect her. It confirmed her fears that she was in serious physical danger if she tried to assert her independence and leave. It confirmed her observation that, for all his strength and the current prestige of his name, Frank was almost as much a captive as herself. And it confirmed the unavoidable and embarrassing perception that this man, starved of women's company for so long, was falling in love with her. That didn't stop her from unsuccessfully trying the windows when Frank wasn't looking.

By Thursday at the latest it was clear that the Great Escape was a Great Disaster. Lennie Books had not received the £500 he had been promised and was missing the pre-Christmas trade in the Whitechapel Road market. John Dickson was seriously alarmed by Frank's repeated insistence that he would not go back to prison, and tried to get Liza to persuade him that he must. It was Liza's clear impression that Dickson was frightened. She was definitely frightened. She doubted whether these villains would let her live when they finally took Frank somewhere else. She knew too much, even though she only knew the men in the flat by their first names, and Dickson had consistently used the name "Patrick". (It was one of the confusing habits of the firm that some members used aliases which might mix them up with other members. Albert Donoghue used his stepfather's surname, Barry, from time to time, which invited confusion with Scotch Ian, or with the brothers Tony and John, who had taken over the Regency Club in Stoke Newington. Scotch Jack, calling himself Patrick, might easily have been mistaken for Patrick Connolly.)

But Frank Mitchell was the most discontented of all. His good temper would suddenly disappear as he demanded to go outside. He was particularly anxious to see his mother and father, after his father broadcast an appeal for him to give himself up. When he insisted that he would go round to Vallance Road and sort the twins out there if they didn't give him his wish, he condemned himself to death. According to Albert Donoghue, Frank had written to the twins at the Vallance Road address, which confirmed that he knew it. The twins would never let anyone to threaten violence around their parents. When Dickson reported on Friday morning that Frank was saying he would blame the twins if anyone came to the flat and caught him, and he would know who to settle with, they decided on instant action. They summoned an urgent lunchtime meeting at Harry Hopwood's home.

Conflicting stories from interested parties immediately surround this meeting. Donoghue says Reggie instructed him to fetch Freddie Foreman from across the river, and the people in the flat were Reggie, Charlie Kray, Freddie and Hopwood. He says that he and Hopwood were sent into the kitchen while the serious business was discussed, after which Charlie Kray came out and gave him instructions for getting Frank out of the flat and into Foreman's van that evening, to be driven down to the country.

Freddie Foreman agrees that the meeting took place. But he denies the presence of both Charlie and Reggie Kray. He agrees that Hopwood was in the flat and was sent into the kitchen so that he didn't know what was being planned. Freddie has admitted that the murder of Frank Mitchell was planned. And he says there were just three conspirators, himself, Albert Donoghue and Ronnie Kray. He and Ronnie Kray put together the details. But Donoghue's conversation in the car showed that he knew what was expected: he certainly knew that Mitchell would never step out of the van alive.

The twins, of course, said that there wasn't any such meeting. Their tendency when discussing villainies to which they did not admit was to have recourse to what the police call "the guilty man's defence". This consists of denying everything, offering no plausible alternative explanation because the accused supposedly knows nothing about the alleged crime, and angrily accuses every prosecution witness of lying. Happily for the truth, Freddie Foreman has now made confessions that expose the twins for what they were. Stupid, barefaced liars, with an inexplicable tendency to whinge when their lies were rejected.

Any lies told by either Albert or Freddie or both, by contrast, are sensible and explicable. And one or both must be lying or completely misremembering, since their stories about the meeting conflict starkly. If Albert attended the inner council in Harry Hopwood's flat, he was party to the conspiracy to murder Frank Mitchell and his subsequent actions might lay him open to conviction as an active participant. He would have a direct personal interest in claiming to know nothing but the emollient cover story about driving Frank to the country for future shipment to the continent.

Freddie has confessed that he was an active participant. His story isn't self-serving self-protection. But it does protect Reggie and Charlie Kray, at Ronnie's expense. Only Ronnie was dead by the time Freddie first gave his account, and dead men can no more be grassed up than they can be libelled. Nobody with a brain in their head would ever believe that Albert Donoghue off his own bat (or, as Reggie hopelessly pretended at his trial, in collaboration with Scotch Jack) set up the escape, harbouring and murdering the Mad Axeman as a private independent venture. Nobody seriously doubts that there was some Kray input to the murder plot. If either Reggie or Charlie Kray, or both, really did participate in the plan to kill Frank Mitchell, Freddie has respected the code of the East End by continuing to protect them and leaving the whole Kray side of the murder plan as a product of poor mad Ronnie's paranoia. The interesting problem raised by Freddie's story, however, is that everybody else has Ronnie rooted in his Finchley safe house listening to his records and refusing to be drawn out.

Why murder in any case? Well, the twins had lumbered themselves with a no-win situation. If Frank couldn't be persuaded to sit tight – and he obviously couldn't – he endangered them and their firm and everybody who enjoyed the advantages of their spy network. And he endangered the promise held out by their supposed American contacts. Let the police catch Frank, and he would be quite incapable of concealing the sources from which he drew support. In any case, he had been bright enough to see that he wasn't a welcome guest any more and threatened to bring the twins down with him if he were arrested. "He's fucking dead," Reggie is alleged to have said to Scotch Jack on learning of this.

There was also a peculiar complaint voiced by Ronnie. Frank was not only a nuisance, he said, he was costing them thousands of pounds. It's not easy to see how this could have been the case. Lennie Dunn's flat came cheap at £500. Liza came cheaper at £100 (later gratuitously raised to £130). If they were having to make heavy pay-offs to buy the silence of people who suspected them, the great thieves' ponces were indeed the biters bit. But it was probably a piece of paranoid miserliness with little basis in reality.

The obvious way to dispose of a rational crook was to send him off to the continent with a satchel of money and arrange a face-lift and false papers for him if necessary. Freddie Foreman had organized just that escape route for Ronnie Biggs. But by now everyone who had met Frank knew that, sooner rather than later, he would trail back again like a great baby, asking for Ronnie Kray to hold his hand. Moreover, Frank was now besotted with Liza and determined to marry her as soon as he could. As a sensible and experienced hostess, she had agreed. Everyone could see she was only humouring him. Getting rid of Liza might obviate the danger of her talking. But how could it be explained to Big Frank, in the grip of his magnificent obsession?

So if he had to go, why didn't the twins arrange to kill Frank

Mitchell themselves? Ronnie was very proud of the shooting of George Cornell and the way he had terrorized everybody into keeping shtum. In Frank's case, however, he couldn't do that because, thanks to the cavalier pre-planning of the escape, the police knew very well that the firm were involved. If Frank's body turned up somewhere, Fat Wally, Teddy Smith and Pat Connolly would be pulled in for starters. And the rest of the firm would probably crumble.

Furthermore, Big Frank was generally seen as a likeable geezer. He didn't drive golf balls into people's open mouths or nail their feet to the floor, as it was averred Cornell had done. There was no prestige to be won in gangland for his murder (and nobody has ever confessed to any part in it with any pride).

The twins were already toying with the old American idea of the outside hit man to increase business. Without necessarily proposing to go as far as murder, they had initiated talks with Glasgow gangs about undertaking each other's serious assaults. It made sense to have Frank eliminated by someone who had no direct connection with the firm.

They had all been rather taken aback by the frenzy of press attention the escape commanded. At first, like the Manson family following the killing of Sharon Tate, they could bask in the fact that their crime had proved more noteworthy than they expected and was enjoying fame comparable with the Great Train Robbery. But it was soon apparent that the panic about a Mad Axeman on the rampage was calling down far more official attention than was desirable. Nobody was concerned that a convict called Lamb made another escape from a Dartmoor working party (and was quickly recaptured) at much the same time. But the Axeman caper brought Dartmoor an immediate visit from Robert Mark, at that time Chief Constable of Leicester and serving on the Mountbatten Commission on prison security. It was a topical subject, because escapes like those of some of the Train Robbers, and the spy George Blake, had already made headline news. It sent the Flying Squad into suspected safe houses and criminal lairs all over London. It was making life more difficult for the whole of the underworld. And such a massive official search for the live Axeman would certainly turn up a dead Axeman if he weren't perfectly concealed.

The twins had no experience of killing anybody quietly and secretly, no experience of "losing" a body so completely that it could never be found. Freddie Foreman had. And the twins had known about the murder of Ginger Marks sooner than anyone else. Jimmy Evans had come straight round to their door with his grievance. The police knew the murder had taken place and they knew where. Like the whole of the East End they knew who was killed and who killed him. But there was no evidence to bring Foreman to book, no body to undergo forensic pathological examination and no good evidence pointing to the means of its disposal. Just all those rumours about Hackney Marshes and the Chiswick Flyover.

So there was every reason to invite Freddie to the meet and ask him to undertake this dirty job. Why did he do it? It was pushed on him at very short notice and at a most inconvenient time. Like Lenny Books, he had a business demanding his attention over the Christmas period when the Prince of Wales would be taking good money. Moreover, his wife was in hospital and he didn't want the addition to his personal worries.

Freddie's own explanations ramble a little. In his memoirs he says it was really like putting down a mad dog. There was, we infer, no other way of removing the intolerable nuisance from Ronnie Kray's life. In subsequent television interviews he recollects a "mad" moment in the Axeman's past which might be expected to strike a clearer chord of public sympathy. Bruce Reynolds was an old friend of Freddie's and he remembered, he says, the way Mitchell stabbed Bruce in the shower, puncturing his lung and putting him in the prison infirmary. Certainly few people would approve the serious injury to Reynolds, one of the best-liked ex-criminals in the country. Except, as we have seen, Reynolds himself said the injury was inflicted at his own request and he wanted it to be serious enough for infirmary treatment as part of a projected escape plan. If anything he was grateful to Frank as the only man in the prison with the nerve and lack of squeamishness to take the job on.

Still, thinking of paying off a debt for Bruce suggested to Freddie that his main motive was returning favours for the twins. It is difficult to see how these "favours" differed from natural shared business interests in their projected joint ventures, at least since the days when the Krays found the flat in Adelina Grove for Fred's years on the trot. But it seems to him a mark of the honourable days of the 1960s that favours were always remembered and returned. And he was quite clear that he was returning a favour, although it is never properly defined. The most obvious friendship and indebtedness to the Krays to emerge from Freddie's various reminiscences seem to relate to Charlie. But Charlie's attachment to and protectiveness of his maverick little brothers had always been marked, and to help them would indeed be a friendly act towards him.

Finally, Freddie suggests that the murder was a sort of mercy killing. Frank Mitchell had nothing more to look forward to, in his opinion, but a lifetime of imprisonment, probably incarceration in a mental hospital and, quite possibly, "the liquid cosh" (disabling tranquillising chemotherapy). So it was really a kindness to kill him.

This excuse really surpasses the effrontery of most previous criminal attempts to postulate a villains' ethos of superior quality to the honest citizens'. There is much to be said against some of the intrusive medical and surgical attempts to treat mania and depression in the twentieth century. Lobotomy, electrotherapy and certain mind-altering drugs have sometimes been used with devastatingly bad effect. But putting patients into quasi-vegetable or catatonic states was never the overt intention and certainly never openly justified by reference to the nuisance the patients were to other people. Where victims' relatives suspected that such callous self-interest had led parents or guardians to risk dubious brain operations, a lifetime's bitterness like that of Tennessee Williams lamenting his little sister might result. Yet Tennessee Williams would not have given higher praise to a moral mobster who boasted of putting her out of her misery once and for all by depriving her of life entirely. Freddie Foreman seems to know that this is not justification to win him much public sympathy. He makes it quite clear that he is not proud of the part he played in Frank Mitchell's death. And he passes quickly to the easier question, why did the Krays pick him and not someone else to do the killing?

His answer is professionalism. He had shown himself competent. They had not. Few people had the skill and facilities to eliminate a person and completely dispose of the body.

But this honest acknowledgement of a manifest truth has its dangers. It comes perilously close to Nipper Read's view of Foreman's role in the underworld. Read once made an unguarded response on television, to the effect that he had been investigating about seven murders of which Freddie Foreman was suspected (This number probably includes several that were actually being ascribed to the Krays at the time). Certainly Read makes no bones about the fact that Foreman was the more dangerous criminal, and the whole pursuit and conviction of the Krays would have been crowned by a much greater success, in his opinion, if he could have put Freddie Foreman away for an equally long time. Asked in 1999 whether he believed Foreman and his gang were contract killers, he replied that there was a possibility, even a probability, although there was no evidence.

This is something Freddie Foreman has always denied flatly. He never, he says, killed for money. He killed Ginger Marks for fraternal revenge and Frank Mitchell to repay a favour he owed the Krays. Albert Donoghue was mistaken, if not lying, in thinking he brought Freddie £1,000 blood money after Mitchell's death.

That death followed the meeting at Harry Hopwood's house with surprising speed. There had been quite a lot of coming and going at the Barking Road flat in the morning, probably occasioned by Scotch Jack's report that Mitchell was threatening to wreak revenge on the twins for grassing him up if he should ever be arrested, and Reggie's over-the-top response. But the definite moves to get Mitchell away did not start till the evening.

Albert Donoghue came to the flat with the news that Frank was to be taken to a house in the country where he would spend Christmas with Ronnie. Frank's delight was tempered by the suggestion that Liza might not be going with them. It looked as if there would be another enormous row, but Albert's instructions were plain enough, whether or not he knew of Frank's intended fate. Get Frank out of the house and into the van by any means, fair or foul.

He was picked for the job because Frank trusted him as one of his rescuers from Dartmoor. Albert assured the Axeman that Liza would accompany him.

There followed a great deal of hasty packing. Lenny Dunn had bought Albert a range of new clothes and a lot of the shirts that went into his suitcase were still in their cellophane wrapping. Frank looked for mementoes to give Liza and came up with two pathetic tributes: a comb in a comb case and a little paper calendar of the past year. He also inscribed a Christmas card to her. Later, when she looked inside her passport, she found £10 that he must have left for her, from money he had been given by the firm. She was sure it was a gift from him as he was the only person who rummaged through her things and looked at her passport.

This was the time at which she says Scotch Jack came into the bedroom and gave her £100 (or a little under) in a paper bag. He seemed upset. And he pleaded with her to persuade Frank to go back to prison.

But it was too late, even had she had a hope of doing that. At around 8pm Albert returned to the flat with a large mackintosh and a hat for Frank. And the news that Ronnie was not coming into the flat himself, but was waiting in the van round the corner. This was the signal for another outburst from Frank Mitchell. But the apparently valid excuse that Ronnie didn't want to break cover while he was in hiding resolved this last denial of "respect". It seemed there would be more serious resistance when Frank was told that Liza would not travel with him. He was not prepared to leave without her. But he was assured that she would follow in an hour. She promised that she would do so, bringing his suitcase. It was pointed out that in the unhappy event that they were stopped, she would be in serious trouble if she were with him. And Frank yielded to that argument. The man really was in love. The gang members were slightly embarrassed as he kissed her, long and lingeringly, before going out to the road.

Albert and Frank left the flat together and, watching from the kitchen window, Liza saw them pass by with another man whom she did not recognize. He may have been one of the two men

Albert said were with the gunmen in the van, though he has never said so.

There was a small panic, or maybe two, relating to patrolling policemen at the time of Frank's departure. John Dickson says two uniformed bobbies on the beat passed by while they were all in the house packing and Frank panicked, believing the house to be surrounded. Albert says one beat officer strolled towards them as he and Albert walked down Barking Road toward Ladysmith Avenue, and he prayed that Frank would not give them away by acting suspiciously. The van was parked in Ladysmith Avenue, one of the straight residential roads running between Barking Road and Central Park Road. It faced toward Central Park Road, and Albert says he saw Jerry Callaghan, the Foreman firm member who had been present at the killing of Ginger Marks, standing outside to let them in through the back doors. Frank got in. Freddie Foreman and Alfie Gerard were sitting on a wheel arch and Freddie invited Frank to sit on the opposite one. Albert went to the front of the van to give the driver directions on getting to the Blackwall Tunnel. He says the car was being driven by Ronnie Oliffe. He climbed in to give the simple directions (turn right, right again and left on the Barking Road which leads straight to the tunnel), and Callaghan climbed in beside him, slamming the passenger door.

This was the signal. The driver gunned the engine and shooting broke out in the back of the van. Albert spun round to see Gerard firing a revolver and Foreman a silenced automatic into the Mad Axeman's head. After four shots, he was still moaning. Gerard said, "The bastard's still alive," and complained that his gun was empty. Foreman finished him off with shots to the heart that made his coat flap.

As soon as the van was in Barking Road Albert asked to be let out. Freddie Foreman confirms that he was very anxious to get away as quickly as possible, which is interesting. For Albert has always declared that, unlikely as it may seem, he had no idea Frank Mitchell was to be murdered. At least, not then, not in the van. He thought he might be assassinated at the house in the country. But he did not know he was leading the man to certain death and he feared that as a witness he would be shot himself if he stayed in the windowless vehicle. He was prepared to make a fight for it to get out if there was any objection to his leaving.

Freddie Foreman has confirmed that Albert's account of the murder was pretty accurate. In particular he described the shooters and the shooting correctly. Freddy insists that he named the wrong men as the driver and passenger, and Callaghan once objected to his presence being aired. (If Alf Gerard had not died abroad, one wonders whether Freddie would also be saying Albert made a mistake in identifying him.) He asks how Albert could have recognized all four men correctly in the dark, windowless van in the badly lit road at night. He also suggests that the proper course for Albert to follow when the case came to trial would have been to say that he could not recognize any of the men at all. Thus had Jimmy Evans followed the code and protected Ginger Marks's murderers. But Freddie also insists that Albert must have – surely did – know exactly what was coming to Frank Mitchell. Which makes it curious that he confirms Albert's anxiety to get away from the van. Albert isn't given to telling stories about times when he exhibited fear.

Back in the house the muffled gunshots created panic. "They've shot him!" cried Liza, and tried to rush out of the door. Dickson held her and restrained her, telling her it was a car backfiring. Being frightened of him, she made no further attempt to get away.

Albert came back and told them all to clean the place thoroughly and take away every bit of their property. He then went to the telephone and Liza heard him give a short message which would become another small bone of contention. According to her, he said, "That dog is dead," and put down the phone. Albert confirms that the gang always used a simple code, saying "that dog," or "horse" "came in" or "won" to indicate that a job was completed. He had done so when he first delivered Frank to Barking Road. He did not believe he had now said, "That dog is dead". The conflict of testimony has been used to suggest that Albert must have been prepared for Frank's murder and the coded message was accordingly worded to report his death. But Liza, certainly, and Albert, almost certainly, were in a state of shock. He might easily have misspoken the word "death" that was in his mind, or she might have misheard him.

The cleaning was thorough. Wet cloths first, then dry. But the gang's clean-ups always were. The police had found Wally Garelick's car so carefully wiped clean of fingerprints that they were sure it had been used for Mitchell's rescue from Dartmoor. They believed their misinformant, who said Garelick, Smith and Connolly had taken Big Frank to Exeter railway station, where Connie Whitehead had taken over and brought him to London by train. Liza, quite unaware that she might be held guilty of harbouring a fugitive (since she did not go to the police) was equally unaware that she might be accessory after the fact of murder when she showed the gang where Frank used to grip the bed's headboard while making love, so that it could be carefully cleaned.

She was very distressed about Frank. She had come to like the big child-minded man and later told a newspaper that wanted a lurid story from her (or allow its hack to write it on her behalf) that he had been a gentle and considerate lover. She was also terrified for herself. If it seemed to her possible that she might be killed for knowing where the Mad Axeman had been hidden, she was sure she was going to die for suspecting where and when he was murdered.

As if to prove that a murder was being concealed, Albert insisted that all Frank's possessions in the suitcase must be destroyed. Liza felt that the gang could do what they liked with the clothes they had bought for their visitor. But, clinging to the faint hope that Frank might have survived, and the gunshots really might have been a car backfiring, she protested against the burning of Frank's beret and nylon mask. Nobody paid a blind bit of attention to her pleas.

Liza expected to wait for Tommy Cowley to pick her up. But when Connie Whitehead turned up in his car, the orders were that she was to go with him and Albert to report to Reggie and then go to a party. The journey was very frightening for her. Connie was cheerful and grinning and she wrongly thought that this was because he knew Frank had been killed and was happy about it. Albert, she felt, saved her life by the advice he gave her in the car. He told her to say nothing to Reggie about thinking she heard gunshots, and she agreed that she would tell Reggie she would never say a word to anyone about Frank Mitchell, because she liked him so much that she didn't want to jeopardize his escape from the country. Albert agreed that this would be a perfect debriefing.

Connie took them to Sammy Lederman's flat in Stepney: a dark and gloomy building to Liza's eye. Reggie came in with Connie and Albert took him aside to say something about Liza. She was quite right to think that he saved her life. The Kray twins really had felt that she might have to be killed. Her agreed speech went down well, however, and in a soft, gentle, but threatening voice, Reggie told her that Frank had "gone against" the Kray firm and joined their enemies, so it had been necessary to get him out of the country. He warned her never to speak about her experience to anyone, ever. If she did, no matter where she went, the gang would "get her". She had no doubt he meant kill her.

It would have surprised Liza very much to know that when Albert reported that Frank "took four injections in the nut, and was still moaning," Reggie started to cry.

The group moved on to the party, which was at Pat Connolly's in Evering Road, Stoke Newington. Billy Exley was there with his wife. So were a lot of very big men whom Liza found intimidating. Reggie asked her if she had received the money he sent her and said she would have some more later. But it was apparent that she would still not be allowed to go home. She got rather drunk and spent the night with Albert in the house. He felt that she wanted his reassurance and he generously offered the comfort of his companionship. But at that stage of his life he was never likely to turn down a bit of nooky if it was available. All Liza could remember was asking him repeatedly whether Frank had been hurt. She couldn't remember his answers. Taciturn Albert probably said little or nothing. It would have surprised her to know that when he got home the following day, and silently bore his wife's upbraiding for staying out all night, he went to the bedroom and, thinking of Frank Mitchell, started to cry.

Liza was sick and hung-over on Christmas Eve when Reggie and Connie came round and took her to a minicab. As she got in to go home and spend her money from Reggie on Christmas things, Connie made a throat-cutting gesture to warn her against saying anything.

On New Year's Eve and on into the New Year, Liza went to a few of the Kray firm's parties and met several of their well-known names, including Charlie and Dolly. At one of these parties, Reggie took her to Vallance Road and gave her a further £30. She never met Ronnie. His response to a description of Frank's death was to demand more details, over which he gloated.

7

"WE ONLY KILL EACH OTHER"

In the mad year of 1967, the twins gave an entirely new spin to Bugsy Siegel's famous utterance. True, they too had only killed other criminals, so far. But Cornell was an "enemy" and Frank (in their eyes) an ungrateful nuisance. From now on, however, their most murderous efforts would be directed toward members of their own gang. They would even be suspected of two killings that probably never happened.

For some years the Kray family had kept a holiday caravan at Steeple Bay in Suffolk. Charlie intended it as a retreat for their parents. Ronnie used it to take boys for weekends. Very shortly after the killing of Frank Mitchell, he had a serious quarrel there, over a boy, with Mad Teddy Smith, who was never seen again. The rumour swept round that the twins had had him murdered.

The rumour was, apparently, wrong. An ex-criminal of unimpeachable reputation endorses the claim of another former villain to have seen Mad Teddy, alive and well – but keeping a very low profile – some time after the twins had started to serve their life sentences. Like their former driver, Billy "Jack" Frost, the subject of similar rumours and similar "posthumous" sightings, Smith seems to have taken himself well out of the Krays' way and never resurfaced under his old identity.

But the twins definitely intended murder with Leslie Payne. They were cold-shouldering "the Brain" since the failure of the Enugu plan, but with the typical circular thinking of paranoia, they then began to suspect that he must be talking to the police, since he was no longer seeing much of them. By September 1966, even before the murder of Frank Mitchell, they agreed that Payne had got to go. A hard man the firm sometimes used was Jack "the Hat" McVitie. A womanizer and a bit of a bully, his nickname came from his habit of keeping his hat on at all times to cover his bald spot. He was given £250 to go with Billy Exley and shoot Payne. The two returned to the Grave Maurice saying that Payne's missus had come to the door and said he was out. Jack did not return the money, and later the firm came to believe that he and Exley had gone no nearer Payne's door than the security pole closing off the private estate where he lived.

Still, Jack was entrusted with another job. He accompanied Reggie, Ronnie Hart and Albert Donoghue to a flat in Hackney where a friend of Connie Whitehead's called Bobby Cannon was invited for a drink with "friends". Reggie and Hart wrapped towels round guns to silence them and hid in the kitchen. Donoghue and McVitie, sitting in the lounge, had no idea what Cannon's offence was. (According to Reggie, who only admits to a frightener, not a real murder attempt, he had incautiously repeated a rather accurate account of the last moments of Frank Mitchell's life, presumably gleaned from Whitehead.) And they wanted to be no part of an unexplained cold-blooded killing. When Cannon turned up they waved him away, mouthing, "Shoo!", then pretended to chase after him, deliberately knocking over furniture in the process. Reggie accepted that Cannon had sussed something. But McVitie was not forgiven for another failure.

During 1967 "the Hat" piled up offences against the twins. Reggie claims that he purloined part of a load of stolen merchandise he was delivering for them, and boasted about it. He caused a disturbance in Freddie Foreman's 211 Club in Balham. He repeatedly made a nuisance of himself in the Regency Club in Stoke Newington. This rather depressing little watering hole had once been run as a spieler by the twins. It lay in Rectory Road, behind Stoke Newington High Street towards the Stamford Hill end, within easy walking distance of the Cedra Court flats and just a little further from Pat Connolly's base in Evering Road, in the other direction. It boasted an upstairs gymnasium, a main clubroom and manager's office, and a basement private club that opened illicitly after hours for the benefit of such as the Krays and their friends. Unlike the Double R or the Kentucky, it held no appeal for West End celebs out slumming, who didn't actually want the real thing. By this time the twins did most of their town entertaining in Astor's and their East End entertaining in the Carpenter's Arms pub in Cheshire Street, which they bought that year. (If they ever thought about Ginger Marks' death just outside it, they dismissed the omen.)

The Regency had been taken over by the brothers John and Tony Barry, who tried to improve its image. They weren't helped by the

Krays' constantly nipping them as well as putting up their "pension". But as they were supposed to be having "protection", they objected strongly to a hanger-on of the firm coming in, drunk and stoned, and kicking up rows which might range from standing on a table and dropping his trousers to carrying a gun and shooting into the walls. Increasingly addicted to pills and booze, Jack the Hat really was, as Reggie later remarked, "a fucking nuisance".

He put his own life at risk when he started seriously slagging off the twins under the influence of drink and drugs. This was the summer when Reggie's wife Frances died and Reggie's genuine grief found outlet in heavy drinking and deep depression. He was all too ready to believe that a man who boasted of cheating him and Ronnie, and who threatened to kill them, might attempt what he said. He also felt that the loss of "respect" entailed by letting Jack say what he liked would seriously damage their business of extortion.

Nor were Reggie's grief and consequent inattentiveness to those around him conducive to smooth relations within the firm. Scotch Jack thought that Reggie, who believed Frances's spirit had entered a robin that came to her grave, was going mad. Dickson also quarrelled with Connie Whitehead, almost came to blows, and threatened to shoot him. Scotch Ian was seen by Donaghue out on a date with Tommy Cowley's wife. Several of the firm's younger members were friendly with Frances's brother Frankie, and this at a time when Reggie spent much of his time drunkenly mooning over the possibility of killing all Frances's relatives. Ron Bender was embroiled in a yet more incredible emotional twist. He was having an affair with Frankie's missus, whom he called "Bubbles". Albert Donoghue and Ronnie Hart were so concerned about the increase in unpremeditated "spankings" for "the naughties" that they devised a warning code to use between themselves. They knew that the twins always sent a trusted friend to fetch a victim for a spanking. They were sure they would be used in each other's case. And they had a special form of words which would actually mean, "Don't come!".

In mid-October the twins ate a Chinese meal with Jack and Albert in the Regency Club. All seemed peaceful and friendly. Most of the other firm members quite liked Jack, while recognizing that his erstwhile gabby liveliness was deteriorating into unpredictability. Nobody knew that Reggie, at this point almost as unstable as Ronnie, had decided that the quiet dinner party would be Jack's "last supper".

The notorious party at which Jack the Hat was murdered came as the conclusion of three other sociable gatherings. 24 October was the twins' birthday, and everybody was invited to have a few drinks with them. On 27 October the celebration was revived in the Carpenter's Arms. Old Charlie and Vi came out for the occasion, happy to be celebrating with their boys, their boys' friends and their boys' friends' wives. Ronnie had two lads called Terry and Trevor in tow, an 18-year-old trainee croupier from the Colony Club and his 19-year-old unemployed friend. Reggie had a new girlfriend, Carole Thompson – "Ginger Carole" to distinguish her from "Blonde Carole" Skinner, a friend of many of the firm who lived in a basement flat in Evering Road, almost opposite the flat where Liza Prescott spent the night following Frank Mitchell's murder. Blonde Carole was expected to have a party at her flat that night and there was talk of moving on there when the pub closed.

Chris Lambrianou was down from Birmingham with a friend called Ray Mills. They had picked that Saturday evening for Chris to introduce Ray to his brother Tony, and Tony to introduce Chris to Ray's brother Alan. The Millses were building themselves form and reputation as a West London "family" based on Ladbroke Grove, but weren't close to the East London gangs. The Lambrianous and the Mills brothers spent the evening in East End pubs getting to know each other, and finished in the Carpenter's Arms. Chris at least doesn't seem to have felt the Millses made a good impression on the Krays. By the end of the evening, he was all for going to a West End club before he kept a date with a girl at Euston. But the Mills brothers wanted to see the Regency Club and Tony wanted to take them there, so the young men piled into Chris's car and went to Stoke Newington.

They weren't the only familiar faces in the Regency that Saturday night. Ronnie Bender had come in with "Bubbles" Shea after an evening at the dog track. Reggie Kray certainly, Ronnie Kray, Ronnie Hart and Connie Whitehead possibly, were around. And Jack the Hat McVitie was there, not in one of his drunken and obstreperous moods, but lively and garrulous. He circulated from table to table in the private basement club, at one point joining the Lambrianous.

Upstairs, Reggie was in an unpredictable "wild" mood. When he learned that Jack the Hat was in the basement, he announced his determination to shoot him there and then and demanded a gun from Tony Barry. Anxiously Barry persuaded Reggie not to do anything so foolish and dangerous, and damaging to the club. But Reggie's foul temper did not subside. Barry was told to take a gun to Blonde Carole's flat. Tony Lambrianou was told to bring Jack the Hat there. And disaster loomed.

At Evering Road, Carole and her boyfriend George Plummer were firmly invited to take their party somewhere else and the Krays' party moved in. Until about half past twelve or quarter to one, it was a perfectly respectable party. Jeff Allen, the former gambler who had warned off Moisha Blueboy, was there with his wife. He was now a successful upmarket estate agent with a mansion of his own in Suffolk. Usually the firm didn't accept awful, lawful wedded wives at social functions, but Pat Whitehead was around keeping an eye on Connie. Among the girlfriends, Vicki Hart was prominent. And as the mixed couples danced together, the only outré spectacle was Trevor and Terry merrily dancing with each other.

It was after that party broke up and all the women had gone home that the famous sub-party leading to Jack the Hat's death occurred. The twins started snipping and sniping at each other. Reggie grumbled that Ronnie wanted nothing but more boys once he'd got a few drinks in him. Ronnie snapped back. Other than Blonde Carole's two little boys, who were asleep in their room upstairs, the only people still in the flat were Connie Whitehead, Ronnie Bender, Ronnie Hart, and Trevor and Terry. Hart had shuttled in some more drinks in Bender's car. Bender went on foot to the Regency to try and fetch Bubbles and, at Ronnie's request, to see if there were any nice boys around. Then the Lambrianous and Millses arrived, bringing Jack the Hat as Tony had been ordered by Reggie in the Regency.

The famous accounts have him bounding down the basement stairs shouting, "Where are the broads and the booze?" They have Reggie levelling a gun at his head, which jammed. Ronnie egging him on with the "I've done mine, now you do yours" taunt. McVitie trying to dive out of the window and Reggie pulling him back by the legs, saying, "Be a man, Jack!" And McVitie responding, "I'll live like a man, but I won't fucking die like one", as Ronnie Kray and Ronnie Hart held him, while Reggie stabbed him repeatedly, finally pinning him to the floor with a knife through his throat.

This familiar scenario essentially combines and abridges two unreliable sources. Ronnie Hart, like any Queen's Evidence witness, was more or less bound to minimize his own involvement and maximize the details that would give the Crown the conviction it sought. Reggie Kray, like nine out of ten impenitent professional murderers, was at pains to make his victim look as despicable as possible. Appendices A to D of this book give four eye- and ear-witness accounts of the murder, which have never been published before, and from which it is possible to draw up a slightly different scenario.

When the Lambrianous and Millses came into the basement, Ronnie came over to shake hands and welcome them, and smashed a sherry glass into McVitie's face. Then he walked quietly away, muttering, while McVitie protested. Reggie grabbed McVitie from behind, pointed the pistol at his head and pulled the trigger. When it failed to go off, he cursed it. The Lambrianous wanted out and had a furious quarrel in the passage, Chris upbraiding Tony for bringing him into this scene before sitting on the stairs, crying. The Greek brothers and the Millses started to go, but were met by Ronnie Bender and Connie Whitehead coming in and let themselves be persuaded to return. There was fighting going on in which McVitie gave a good account of himself against the twins, Ronnie Hart, and possibly Bender and Trevor or Terry or both. During this, McVitie smashed the window, either in sheer rage, or accidentally in defending himself. He did not try to dive through it, though at one point he tried to walk out of the door and was shouted at to come back. And the Krays ordered that no one was to leave the flat.

It has been persuasively suggested that the first attempt to stab McVitie was made by Ronnie Kray. But the ordinary table knife he had snatched up was useless. Somebody – almost certainly Ronnie Hart – fetched Reggie a carving knife from the kitchen. And while the two Ronnies held McVitie, Reggie stabbed him repeatedly in the abdomen, twisting the knife fearfully. Chris Lambrianou offered to go home and fetch another pistol. Connie Whitehead was assigned to drive him. Tony Lambrianou had found Carole Skinner's little boys starting to come out of their bedroom and took them back out of harm's way, before himself wandering out into the garden. Trevor and Terry were hurried out of the house, followed by the Millses. The twins, their arms covered with blood, started abusing Ronnie Hart, gathered up the pistol and the knife, and hurried away, telling Ronald Bender to get rid of the body by throwing it on the railway lines by Cazenove Road, so that the injuries would be taken for the result of an accident.

To Bender's relief, Chris Lambrianou returned shortly, looking for Tony. He had picked up a gun from his house, resisting Connie Whitehead's urging that they forget all about going back to Evering Road. He was shocked to learn that Bender had been left to cope with everything himself and persuaded his brother and Whitehead to help clean up the flat. The carpet and lino were covered with blood and had to come up. Blood splashes had sunk into the wooden fireplace surround and had to be burned. Carole Skinner and George Plummer arrived home to find Chris coming up the basement stairs with a basin of blood and pieces of liver to pour down the lavatory. George was drunk and was put to bed in the little boys' room. Carole was urged not to come downstairs for the time being.

They got the worst of the blood up and took McVitie's body, wrapped in a candlewick bedspread, out to his car, a battered Ford Zodiac with one headlight missing. The boot was full of junk, so they put the body on the floor in the back. Deciding that the

Cazenove Road railway line was a stupid place to dump it, they agreed to run it down to the Richardsons' manor in Camberwell. Whitehead refused to accompany them, saying he had to make some telephone calls, but would return to the flat. Tony drove the Zodiac. Bender and Chris followed in Chris's car, but lost Tony between Cambridge Heath Road and Commercial Road. They found him on foot on the other side of the Rotherhithe Tunnel. The Zodiac had run out of petrol and he had chugged its last splutters into the maze of tiny back streets between the tunnel exit and the river, abandoning it outside St Mary's Church in a pool of confetti left by a wedding that day.

Tony Lambrianou then went home. Chris picked up his date from Euston and went back to Evering Road for his gun. He helped Whitehead, Plummer and Carole continue cleaning up, and left around 4am when he thought it was all shipshape and Bristol fashion again (a bachelor opinion Carole did not share). Bender, meanwhile, made his way to Charlie Kray's to tell him what had happened.

But Charlie already knew about the murder. A telephone call in the small hours had summoned him to Harry Hopwood's house where the twins and Ronnie Hart told him about it. In 1997, Charlie's revised memoirs still pretended that he groaned at the news, went home and told his wife a cock-and-bull story to explain why he been called away, and went to sleep, only to be framed later for supposedly helping get Freddie Foreman to dispose of the body. Maybe Charlie is still unaware that Ronnie Bender's secret confession, made in 1969, reveals that he told Dolly the truth while Charlie was still out. She called in Tommy Cowley for help. When Charlie got back, he and Tommy dismissed Bender and conferred together. There is no reason to suppose that Charlie simply washed his hands of the twins' latest foul-up. (See Appendix C.)

The meet at Harry Hopwood's involved that unfortunate friend of the twins' parents in more than he bargained for, much more than had happened when he was excluded from the discussions over Frank Mitchell. The twins, as usual, behaved like Napoleon in a crisis. They ran away and left the army to get itself clear if it could.

They were hurried out to a safe house in north London. Other gang members said it was Tommy the Bear's flat in Tottenham, but he and his missus denied this fervently. From there they went off to Jeff Allan's new mansion near Lavenham and thoroughly enjoyed themselves. They found a Victorian mansion called The Brooks at Bildeston, near Hadleigh, where they had been evacuated during the war. It was for sale for £12,000 and they snapped it up. Vallance Road was now scheduled for demolition and old Charles and Violet were being moved to a council flat in Bunhill Row. They were happy to enjoy the country life in greater luxury than the caravan at Steeple Cove. The twins had the house put in Violet's name so that, although they enjoyed playing country squires from time to time, they had few enough assets to be entitled to legal aid when they needed it.

Ronnie Hart spent a week in Suffolk with them. He also had to hide out until it was clear whether they were all wanted for murder. He also felt that he deserved a holiday, having undertaken much of the immediate clearing up of the kind Reggie had done after Cornell's murder.

Problem number one was the body. Far from being an obviously better dumping place than the Cazenove Road railway line, St Mary's Church Street, Rotherhithe, left it right on Freddie Foreman's patch. And nobody wanted to quarrel with Freddie.

It has never been reliably revealed exactly when the twins learned of this crisis. It has been reported that Ronnie threw a massive tantrum at Tony Lambrianou. The likeliest time would be after Charlie Kray got home and learned from Ronnie Bender exactly where the Zodiac had been dumped. Bender places Charlie and Tommy together at that point. Ronnie Hart testified that he drove Charlie over the river to warn Freddie before dawn. Charlie and Freddie both deny this and say it was Tommy Cowley who went with Hart. Freddie says he didn't see the driver of the car (Bender's mini, which was borrowed by Hart for much of the night of 27–28 October, and was parked around the corner). But Freddie says it was Tommy Cowley who came and told him the bad news in the small hours of the morning.

Harry Hopwood, on the other hand, swore that Hart never left his flat until morning. Hopwood also swore that he was allocated specific tasks to carry out with Hart. They washed the twins' gun, knife, jewellery and loose change to get the blood and fingerprints off them, then threw the gun and knife into the canal at a point in Queensbridge Road. (When the police recovered the gun, they noted the missing spring that caused the mechanism to jam.) Hopwood also bagged up the twins' bloodstained clothes and gave them to his distant cousin, elderly Percy Merrick, to be burned on his allotment in Kent. Hopwood's story has the persuasiveness of a man whose evidence convicts himself as well as his accomplice. Percy Merrick corroborated the detail about the bloodstained clothes.

Now, look at the known facts. Freddie Foreman has acknowledged a feeling of some contempt for Tommy Cowley, whom he suspects of grassing while the gang were all in prison. On the other hand, he was a good friend of Charlie Kray, and Charlie staunchly went to prison for something he swore he hadn't done. Charlie Kray would be both a more probable friend to send knocking on Freddie's door with very bad news at some ungodly hour and, as both followed the East End code, a friend whom Freddie would not want to implicate. Tommy Cowley was dispensable.

Ronnie Hart, on the other hand, abandoned the code completely, turning Queen's Evidence. And with the police as his only protection, he really had to be as helpful to the prosecution as he could. To say, as Harry Hopwood did, that Charlie Kray was instructed to do something about the body was not evidence that he carried out his instructions. To say, as Ronnie Hart did, that he drove Charlie across the river and saw him go round to Freddie Foreman's was much more incriminating, and had the added advantage of putting Foreman in the frame, which Hopwood couldn't and didn't do.

Now that we have Ronald Bender's full account of Charlie Kray's return home to find Tommy Cowley and Dolly well aware that McVitie had been murdered, it would not surprise me in the least to learn that it was actually Charlie and Tommy who drove down to Southwark, and Ronnie Hart who was perjuring himself in confessing to that little piece of conspiracy.

Freddie drove out to St Mary's Church to survey the damage. He was decidedly unimpressed by the Kray firm's lack of professionalism. And he removed the car and body to a lock-up, to await permanent disposal. He also cleaned Ron Bender's mini, to get rid of the bloodstains left by the twins' clothes. When the police found it, the forensic lab reported that there was blood in it, but it was not Jack the Hat's. The police never found Chris Lambrianou's car, which the firm disposed of without asking his permission. It was a silly move, as its disappearance led to serious suspicion that Lambrianou had got rid of it for some sinister reason.

Albert Donoghue, who had plastering skills, was sent to redecorate Carole Skinner's flat from top to bottom. Freddie Foreman, for his part, hoped he had made it clear that he was doing the Kray family no more favours. Whether he would have been able to stick to that had they remained at liberty more than a year, must be uncertain. That pair of chancers, Ronnie and Reggie, would have been quite liable to run back to efficient Freddie had they succeeded in rubbing out any more of Ronnie's list.

For the list went on. There were more internal threats to gang members. Connie Whitehead was to be rubbed out for causing trouble with John Dickson. Wally Garelick quietly warned him not to come into a room where gang members had been given hidden weapons and ordered to kill him. The twins worked out that Wally must have done this. He went on the list.

There were even wilder plans. The favours done by Freddie Foreman were to be repaid by rubbing out Jimmy Evans. Allan Bruce Cooper got the former speedway rider, Split Waterman, to construct a lethal briefcase, with a hypodermic needle hidden in the fabric lining. Spring-loaded and filled with cyanide, it could jab and inject a victim through a pin-sized hole in the side when a release by the handle was pulled. Evans' almost instantaneous death would almost certainly to be taken for a heart attack. "Mr ABC" introduced a supposed American hit man called Paul Elvey, who was given the device to use on Evans, either in Winston's Club or in the foyer of the Old Bailey. Elvey failed. He was given a new task, to shoot Evans at his home while pretending to be a magazine salesman. Despite some desultory practice with a crossbow, he failed again. Finally he collected a quantity of gelignite from Scotland to car-bomb George Caruana. There was a double purpose in this: belated revenge for the murder of Tommy Smithson, and a favour to Bernie Silver as a consequence of which the twins hoped he might be blackmailed into letting them have a slice of the Soho pornography and prostitution rackets. They were toying with the idea of expanding into pimping and drug dealing.

Elvey got himself caught in Scotland with enough gelignite to blow up half a street. Cooper, the self-advertised gun-runner who had supplied two duff guns, one which didn't kill George Dixon and another which didn't kill Jack McVitie, lost so much credibility with the twins that he had to organize Ronnie's trip to New York via Paris in 1968 to regain face.

But while their actions grew stupider, the twins were blithely confident that they really were above the law and had the police under their control. Scotland Yard's files show how they or their contacts could use misinformation to keep the police looking in the wrong places. When Frank Mitchell escaped, the police followed up rumours that he had gone abroad, especially a recurrent one that he was in Tangiers. Interpol was given a full description, including his tattoos ("Dad" in a heart and "Mum" with a butterfly, on his right arm). The Kray connection didn't lead them to suspect a Kray killing.

Then, in October 1967, Norman Lucas of the Daily Mirror printed a story which subsequently proved true in every detail. The Axeman, he said, had been shot in a gangland killing and dumped in the sea off the south coast. Detective Chief Inspector Harris promptly wrote a memo to the Commander of C Branch (head of the CID) to quash the story for good and all. It was, he said, "undoubtedly started by…the licensee of the Barley Mow Public House in Headlam Street E1, with the intention that it should be passed to me". The Barley Mow was one of the Quill brothers' pubs and the landlord was said to claim distant relation to the Krays. Harris insisted that the whole story was intended to cut down on police investigation into Mitchell's whereabouts. "Detective

Superintendent Frank Williams and I," he wrote, "have received information from two entirely separate sources that Mitchell is in Eire, and this is undoubtedly correct. We are constantly in touch with the Garda Siochana respecting him."

Now, Frank Williams was deputy head of the Flying Squad. And he had a special relationship with Freddie Foreman which Freddie felt had proved very useful to them both. It had helped, for example, negotiate the surrender of Great Train Robber Buster Edwards and the return of a substantial part of the cash he stole. Freddie Foreman has said on television that Williams seemed very disappointed when the personal intervention of his chief, Tommy Butler, at the last moment, meant that he could not take any cash as a reward for his part in this prestigious arrest. Freddie has also said that he believed in the useful story, "gone to Ireland", to explain embarrassing disappearances.

In the hands of a rigidly straight policeman, informants would ultimately break the Krays. But until that happened they had some reason to believe that the system was working for them.

8

RATS, REVELATIONS, RETRIBUTION

Some police officers mistrusted the system by which the CID in general and the Flying Squad in particular cultivated major active criminals for information. Sir Robert Mark's famous crack, "A good police force is one that catches more crooks than it employs", was thought to be directed at the proud body of men with the flying eagle on their ties. Mark called the CID "the most routinely corrupt body of men in London". But that didn't mean all of them. Bert Wickstead, who was to clean up the remaining East End gangs after the Krays had been put away, had his personnel file endorsed in red, "Not Flying Squad" to avoid a promotional transfer he didn't want. And Nipper Read might enjoy a cup of tea with a retired villain like Jack Spot, but did not mix socially with the artful dodgers he was trying to catch. True, he had been embarrassed to be caught noting car numbers outside the Krays' celebration party after their acquittal in the Hideaway Club case, and he had accepted the invitation from the twins' private detective to step inside for a moment rather than skulk in a telephone box across the street. But he had not, as the press chortled, been caught drinking champagne with the twins. The man they photographed and wrongly identified as Read was the actor Edmund Purdom, another of the sixties gangsters' fans.

Read was poison as far as Ronnie Kray was concerned. Ronnie knew that in 1968, after sterling service on the Train Robbery and promotion to the Murder Squad, Read had been given the special task, "Get the Krays". Ronnie showed writer John Pearson the pet snakes he had named Gerrard and Read. Somewhere his inside information service to the most routinely corrupt body of men in London had let him down. Read had a new boss. Not Fred Gerrard, who had always been in danger of being overridden by Billy Hill's pal Ernie Millen. But Big John Du Rose, fresh from the triumph of solving the "nudes in the Thames" mystery and driving "Jack the Stripper" to suicide.

Du Rose was an old-fashioned copper who certainly used active crooks for information. But he was also the Yard's chosen man for dealing with sensitive and potentially embarrassing matters, like the official investigation into the mentally deranged Detective Sergeant

Challenor, who was caught bang to rights framing innocent citizens. Big John was now in charge of the mission to get the Krays. And without hands-on interference, he fully approved Nipper Read's insistence that his team be based in Tintagel House, a Metropolitan Police office property south of the river, which today houses the Complaints Bureau. Very appropriately, since Nipper disguised his operational use of the outpost as an investigation of police corruption (Which in a way it was, wasn't it?). He ordered his team not to socialize at New Scotland Yard. And he listened to complaints.

The Krays brought it on themselves. They really shouldn't have tried to kill people and at one and the same time insist that the "code of the East End" must prevent their victims' seeking police protection. Even Jimmy Evans finally gave up taking the threats to his life as a natural hazard. But that was after the twins were locked up out of harm's way.

Nipper Read got his first complaints from Leslie Payne. The fraudster might have found the threat of muscle useful to enforce deals like the part-ownership of Esmeralda's Barn. But he was not into killing people. And he was not putting up with attempts to kill him.

And so Nipper Read found his investigation starting in the unglamorous area of crooked financial dealings and long firms. It seemed a lot less colourful than examining the striations on spent bullets. But following the money is one of the best ways of unravelling a crook's web and catching the spider at the centre. It was tax inspectors who brought down Al Capone, not Eliot Ness's famous "Untouchables". It was the money trail that linked Richard M. Nixon to the "third-rate burglary" at the Watergate building. J. Edgar Hoover was no fool when he insisted that every FBI agent must hold a degree in either law or accountancy.

The unravelling of Leslie Payne's activities brought a lot of low-grade informants out of the woodwork. Front men for the long firms and the like. Men whose previous form was likely to be at most a little theft or handling small amounts of stolen property. It was peanuts, but it pointed back to the Krays.

Their more recent financial dealings were more hopeful. Uncle Alfie Kray was picked up and charged with handling forged travellers' cheques in association with Charlie Kray's former partner, the receiver Stan Davis. Some curious cross-referencing in The Times index suggests (without explanation) that somebody thought this was connected with a Mafia operation to steal travellers' cheques from Kennedy Airport. Certainly Nipper was starting to connect the Krays with the Mafia. Following the money had led to the sale of stolen bonds and the transatlantic connection. This was fine as long as Leslie Payne was involved. Genuine grown-up crimes earning genuine money would stand up in court. But from Payne, the business dealings passed to the two American flakes, Mr A. B. Cooper and Mr Joe Kaufman.

They had been pretty useless as Kray associates. They seemed pretty useless as witnesses. Mr ABC stuttered and claimed to be an international gunrunner. And a covert FBI agent. Or CIA agent. Or (check it out, Mr Read) an informant working for Big John Du Rose himself! Read was flabbergasted and feared he had been double-crossed after all. Du Rose unwillingly confessed that he had used some information received from Cooper. But he had not used Cooper as a planted covert operator running parallel to Read's investigation.

Joe Kaufman hadn't got any Scotland Yard links to make him look good. But he tried Cooper's ploy and claimed to be working under cover for the FBI. That little story didn't check out. The FBI told Read that Kaufman was no undercover agent of theirs, he was just a low-grade Mafioso.

Working with these flakes tended to make the investigation flaky. Cooper rightly feared that the twins were plotting to have him killed. He pretended illness to explain his inability to attend meets with them and had himself put into hospital under police protection. Somebody had the bad idea of wiring his room and getting him to lead the twins into incriminating conversations when they visited his sickbed. The scheme was a total failure. The twins didn't visit him, they sent Tommy Cowley. Tommy didn't believe Cooper was sick and refused to take his baited conversational gambits seriously. The gangsters believed that a nurse who clumped in and asked Cooper to pick his supper menu was really a disguised policewoman asking him to turn up the microphone under his bedclothes.

As for Cooper's tales of murder plots, they seemed utterly ludicrous. The men who had ruthlessly marched into the Blind Beggar, shot their chosen victim in public, and terrorized a whole neighbourhood into silence, were now messing about with poisoned briefcases and a hit man who went all the way to Scotland for gelignite that they could have been obtained for him in London at no expense And he had got himself caught with enough to blow up St Paul's. The Krays sounded more like Ealing Comedy villains than the vicious gangsters fictionalized as "Scotchyanks" in "Big Breadwinner Hogg". (Somebody scriptwriting for "Hogg" kept a pretty close eye on the Kray firm exposés, as the series proposed that the most feared firm in London were Scottish hard men with American Mafia connections and methods. The series also introduced a low-level criminal loner called "Ackerman", the relatively unusual name of one of the Krays' actual gofers.)

The crime that really interested Read and his team was the murder of George Cornell. The springing of Frank Mitchell was less important and might even be popular with a public who seemed not to resent the escape of George Blake and the Train Robbers. Mitchell's murder, like Jack McVitie's, was a deep rather than an open secret. But the open killing of George Cornell was a public outrage, comparable with Ginger Marks's death on the street outside a pub full of people. London must not turn into 1920s Chicago.

Rumour ran round the East End that a big Irishman was asking a lot of questions about the Krays. He was Chief Inspector Henry Mooney, doing the legwork for Read's team and, frankly, not getting very far. Fearing that he might be investigated as a known friend if the heat was on the Krays, Freddie Foreman asked his Scotland Yard contact, Frank Williams, whether he should quietly go abroad for the time being. Williams told him he had nothing to worry about.

Following the money had, however, produced some evidence of the threats by which the hard men kept everyone in line. Du Rose and Read decided to pull in the central members of the firm. And then, with the threateners under lock and key, it was just possible that somebody might start to tell the truth about the night in the Blind Beggar.

And so the famous dawn raid took place in May 1968. It was a deliberately high-profile operation. The police wanted everyone to know that the Kray brothers and 18 members of the firm were locked up. The Krays' parents' flat in Bunhill Row, where the twins were sleeping that night, was the scene of the most intense operation. Armed police broke down the door and rushed into the bedrooms. Ronnie, in bed with a boy, managed the cheeky cool that endeared him to those who liked him. "Be careful with those things, they might go off," he warned the police. Reggie, in bed with Chris Lambrianou's former girlfriend, June Macdonald, was much wilder. He raged at the "liberty" the police took in making them get out of bed and stand naked in front of them while they searched the room for weapons.

Charlie went quietly from his home, surprised that the police wanted to handcuff him and perhaps even more surprised that his wrists were too big for their 'cuffs.

The long list of other names, however, was a bit of a disappointment. Too many complete unknowns, who had been involved in the long firms and the bearer bond sales. Too many non-violent firm members, like Tommy Cowley and Sammy Lederman. Among the firm's hard men still at liberty were Dickson and Barrie. The big and menacing-looking Lambrianou brothers were also free. Freddie Foreman has revealed that he was lucky not to be arrested with the twins. He went to Bunhill Row to see them that morning and found the place swarming with police who, to his great relief, didn't recognize him. It would have caused real tremors in the underworld if he had been taken in the raid.

The charges the police were bringing seemed absurd. A lot of alleged frauds concerning companies the public had never heard of. Nothing about extortion and uttering threats, let alone assaults and violence. The Richardsons' arrests for the Mr Smith Club affray and the torture trials were much more colourful. But there was one charge that worried the Krays quite a lot: "Conspiracy to murder". The indictment didn't say who this referred to. If the police were on to the truth about Frank Mitchell or Jack McVitie, or had persuaded a witness to stand up and tell the truth about George Cornell, then the twins were unlikely to be at liberty and controlling things again by the summer. Their lawyers hammered away at every custody hearing. Just who were the Krays supposed to have conspired to murder?

The answer was a huge relief, when it was finally forced out. George Caruana. Nipper's team hadn't got anything stronger than the antics of Mr ABC to go on. The twins anticipated a slap on the wrist for taking money from long firms - and the strengthening of their reputation for legal invulnerability.

But the police went on stolidly with their case. And two breakthroughs opened it up for them. When the evening papers reported "new revelations", Lennie Dunn panicked. He had expected to be arrested at any moment for his part in harbouring Frank Mitchell, and probably charged with being accessory after the fact of the Axeman's murder. This, he assumed, was the new revelation. He went to the police, and soon Read was hearing what was, in fact, a revelation to him. The true story of Frank Mitchell's sad end.

Now there was renewed vigour in the investigation. The Krays were in the frame for a murder and they had led the police to Freddie Foreman.

Inspector Mooney enjoyed a triumphant success with "Mrs X", the barmaid at the Blind Beggar. The police had left her alone since her evidence at Cornell's inquest. Now Mooney started visiting her and questioning her gently. Mrs X was understandably afraid that if she told the truth now she would be charged with perjury. And no police officer had the power to promise her immunity. After winning her trust over several visits, but extracting no admission of what she had seen, Mooney finally suggested to her that she visit a solicitor to look after her interests. And the solicitor immediately assured her that there was no realistic likelihood of her being prosecuted for having been intimidated by the most notorious witness tamperers in London. Encouraged by an actual villain who was a friend of her husband's and who felt that the shooting in the Blind Beggar risked changing the face of gangland for the worse, Mrs X made her statement. And the murder of George Cornell was set down against Ronnie Kray and Ian Barrie.

The twins promptly decided a strategy that cooked their own goose. In a defendants' prison conference from which solicitors' clerks Ralph Haeems and Manny Fryede were carefully excluded, the twins announced that they would go free because the others would have to cop guilty pleas for them. Scotch Ian could take the rap for killing George Cornell. Albert Donoghue could confess to murdering Frank Mitchell. And Ronnie Hart would take sole responsibility for Jack McVitie's death. The twins would walk free. Q.E.D.

The plot backfired. The underworld generally agreed that there was some animus between the twins and Ronnie Hart that might just entitle them to make him go down for them. In any case, Hart was definitely liable to be convicted of that murder. He had been involved in the final struggle that led to McVitie's death and some witnesses would suggest that he brought the fatal knife from the kitchen. Scotch Ian's rights never became an issue as he chose to stand "staunchly" alongside the twins, and ultimately accepted a long sentence. But the twins were taking a liberty with Big Albert. Even Freddie Foreman, who stood to gain most if Albert pretended to have shot Mitchell, and who still insists that Albert knew perfectly well he was leading Frank out to his death - even Freddie thought the demand was unreasonable.

In the magistrates' court, a little crook that practically no one had ever heard of led the way in testifying from the dock. Charles Mitchell was part of the minor fraud cases. The twins made the mistake of having Tommy Cowley try to nip him for £5,000 while they were in the exercise yard. The money was to be put into eliminating a witness. Mitchell wanted no part of this, and to the shock and horror of his co-defendants, he moved from the dock to the witness box and testified against them.

One by one, other defendants and associates got messages to Nipper Read and made statements. He was handicapped by their fearful insistence on absolute secrecy. There were still men on the outside who would threaten their families on the twins' behalf. But the small players came clean when they realized how much of the truth the police already knew, even though they couldn't be assured that they were in good company in spilling the beans. One by one, men were shifted to other prisons, away from the twins' influence. Harry Hopwood, Percy Merrick, Billy Exley, Alfie Teal, Wally Garelick and Ray Mills would all give evidence against the Krays. And the big players gave the decisive evidence. Albert Donoghue got his vital message smuggled out to Nipper Read, pleaded guilty to harbouring Frank Mitchell, and told the courts what he knew. Ronnie Hart couldn't pretend to complete innocence of murder. He turned Queen's Evidence. And Scotch Jack Dickson, unwilling to see his old friend Ian Barrie sent down for something he didn't do, joined Albert Donoghue in copping a guilty plea to harbouring Frank Mitchell and gave the evidence the police needed.

The trials themselves were rowdy. The twins' pretence in their later books that they behaved with dignity under provocation is utter rubbish. They shouted abuse from the dock at hostile witnesses. They called the prosecuting counsel "a fat slob" and bellowed accusations of lying at Dickson and Hart. It was an awkward case for both sides. Ronnie Hart, as the prosecution had to admit, was not a very appealing witness. But the argument that he was only trying to save his own skin didn't really help the defence. Shouting, "You're another!" doesn't go to show that a man is lying. The defence had equal difficulty with Mrs X. She was so obviously quite different from the trail of villains giving evidence about their wrongdoings. She was an honest citizen who had overcome serious intimidation to tell the truth. And counsel who had no compunction about tearing into the character, truthfulness and reliability of Scotch Jack Dickson, had to use kid gloves in putting before the jury the fact that Mrs X's statement now was not what she had said previously.

Scotch Jack let his hostility to Ronnie Kray show in the magistrates' court, when he was asked to identify him among the prisoners in the dock and called him "the fat one with glasses". Reggie's one useful intervention came in front of the magistrates, when he interrupted testimony about Split Waterman's lethal briefcase with the shouted question, would James Bond be next in the witness box. The magistrate agreed that the wild pranks of Allan Bruce Cooper and Paul Elvey were simply too outrageous for a jury to take seriously and declined to send the case on for trial.

With the murder of Frank Mitchell held as a separate trial from the joint one for the murders of Cornell and McVitie, the jury did not hear queues of villains giving evidence about the twins' actions before and after the murder. They had, as the judge said, to make up their minds on the basis of Albert Donoghue's evidence alone. It is most unlikely that any jurors believed the defence's far-fetched suggestion that Billy Exley, John Dickson and Albert Donoghue planned Mitchell's escape and subsequent murder behind the twins' back, in order to increase their own standing in the underworld, any more than they were likely to believe Freddie Foreman's preposterous suggestion that Ronnie Hart and Donoghue had been "nipping" him at the Prince of Wales. But since Albert's insistence that he had no idea Frank was to be shot was manifestly vulnerable to the cui bono test, or even Mandy Rice-Davis's ("He would say that, wouldn't he?"), there was reasonable doubt about accepting his testimony. The twins, who in the other trial had dragged down with them all their fellow defendants except Tony Barry, used this unjust acquittal to perpetrate continuing absurdities about Frank's fate. Billy Exley (dead by the time Ron wrote the words) was probably responsible. Or, as Reg claimed, the Axeman was probably still alive and well abroad. Charlie plumped for the silly defence idea of a Dickson-Exley-Donoghue plot.

Those who stood in the dock with them at the double murder trial were compelled to go along with the Krays' stupid "guilty man's" defence. All the defendants knew nothing about any party at Evering Road. So the twins couldn't have been there. Ronnie was drinking with the firm in the Widow's pub the whole evening that George Cornell was shot. The gang all took off to Walthamstow suddenly because they wanted a change of pub. It wasn't really very far from Whitechapel.

Tony Barrie refused to go along with this nonsense. He admitted taking the gun from the Regency to Evering Road, pleading that he did so under duress because he feared Reggie Kray. The jury had no difficulty believing him and he was acquitted, the only defendant to walk free. Ronnie Bender, and Chris and Tony Lambrianou, knew they looked absolutely ridiculous stonewalling counsel with their support of the twins' mutton-headed denial of everything. When they found themselves convicted and with long sentences ahead, they promptly told the truth. (See Appendices A, B and C.) It was too late. The Appeal Court could not hear their evidence. After they had served their sentences they went in rather different directions. Tony reverted to crime and gloried in his days as a Kray mobster. He wrote memoirs boasting of his staunch loyalty to the twins and the underworld code, little thinking that his statement for the Appeal Court would resurface to tell a different story. His memoirs were staunch enough, making the rock-solid assertion that to his certain knowledge Freddie Foreman had nothing whatsoever to do with the disposal of Jack McVitie's body, which was decently buried with some sort of last rites not 50 miles from London. He can never have imagined that Freddie himself would blow that story to smithereens and leave Tony Lambrianou, self-styled Kray gang boss, and all three Kray brothers, without a shred of credibility.

Chris Lambrianou, by contrast, had always retained something of his honest father's awareness of how his misdeeds appeared in reality. He was bitter and violent throughout his prison sentence, knowing he was being punished for something he hadn't done and hadn't remotely approved of. After his release he converted to evangelical Christianity and took up the invaluable work of counselling young drug-offenders.

Connie Whitehead, who had struck Nipper Read as a fence-sitter, retained his posture. His appeal did not make a full statement of all he knew about the party in Evering Road. But it described the pressures brought to bear on him to make him stay with the twins' chosen solicitors and to withdraw the statement he wanted to make to his counsel which told some of the truth. His appeal, like all the others, was turned down.

As the twins used their time in prison to write books, and Charlie, on his release, kept their memory green and their bank accounts solvent with authorized sale of their image on T-shirts and gewgaws, stories about them spread. They or their firm were rumoured to be involved in other gangland killings of 1967. That of Jack Buggy, murdered in Teddy Machin's Mount Street club and thrown into the sea, from which his body, trussed with chicken wire, was washed up. That of Tony "the Magpie" Maffia, shot in his car, which was then mysteriously driven some distance along the Southend road before being abandoned. Most remarkably, the Krays were alleged to be responsible for the death of Freddie Mills whose body, shot through the eye with a rifle that lay beside it, was found in his car outside his own night-club. The police and the inquest decided this was suicide. The Mills family doubted it, and the story went round that the Krays had murdered him as a warning to other club owners that they had better pay pensions or accept nipping. The Krays volubly denied this, insisting, almost certainly truthfully, that Mills was a hero to them and they would never have contemplated trying to extort money from him. The police agreed that there was absolutely no Kray involvement in Mills' death. Pointing to the fact that he had unquestionably borrowed the gun that killed him, that his marriage had recently undergone some stress, and that his bank accounts were inexplicably empty, they were and are convinced that he committed suicide. It is not true, as has been sometimes suggested, that the Mills' file in the archives of Scotland Yard contains Freddie's confession to being "Jack the Stripper". But it is true that, well after the event, a police officer received a letter accusing Mills of being both notoriously bisexual and the Stripper - a rather unlikely combination, in fact. It is also true that the homosexual world believed Mills' bisexuality was about to be exposed, by a charge for cottaging. The underworld, "staunch" or not, tends to think he was murdered, but completely clears the Krays of any responsibility. The underworld thinks somebody much closer to Mills and with possible access to his missing funds could give a full account of the ex-boxer's last minutes.

The beginning of the seventies should have seen the end of effective gangland in London for some time. With the Krays, the Richardsons and Freddie Foreman in gaol, and the Mifsud-Silver axis exposed in the wake of the Obscene Publications squad trials, Sir Robert Mark gave the solidly reliable Bert Wickstead the task of cleaning out the last of the extortion racketeers. And Wickstead carried out his task with efficiency and relish. Unfortunately for him and us, an irresponsible newspaper campaign led to changes in the law, and organized crime got a really strong footing in Britain which had previously been impossible. Prior to 1967, drug addicts registered with their doctors and could be prescribed their drug of addiction on the National Health Service. There was no opening for professional drug dealers to break in, although crooks like the Krays, and the American Mafia who had previously eschewed drug trafficking as too sensationally unpopular, were starting to be tempted by the possible profits. A whole generation discovered that "reefers" or "hashish" were not instantly addictive, and celebrities experimented with harder drugs. About half-a-dozen doctors in London tended to over-prescribe, some probably corruptly, others certainly from a pig-headed belief that they were giving essential "treatment". Some of this heroin found its way onto the streets and was sold around Piccadilly Circus, where young people congregated around midnight in the sixties. And the popular press demanded that this scandal be stopped, and Britain come into line with other, more "responsible" nations, which disallowed the prescription of drugs and refused all treatment for addiction except "cold turkey". At that point there were at the very most a couple of thousand addicts in the whole country, and nobody at all was pushing dangerous drugs to schoolchildren. Most of those who were addicted were able to hold down responsible jobs and support themselves; after all, mandarin China survived perfectly well under educated bureaucrats who enjoyed a pipe of opium in the evening as a Westerner might enjoy a scotch and soda. But, just as professional crime was facing a devastating crackdown, Parliament yielded to the newspaper pressure and passed the Dangerous Drugs Act, 1967. We all know the results. We are living with them.

Until recently the most fascinating question about the Kray case remained the whereabouts of Mitchell's and McVitie's bodies. Then, after Ronnie Kray's death, Freddie Foreman rocked the underworld and completely undermined the credibility of other villain' memoirs with his own book, *Respect*. It didn't grass up anyone who was still living. It didn't categorically acknowledge that he had murdered Frank Mitchell. But no alternative could be inferred, and he didn't deny it when Duncan Campbell drew the inference in an interview about the book. He admitted it without concealment when interviewed by Carlton Television. And he said where the bodies were.

The Foreman firm first needed somewhere safe to dispose of a body in 1961, when a raid on a bank security van in Bow went wrong. The guards turned out to be armed – something previously unknown in London – and one of the thieves was lethally injured. The gang couldn't leave his body to be found, it would have brought the heist straight home to them. They accepted advice from American associates that the best way to get rid of it, once and for all, was to weight it down, using chicken wire to secure the weights, and throw it out at sea. Feeding the fish, said the Americans; feeding the crabs and lobsters, said Freddie and his friends, as becomes members of a knowledgeable seafaring nation.

The Foreman firm had contact with a Newhaven fisherman through whom they had previously smuggled Swiss watches. They ran the body down to Newhaven, and it has never been seen since. In the Channel, too, lie the bones of Ginger Marks, and Frank Mitchell. And others, one wonders? John Buggy's body, tied with chicken wire, turned up off the Sussex coast. Tony Lambrianou, childishly boasting, "I know something you don't know", adds that it was weighted with iron when it went down. More interesting still, the car Lord Lucan was driving when he was last seen alive was found abandoned on the edge of Newhaven. It has long been rumoured that Lucan did not escape abroad or commit suicide, but was himself disposed of after the hit man he had hired to kill his wife killed the wrong woman, and the professional villains involved realized, by his flaky conduct that night, that he would be very unreliable under questioning.

Am I saying Freddie Foreman killed Lord Lucan? Of course not.

He couldn't have. He was still in prison serving his sentence for standing firm with the Krays. But I do suggest that Freddie's revelation about famous missing bodies leaving the country from Newhaven, rather than going into building foundations and roadworks, gives food for a lot of thought. And his revelations, together with the confessions of the Lambrianou brothers and Ronnie Bender, completely expose the self-serving lies and evasions littering all the books the Kray brothers have written about themselves.

The constant question about Reggie Kray, now, is whether he should be released. The question really amounts to asking whether he should have been hanged if capital punishment still existed, since "life meaning life" is the substitute the public may accept.

There are three persuasive justifications for capital punishment. To protect the public from the prisoner's continuing violence. To assure the public that the law will undertake so severe a penalty as to eliminate the risk of continuing vendettas, with victims' relatives taking the law into their own hands. And, as the great French moral philosopher Simone Weil suggested, to put the prisoner under such extreme mental pressure that he may come to view his crimes as right-thinking people do. (Of course, Simone Weil believed in an afterlife when proposing this rationale.)

Is Reggie Kray still a danger? He says not (Well, he would, wouldn't he?). It's unlikely that he's rich enough to retire like Freddie Foreman. And it's likely that, like his brother Charlie, he doesn't have any skill other than crime to make his living once the entertainment industry loses interest in him. So while I don't think for a moment he would ever kill in a frenzy again, I don't think his activities would be necessarily desirable.

Would other people try to kill him? I doubt it. The Mitchell family are law abiding. McVitie didn't leave male heirs to avenge him. Cornell's brother may once have threatened revenge, but is probably too old.

Has Reggie come to see himself and his own actions in a proper light, reached that frame of mind which I call "remorse", without Uriah Heepish humbug? There's not a trace of it. He feels that he has suffered and lost more than those he killed or had killed. He is hopelessly self-pitying, hopelessly convinced that he had the right to kill Jack McVitie. His is not an attitude of mind I should want to see accepted by the law as fitting him for pardon. You can't forgive people who don't want to be forgiven. Reggie doesn't yet seem ready for parole.

APPENDICES

APPENDIX A: TONY LAMBRIANOU'S
SECRET CONFESSION

In 1988 Reg Kray confessed. "Yes," he wrote in *Our Story*, "I killed Jack McVitie. I denied it at my trial and I've wished ever since that I hadn't."

According to Tony Lambrianou, this confession freed him to speak for the first time about the murder. In 1991 in *Inside the Firm* he claimed that, 'Up until the time that Reggie Kray admitted his part in the killing of Jack the Hat McVitie, every loyal one of us held our silence of a unique era in British crime'.

Ronnie Kray was less than convinced. In 1993, he wrote in *My Story*, "Tony Lambrianou is nothing but a lackey and a grass. He grassed us when we were all locked up waiting for trial. Nipper Read went to see him when we were on appeal and Lambrianou said to him 'The Krays done the murders. It was nothing to do with me and my brother.' That's what he said and so did his brother Chris. And I can still get the statements to prove it. They both put all the blame on me and Reg, they both said they were innocent. They both grassed us'"

There is nothing sinister about Ronnie's claim that he could get the statements: no implication of corruption in the criminal justice system. The Lambrianous' statements were not part of a confidential police investigation. They are depositions with legal implications for the Krays, who consequently have every right to see them. And that justice may be seen to be done, they have been preserved and now come into the public domain.

Ronnie's habitual inaccuracy is apparent when he says the statements were made while they were all in prison awaiting trial. They were actually made (as he also says) when they were making their appeal after conviction. They existed, and Tony's in particular is a revelation about the man who has counted himself among the "staunch" chaps who respected the "East End Code"; who has called himself "a member of the Kray twins' notorious firm;" and comes second only to the mad "Colonel" in swaggering about those glory days of the mid-sixties. Tony Lambrianou let his publishers describe him as "the former Kray Boss".

Here is what Tony Lambrianou had to say from Durham Prison

when given leave to appeal against his conviction in June 1969. (Typist's occasional punctuation errors and omissions, and occasional mis-spacing, reproduced without comment).

The grounds upon which the appellant seeks to call fresh evidence are

1. That he was precluded from telling the truth in the witness box through fear of Charles Kray, Reginald Kray and Ronald Kray.

2. That his defence was not presented by his Solicitors as a result of pressure being exercised upon their clerk Ralph Hyams [sc.Haeems] by Charles Kray, Reginald Kray and Ronald Kray.

The witnesses the appellant seeks to call are

1. Chief Inspector Cator [sc.Cater]

2. Terry (surname unknown) and Trevor (surname unknown) whose statements will be attached to that of Chief Inspector Cator.

3. The appellant himself who desires to give fresh evidence in accordance with the statement attached.

During 1967 I was living in Bethnal Green, London E.2.

On the 28th October 1967 I met my brother Chris. at about 7.30 p.m. and went to various Public houses as he describes. We went to the Regency Club and upstairs Jack McVitie joined us. My younger brother Nicky was also at the Club and he told me sometime after we had arrived that Reggie Kray was in the Club. Sometime after midnight when we had gone downstairs to the lower Bar I decided to get some cigar[e]ttes from the machine near the office. I went upstairs and while there Tony Barry came out of his office and then walked back in again. He then re-emerged and asked me into the office; Reggie Kray, Ronnie Kray, Bender and Hart were there. Whitehead was I think also in the Club but I don't think he was in the office. The conversation was to this effect. Ronnie Kray 'Is McVitie downstairs?' I said 'Yes, he's drinking with us.' The[n] something was said about getting him up to the office and either Hart or Reggie said 'We're going to do him.' I said 'What's it all about?' and I did not really get any reply. I never really thought much about what was said because I knew that the week before

Reggie, Donaghue and McVitie had all had a meal together and Reggie had paid and McVitie had told me he was therefore back on the Firm. I was asked if I had a car and I said I had; Hart told me to bring him [McVitie] round to Carols and I said that there were the others and he said that they could all come and then there was a discussion as to whether the others could come. I also asked, 'what he had done'. Reggie just said that he was a fucking cunt. Then they argued among themselves and I was standing in the doorway; finally they said that there was a party going on round at Carols and Hart, I think, said 'Bring him round, we'll have a talk with him.' I saw no gun at this stage.

I went downstairs and invited the Mills and McVitie to the party. This was not unusual because normally when they had a party they would invite everyone around. We went to Skinners in McVities car and when we arrived I was the first one to go down the stairs. There was music playing. McVitie followed me. It was about 12.30 or so. I saw Whitehead and Bender coming out of the back. I was the first into the room and Ronnie Kray was standing in front of the fireplace with his thumbs in the waistband of his trousers. The two youths were dancing. Ronnie Kray shook hands with me and almost immediately Reggie jumped on McVities back and put a gun at his head. It would not work. Ronnie hit him with a glass and cut his lip. McVitie protested. I cannot remember the words. The Mills were by this time in the room and Hart and Bender. I was terrif[i]ed and I left the room. On the stairs my brother Chris was sitting weeping. We had an argument about it because we realised then what was happening. Chris started to go. Hart came out and I quieted Chris because of him. Then Ronnie Kray said, 'Whats the Matter with him' – meaning Chris, and I said he was upset. The Mills wanted to go, but no one was allowed to go. McVitie had come to the door of the room he had his jacket off. Reggie hit him and pulled him back into the room. I was just outside, the door was ajar. Reggie had a knife at McVities' throat, Hart was holding McVitie. The knife would not penetrate. I was terrified. I ran again up the stairs, as I did so I met two children on the stairs and I pushed them into the bed-room. I stayed there what seemed a long while, but was probably only a moment or so. I came out of the room and started going down again. They were all going out. Bender was talking to Reggie, who said, 'get rid of him'. I remember both Ronnie and Reggie's arms were covered in blood. The Krays and Hart left. Bender persuaded me to go into the room. McVitie was lying under the window with his legs underneath him and with half his stomach hanging out, his head was almost severed and his eyes were open. Bender said 'Its all over, its done'. I couldn't believe it.

Later my brother Chris returned. He has described how we cleaned up and disposed of the body and it is true. Bender and I had an argument as to who should drive the car and it was decided I should. Afterwards I took the keys of McVities car and threw them in the canal. I was present when the Krays spoke to my brother the following Monday in the Carpenters Arms. They had told me they wanted to see us; I did n't want to go but my brother was in such a state that we thought it wiser to comply.

I never knew that this was going to happen to McVitie. It passed through my mind that he might get beaten up but I had dismissed it when I realised he was on the Firm again and when Hart had said they were going to talk to him. I know we should have come to his assistance but I was terrified that without a weapon the same would be meted out to us too.

Relationship with the Krays.

I have never belonged to the Kray Firm. I met them at the same time as my brother Christopher and only really started to see much of them about eight weeks prior to the murder of McVitie; this was primarily because I was also a member of the Regency Club and also drank in the same Public house. I personally was never asked to do anything by them but I knew only too well their reputation.

As regards the Solicitors the same occur[r]ed to me as to my brother. We knew that false statements had been made to Sampsons by witnesses and that it was more than our lives were worth to try and change Solicitors. I told Ralph Hyams [sc.Haeems]what had happened but he told me that the Krays would have to be told if I p[e]rsisted and so eventually I signed a statement for Sampsons that was quite untrue. I was in Brixton on remand with the Krays and when they found out that my brother had made a statement to Sampsons that involved them they constantly threatened me and my family. I was present at the joint conference in Brixton with my brother, the Krays and Bender and Ralph Hyams. Ronald Kray was almost apoplectic with rage over what my brother had said and we both re[al]ised we had to support the Krays to stay alive. I never wanted to go into the witness box but such pressure was put upon me in the trial that I had to do even that.

Lambrianou seems self-interested and unpersuasive in pretending that he dismissed the idea that McVitie was likely to be given at least a beating or striping, even though he heard Hart say they were going to"do" him and Reggie said it was for being "a fucking cunt". In his memoirs he admitted knowing that McVitie was going to be beaten – (something he had never really admitted to his brother Chris, whose conviction depended entirely on the assumption that Tony had asked him to help lure McVitie to what they both knew was going to be a very unpleasant meeting). Otherwise, this statement, reducing Tony Lambrianou from his preferred "hard man"insider role to a terrified outsider buckling under pressure from Ralph Haeeams and the Krays, seems honest enough. Comparing it with his later memoirs shows a good deal of "East End Code" surviving. He doesn't mention Terry and Trevor, Bender and Hart all joining in beating or manhandling McVitie at some stage. And he shields his brother Chris from the damaging admission that he left the party to fetch a gun. But his whole recollection of the fight is briefer than the accounts given by Chris Lambrianou and Ronnie Bender, and most of the abbreviation reads like the completely unconscious editing and abridgement carried out by memory as it tries to recall a rapid and alarming sequence of events.

APPENDIX B: CHRIS LAMBRIANOU'S
SECRET CONFESSION

Although, like his brother, Chris Lambrianou hoped to introduce new evidence from Terry and Trevor to support this new statement, his memoirs remark that only points of law could be heard in the Appeal Court, and so beyond admitting through his lawyer that there had been a party and he had been present, there was nothing really new he could say. So it has never been revealed that he made the following relatively full statement of the facts as early as June 1969.

Ronnie Kray felt justified in grumbling that Chris put all the blame on him and Reggie. It is possible that the "grassing up"while they were all on remand, which Ronnie was still raging over 25 years later and ascribing to Tony, was the statement Chris Lambrianou here describes making to Ralph Haeems which admitted that there had been a party and the twins were present at it. Neither Ronnie, Reggie, or any of their admirers, however, can point to anything in this statement which falsely implicates them or exonerates the Lambrianous. The Krays' twisted morality is well revealed in their fury that the Lambrianous finally told the truth,while their own whining about their own long sentences exhibits no recognition that their insensate folly and ruthless threats forced their followers to draw down even less deserved long sentences because they infuriated Melford Stevenson with their transparent lies on the Krays' behalf. Like Tony, Chris might well be seen as deserving praise from those who respect the "East End Code", since he minimised the possible inculpation of Ronny Bender, Ronnie Hart, Trevor and Terry.

The grounds of appeal are identical with those submitted by Tony Lambrianou (Appendix A). Chris Lambrianou's statement is as follows. Again, corrected typos are marked by square brackets, but punctuation errors are reproduced.

At the material time I was living in Birmingham. I used to come down to London to see my father and brothers from time to time. On 27 October 1967 I went to a club called the Dolls in Digbeth, and Ray Mills was there. We agreed as we were both going to London the next day to meet at an old pub in Leamon [sc.Leman] Street. On the 28th Oct. I came down in my car, a

Ford Corsair and went round to Tony my brother at about 7.30p.m. I told him I was meeting Ray Mills for a drink and asked him if he fancied one. Tony knew Alan Mills but not Ray, and I knew Ray but not Alan. We went to the Pub in Leamon Street [the White Bear in Aldgate, according to Tony's memoirs, and then on to Wapping] and the Mills came in and we had a few drinks. We decided to go elsewhere and went to the Carpenters Arms which is a pub owned by the Krays. We had a couple of drinks and I met Ronnie and Reggie Kray. I introduced them to the Mills. We were there about thirty minutes and Hart, Whitehead, Connolly and old man Kray were also there. From there we went to the Queens in Hackney Road, that is the Mills and Tony. It was then decided to go to the Regency, a Club in the East End owned by the Krays.

Once the four of us were at the Regency in the upstairs bar we noticed Jack McVitie in the corner with some one else I did not know. I had known McVitie for some three years and he joined us for a drink and was introduced to the Mills. McVitie was dodging about at the bar and when it closed at mid-night he suggested we went downstairs. We agreed, but I personally did not want to be too long because I had to meet a girl at 3.30a.m. at Euston. While downstairs I noticed Hart coming into the Club, with Whitehead and he picked up a box with drink in it. Tony left us for a while. When he came back he said that there was a party going on and there seemed to be a general invitation all round. Bender said the twins were having a party. I was not very keen but as the others wanted to go, including the Mills I went along. I was going to get my car. McVitie said we could all go in his car, and we all got in. McVitie was driving. I was next to him, Tony and the two Mills brothers were in the back. McVitie had had some drink but he was certainly not drunk. The journey took three to four minutes and then we parked outside an all night bakery in a road opposite Carol Skinners. We all got out and walked across the road. I did not know if it was all right to bring the Mills in view of their (the Krays) animosity towards them, so I asked them to wait. Tony and I followed McVitie down the stairs and by the time I got into the room McVitie was already there. I noticed there were only the two Krays, Hart and two youths dancing. The music was loud. Suddenly I saw Reggie Kray jump up on McVitie from behind and put a small gun up to the back of his head, frankly I thought it was a toy pistol. I heard him pull the trigger a number of times without success. Reggie turned round to Hart and said 'It doesn't fucking well work, you gave me a dudon [dud 'un].' The Mills were in the room by this time having been brought down by Whitehead. I realised then the import of what was happening and I was right choked and upset. I left the room and had a terrible argument with Tony on the stairs outside accusing him of setting McVitie up. Great confusion followed with comings and goings and I sat down on the stairs and wept I told Tony words to the effect that had I known about this I would not have come.

Reggie Kray came out of the room and asked what the trouble was and I told him I thought it was a fucking liberty bringing me over like this and he said 'don't be stupid' and went back into the room I saw McVitie in a chair talking to Ronnie. I said to Tony 'Who do they fucking well think they are – God – I'm going to get a shooter.' We went upstairs and just got outside the front door when we met Bender; he said 'is the party still on' and I told him what was going on and he said 'don't be a silly cunt, go and have a drink, this is all a joke.' so we went downstairs again and I saw the Krays and McVitie still shouting and again I tried to leave and then I heard one of the Krays say 'don't let anyone leave the house.' There was a general argument and Hart and Whitehead stopped me going and then Reggie Kray came out of the room and said 'what is the matter with you?' and I said I wanted to leave, and then I said I'd go and get another shooter. This was a ruse, by this time I was terrified. Reggie told Whitehead to drive me round to my house and pick up a shooter. I thought the Krays had gone mad. I went in Whiteh[e]ads white Jaguar and he dropped me off at my house and I got a .38. I was in a hurry to get back because my brother Tony was there together with the Mills brothers and I thought anything could happen to them. Whitehead was not anxious to go back and we had an argument lasting about ten minutes. Eventually he took me back and I rang the bell of the house and

Bender opened the door; he said 'its all over' I said 'fucking hell whats happened' I went into the room and saw McVitie lying on the floor under the window, dead. I couldn't believe he was dead I thought at first he was just badly injured. The Krays had gone and Tony and Bender were in a terrible state, and I was terrified. Bender said 'WE've been told to sling him over the railway at Cazeno[v]e Road,' and I said 'You can't its fucking stupid' and then I thought and I said 'We will put it in a motor and put it the other side of the water.' We rolled the carpet up and I got a candlewick bedspread from upstairs and rolled McVitie up and we put him in the passage. Where there was thick liver on the floor I cleared it up and emptied it down the W.C. McVitie had been lying under the window on his back with his legs doubled up underneath him his eyes were open and his head was nearly severed; from his stomach there were pieces of dark brown liquid oozing. Carol Skinner was standing at the top of the stairs with Ronnie [sc. Georgie] Plummer. Bender told them that there had been trouble downstairs and she was to go into the bed-room and stay there. We cleared up as much as possible. I put my gun in a pram in the spare room; Tony went out and got McVities car and I walked round and got my car from the Regency. McVitie's body was put into his own car, Tony drove it with a pair of socks on his hands while Bender and the body were in the back. I followed in my car. We went through the Rotherhithe tunnel and then round the one way system and eventually we stopped outside a Church where there was a lot of confetti, opposite a new block of flats We left the car and the body there. Bender and Tony got into my car and we returned North of the River and then dropped Bender off at the other end of the tunnel. We went to Tony's house and had a cup of tea and then I remembered I had left the gun in a pram in Carol Skinner's flat. We went to Euston and picked up the girl I had to meet and then to Skinners flat. The girl stayed outside. It was around 4 a.m. and Tony had not wanted to come. Skinner opened the door; Vickie, Whitehead and Plummer were there. They were washing everything in sight, the floor, the walls, but there was thick blood under the lino and I cleaned this up. I then asked Carol Skinner to make some tea and while she did I slipped out and got the gun. Then we left.

The following Monday week I went down to London again from Birmingham and Tony gave me a message that the Krays wanted to see us. Needless to say I was scared stiff, because I felt that if they had done this to McVitie they could equally do this to us. Tony did not want to go, but I felt that if we didn't the Krays would suspect us. We went to the Carpenters Arms and Ronnie and Reggie were there with Dickson, Donaghue and Hart. Reggie I remember asked me if I wanted a drink, and although I was scared I said to him 'It was a fucking liberty what happened' I asked him what was wrong with McVitie, was he a grass, or a bad man and Reggie said 'No, he [was] none of those, just a fucking nuisance,' and said that it was just unfortunate that it had happened like that and I was to forget it. Then he said 'Don't worry we had to get rid of your car because your prints were all over it with Tony's and the Mills brothers.

Relationship with the Krays.

I first met the Krays casually in 1963, but not until August 1967 did I drink with them; this arose when Hart told me the twins wanted to see me and I went to the Carpenters Arms with Tony as a result. They told me that if I should take gambling parties to their gaming Club at the Grand Hotel, Leicester I would be paid a commission. They invited me to drink at the Carpenters Arms when I was in London. I was aware of who they were and the power they held; I was at no time a member of their Firm.

After I had been questioned by the Police about the McVitie affair I was very upset and the Kray twins knew this and told me not to worry and got Carol Skinner to take me to Sampsons.

I saw Manny Frede, and he wanted to refer me to Ralph Hyams [sc. Haeems]; since he was not there I was asked to return at 5pm which I did. I made a statement to him at his request and I was asked what the Police had said and how they had treated me. I was asked to come back the next day and swear it before a Commissioner for Oaths. Hyams said 'You will never be charged, the twins have it all O.K.' But I did not go back.

After my arrest, I asked to see a Solicitor and the Police were told it was Sampsons because I had already been to see them.

Eventually I saw Ralph Hyams at West End Central, and he told me to tell the Police nothing. The next day at Bow Street, Manny Frede came into the cell and he said 'It will never get passed [sic] the Magistrates' and warned me to say nothing. I was sent with Bender to Wandsworth and my brother Tony was sent with the Krays to Brixton. On the following Wednesday I made a statement in my own handwriting on three foolscap lined pages. This did not set out the account as I have put it down truthfully above but involved the Krays and told the essence of what happened. I gave it to Ralph Hyams and he read it and said that he would have to show it to the Krays. I told Hyams not to show it to the Krays, but he said he would have to. Two days later Hyams came back and said that the twins had said that it was not to be used. I went on about it to Hyams and he kept on reminding me that Tony was in Brixton with the Krays. He said you have got to do it their way, the twins say that they weren't there and you have got to help. He then told me that I had nothing to worry about because the twins had a lot of power. He altered the statement and I was told what to say. Just before the trial we all went to Brixton for a joint meeting with Hyams the Krays Bender and my brother Tony. Hyams told me again that the twins were very upset about my statement, and inferred that this meant angry with me. When I saw Ronnie he was livid with me and said 'are you fucking well putting us in it?' He was swearing and shouting and I quite honestly thought I was going to get done. Hyams was present during the whole out-burst.

What ever I said always went back to the Krays and whenever I saw Counsel someone from Sampsons was always there. I knew I could not change solicitors because the Krays had told me that I had got to think about my family. I knew that their power extended well beyond prison walls and I thought it was more than my life was worth to go against them.

I asked Hyams to call witnesses Vickie Hart, Georgie Plummer and the two youths, Terry and Trevor whose names we gave them and whose address they alrea[d]y knew, but he refused and said that he could do nothing that would affect the twins. It is only now that I realise that something can be done.

APPENDIX C: EXTRACTS FROM RONALD BENDER'S SECRET CONFESSION

Ronald Bender's statement to his solicitors at the time of his appeal was extremely long and detailed, with a mass of plausibly half-remembered conversation. Much of it concerned his problems with 'Bubbles' Shea and her refusal to go to the twins' party. Much of it dealt with his anger that Ronnie Hart said in evidence that Bender's brother Terence, rather than his brother-in-law, had driven them from the meeting at Harry Hopwood's house. Bender detailed the ways in which he was deterred from putting forward evidence to refute this, even though he had promised to be economical with the truth about the twins' presence at the party in Evering Road. About 7000 words detailed ways in which he felt he and other defendants were not adequately legally represented by Ralph Haeems, and how they felt their families to be under threat from Dickie Morgan and the Lambrianous and other Kray associates as long as they were at large, so that they dared not change their solicitors. Like Christopher Lambrianou, he complained that his legal representatives never sent for the witnesses he wanted to appear in his favour; that he was not given access to his counsel without a representative of Sampsons' being present; that Ralph Haeems was present at the defendants' joint conference in Brixton, when the twins' determination that everyone should back up their 'guilty man's defence' was steam-rollered over any suggestion that anyone should admit to knowing anything about the party. Bender believed that Haeems was passing the proofs of other defendants' evidence to the twins so that they could have testimony changed to what they wanted. One paragraph from several hundred succinctly goes to the heart of his accusations, suggesting a cunning and legalistic ploy on the part of solicitors' clerks who had started their representation by insisting that other defendants would not be compromised because they also represented the twins:

Hyaeems [sic] acted as a sort of messenger from the twins. He would never say, "You have got to say this, or that", to me. He would put it in a more subtle way by saying, "I can't tell you what to say but the twins want you to do this, and that, and if you want to, I will write it down". Hyaeems, on a number of occasions during the interviews with me would tell me – "Ronnie (meaning Ronnie Kray) sends his regards, and is asking about your boys". Before my arrest Ronald Kray had expressed no interest whatsoever in my family, and I took whatever Hyaeems had said as the clearest possible message, and/or threat, that I was to put forward a defence that suited the Krays.

Independent statements from several of Bender's relatives confirm the occurrence of threatening telephone calls and visits from members of the Firm, demanding that Ronnie Bender stick with Sampson and Co as his solicitors, and back up the twins' story that they knew nothing about any party at Blonde Carole's.

Of the greatest interest, however, are the passages which give the clearest corroboration of the Lambrianous' account of events in Carol Skinner's flat; an independent corroborative account given privately to different solicitors and recorded in a different way. There are possible self-serving touches. He denies being actually in the office at the Regency with the Krays and Ronnie Hart, which eliminates him from hearing the conversation Tony Lambrianou reported in which Hart or Reggie said they were going to "do" McVitie. By his own account, Bender took no part at all in the struggle in the flat, though others recalled him joining the Krays, Hart and Trevor in (at least) pushing Jack the Hat around. But his explanation of his movements between the flat and the Regency Club accounts for Chris Lambrianou's meeting him coming in the front door just too late to see McVitie glassed by Ronnie and unsuccessfully shot at with Reggie's duff pistol. While they remember actual words differently, Bender and Chris are at one in agreeing that a distraught Chris was jovially reassured and persuaded back to the basement by Bender. And this same late arrival when the secondary players made the re-entry to the basement is evidently what Tony Lambrianou, (who admits being distraught himself), misremembered as Bender and Whitehead "coming out of the back" when McVitie first arrived.

Bender starts by saying that he took Mrs Shea to Clapton greyhound track on the night of 27 October and then on to a pub. After closing time she asked him to take her to the Regency Club to see a friend of hers called Maureen. At the Regency he was invited to go on to the party at Carole Skinner's, but Mrs Shea didn't want to go to a Kray party. Reginald Kray, Anthony Barry and Ronnie Hart came out of the office, Reggie looking angry and Barry worried. Reggie intimated strongly to Bender that Ronnie Kray would be annoyed if he didn't show up at the continued birthday party. So to Mrs Shea's irritation, Bender went with Reggie and Ronald Hart to Evering Road, where the party was in full swing, and everyone except Reggie seemed to be in a good mood. He saw Jeff Allen and his wife, Big Pat Connolly, Vicki Hart, "Ginger Carole" Thompson, Pat (Mrs Cornelius) Whitehead, (who asked him where her husband was), and two elderly couples he didn't know. Ronnie Kray was in a good humour, drinking with with Terry and Trevor, and he asked Bender if there were any nice boys down at the Regency.

At half past twelve the party started to break up. Big Pat Connolly asked Bender for a lift home, but he had lent his car to Ronnie Hart who had gone to fetch more drink. (Cf. Chris Lambrianou's seeing him and Whitehead with a case of drinks in the Regency at that time). Bender wanted to leave, but Ronnie Kray insisted that he should fetch his girlfriend from the Regency and see if there were any nice boys for him there. Reggie tried to make Bender dance with Trevor or Terry, and when he refused, with Vicky Hart. Although Ronnie Hart returned with his car, he was relieved to slip out and walk over to the Regency. Mrs Shea was very annoyed that he wanted to go back to the twins. She and her friend had been refusing invitations to Evering Road from the Lambrianous and the Millses for some time, and when Connie Whitehead came in and said the twins definitely wanted Bender, she stormed out and walked home.

Bender went back to Carol Skinner's flat in Whitehead's car, and from this point his statement corroborates Chris Lambrianou's:

As we were walking up the pathway to the front door of the house, Christopher Lambrianou was coming out of the house and the front door was open. I said, "Alright Chris?" and he replied, "There has been some trouble downstairs", or words to that effect. He also said "Reggie Kray and McVitie have been fighting". He said Reggie Kray had been threatening McVitie.

He said something to the effect of "Who do they think they are, gods?" (referring to the Kray twins) and I thought to myself that I did not want to go downstairs on my own with Whitehead and said, "They want to see me, Chris, come down and have a drink with me. I didn't have a chance to have a drink with you at the Regency," and I said, "Don't take any notice of them fighting, they are always hitting some one on the chin". I said "Come on down with me". I should say here that Christopher Lambrianou was the first person I saw coming out of the front door and down the path as I and Whitehead were going to the door, but that as we reached the door we were joined by Tony Lambrianou and the two Mills Brothers. These men were congregating in the passage of the house. We all of us then went down stairs towards the basement. Behind me were Christopher Lambrianou and Whitehead and the others were in front of me as we reached the basement.

I remember that the two Mills Brothers went into the basement room with Anthony Lambrianou. The door of the room was open and I could hear what seemed to be a scuffle going on in the room. I was standing just outside the door and Ronald Kray and Ronald Hart came over to me and I said to Ronald Kray – "What's going on Ron, what's happening?" He replied, "I will give him challenge me". He then walked across the room and struck McVitie in the face. I remember saying, "Don't Ron, don't Ron". As the fight was going on McVitie had his back to the window and I heard the sound of breaking glass. I was watching, and I am quite sure that when the window was broken as it was, it was not through McVitie trying to escape through the window but because he was forced back into the window by the blows being struck by the three men, Ronnie Hart and the Kray twins. I assumed when I heard the glass break that McVitie's elbow had gone through the window. I would add that at this stage McVitie was still fighting back. All the time this was going on I was still standing in the doorway of the room.

As McVitie was moving forward, punching away from the window I saw Ronald Hart produce a knife and hand it to Reginald Kray. So far as I could see, the knife was under his coat. Reginald Kray immediately stabbed McVitie violently, twice in the stomach, and then once in the left side of the face and once in the neck. As this took place McVitie keeled over and fell across towards Ronald Hart's legs, over by the window. Hart had been holding McVitie with one hand at the time when he produced the knife and handed it to Reginald Kray. As this incident took place the people in the room rushed to the door and I can remember that I was nearly knocked over by Anthony Lambrianou as he ran to the door, and towards the stairs. The two youths also ran towards the door and as they did so I can remember saying to them, "Don't run, d[o]n't run, walk, for your own sake". I was petrified at what had happened at this stage, and when I said this to the youths I was frightened that Reginald Kray might stab them. I did not know where he would stop, because he seemed completely berserk. As I said this to the youths I ran forward to where Reginald Kray was standing, about six feet from me. I struggled with him for about 10 seconds, got hold of him by the wrist of the hand in which he was holding the knife, and I remember him struggling with me and succeeding in transferring the knife into his other hand. I managed to get the knife out of this other hand and I jumped backwards. I can remember Ronald Kray saying to me, "What are you doing, what are you doing?" Then I realised that in taking the knife from Reginald Kray I had put myself in danger. Reginald Kray said, "Look what you have done". The palm of his hand was bleeding where the knife had cut it as I took it from him. I can remember saying, "I never done it". Ronald Kray said, "He never done it, he never done it" (meaning that I had not been responsible for the cut on Reginald Kray's hand) and he then started an argument with Ronnie Hart. I heard the knife mentioned, but I left the room immediately, got hold of a towel and handed it to Reginald Kray to stop the bleeding on his hand. He wrapped it round his cut hand. I remember at this time that Ronald Hart re-entered the room (I do not know where he had gone), carrying a gun and Ronald Kray said to his brother, "Show him your hand". He took the towel off and handed it to Ronald Hart and said "Wrap the things up in that, we are taking them with us".

I know that when I left the room to get the towel I had not got the knife with me and, so far as I can remember, I gave it either to Ronald Hart or Ronald Kray. I can remember the knife and gun being wrapped in the towel that had been put round Reginald Kray's hand. I would emphasise here that when Ronald Hart came back into the room with the gun it was the first time I had ever seen it and I am quite emphatic that at no stage whatsoever during the fight with McVitie did I ever see a gun or ever see anyone attempt to shoot McVitie.

I got the towel from the kitchen. When I went back into the room, Reginald Kray said "What did you take the knife out of my hand for?" I said "I didn't want you to hurt yourself". I said "I never done that to your hand Reg, you done that when you were killing him". I said all this because I was terrified of the way he was looking at me, and I realised the position I had put myself in.

Ronald Kray said to Reginald Kray, "It's not him you want to have a go at (meaning me), it's him", pointing to Ronald Hart. Ronald Kray said, "We have got to get the body out of the house". He said to Ronald Hart, "You come with us" (meaning himself and his brother). I said, "What can I do with it, Ron?" He said, "Chuck it somewhere, chuck it over the railway somewhere". I said, "Where?" He said, Put it over the Railway at Casanova [Cazenove] Road, opposite Coral's". I said, "Yes, yes, I will do it, I will do it". I wanted to get them out of the house, and the Kray twins and Ronald Hart went up the stairs and presumably then left the house.

I then went into the kitchen, got myself a drink, and so far as I know, I was the only one left in the basement of the house.

And so he was, when Chris Lambrianou came back, found Tony outside the house, and came downstairs with a gun in his hand; said 'Oh, the fucking bastards.' as he realised the twins had callously left Bender to deal with everything on his own, and persuaded Tony and Connie Whitehead (when he turned up) to give him a hand. Bender's statement continues for another ten pages, confirming everything the Lambrianous later said about the great clean-up and the removal of the body. His revelations about Dolly Kray's knowledge of the truth at the time when Charlie pretended she still knew nothing and he was not implicated in disposing of McVitie's body run as follows:

> I went to Charlie Kray's house. His wife (Dolly Kray), opened the door. She said "Who is it?" I said "Ronnie Bender, I want to see Charlie, it's important". I remember she took a chain off the door and let me in. She told me, "Charlie's out - what's he had to go out for" and I replied "I don't know". She said, "What's happened?" I said "They have killed Jack McVitie". She said "Oh, no, no," and seemed to be about to faint. She seemed concerned about Charlie and picked up the telephone and made a call. I heard her say - "Is that you Tom? - you had better come over, they've just done McVitie." She said - obviously in response to a question from the other end - "He's out" and then a little later she said, "Alright". She gave me a cup of tea, asked me what had happened and I told her I didn't want to talk about it.
>
> About 20 minutes after I had arrived, Tommy Cowley came. I told him what had happened and explained to him where the body was. I didn't mention the Lambrianous to him, and then Charlie Kray came in. He told me to go home, I asked him for a lif[t], he said he couldn't give me one, and Tommy Cowley similarly refused.

Bender then walked to his sister's house in Millwall and spent the night on her couch. In the morning, when he rang Ronnie Hart, Vicki asked him to go and pick up Ronnie from Harry Hopwood's. Bender and his sister persuaded his unwilling brother-in-law to drive him there, and after taking Hart home, accepted his instructions to go back to Evering Road and tell Blonde Carole everything would be made good.

At this point Ronnie Hart evidently felt himself to be in a commanding position in the Firm, as he told Bender it didn't matter that the body wasn't in Cazenove Road; his place for it was even better. Vicki Hart was with Carole Skinner, helping her clear up the remaining mess, and Bender took away the bloodstained carpet to a scrap yard in Poplar High Street whose owner agreed to burn it.

And in the afternoon, Bender, his sister and his brother-in-law all went to visit Bender's father's grave a normal family making a Sunday cemetery visit.

APPENDIX D:
TREVOR'S UNSIGNED WITNESS STATEMENT

The police traced the boys Trevor and Terry once the various gang members started to crack and reveal what had happened in Carole Skinner's flat. They had no wish to damage the future of lads who were in no way involved in the Kray Firm's vicious activities, and their surnames have never been made public. When Trevor made a statement to Detective Inspector Cater, no attempt was made to force him to sign it, and he was not required to appear at the trial. The statement itself is valuably free from the intrusive police formulations and slightly archaic grammatical corrections which all too often reveal the hand of the officer making sure a witness's words are improved into a suitable form for evidence (though questions for clarification can easily be envisaged).

Trevor's observations contain omissions – (by his account he should have been present to see Ronnie start the violence by glassing McVitie) – and confusions – (he rather doubtfully brings Tony Lambrianou into the room much too early, and overlooks Bender's absence at the start of the fighting: in fact, he seems to start the violence from the point at which the Lambrianous re-entered the room, bringing Bender and Connie Whitehead). I should never accuse a 19-year-old of self-serving evasion for being frightened to admit to the police that, encouraged by older, violent men, he may have joined in a little roughhousing just before hearing a man being sickeningly murdered in the next room. Trevor gives a compelling account of that evening's mayhem as it appeared to a lad who knew few of the principal actors, and had no idea what it was all about. Trevor also reveals the sort of pressure brought to bear on potential witnesses, even when they would seem to have been satisfactorily terrorized into silence.

I remember the party you are talking about. That night me and Terry was asked to go over to the Carpenters Arms for a drink and we went there. There was a crowd there. I remember Bender and Hart were there and Ronnie and Reggie Kray. Somebody said did we fancy coming to a party and we said yes.

We went to the party in a motor. I don't know the people

who were in the motor, but we went round to a house on the corner and we had to walk up a path to the front door with a garden to the right of the path. I don't know the name of the road it was in.

We went in the front door, along a passage and down some stairs into the basement. We had to turn to the left on the stairs to get down to the basement. At the bottom of the stairs to the left there was a room with a party going on in it. Next to this room, but further away from the stairs was a kitchen or a fair sized room with a sink in it.

There were quite a few people, as I remember it, at the party when we first arrived, including women, I think about four women. They were dancing to music from a radiogram in the far corner of the room from the door next to the window. I put some records on it and played them.

It wasn't the sort of party I enjoy, so I had a few drinks and after about three quarters of an hour after we got there, everybody seemed to leave. All the women left and there was just a few fellows there. There was me and Terry, Ronnie Hart and Ronnie Bender and about five or six others whose names I don't know. I think Tony Lambrianou was there.

Ronnie Kray then asked me and Terry to make some more noise. He didn't say why, but I thought he wanted us to do this because he was going to hit someone and we turned up the radiogram loud and danced about singing loudly and all that to make it sound like there was a party going on.

Ronnie and Reggie Kray, Ronnie Hart and Bender were standing by the door while we did this. The next thing was, a fellow came into the door of the room. I don't know why, but I had the feeling he might have been pushed into the room. I looked at his face at the time and I think I would recognise him. I had never seen him before.

As he came into the room, Ronnie and Reggie grabbed a hold of him and I guessed this was the feller we had to turn the music up for and they were going to set about him. I ran from the middle of the room to the wall.

You have shown me a photograph and I have no doubt at all that this is the man who I saw coming into the room that night and who the Kray brothers grabbed hold of.

Anyway, after running to the wall of the room, I ran round the back of them and out of the room into the passage outside at the bottom of the stairs.

As I did this, everything seemed to happen at once. Someone came downstairs, I think two fellows together and at the same time somebody came out of the room I had come out of just beforehand. I was afraid to look at who was there. I was scared and looked at the floor. I heard voices from the livingroom where I had been previously and they were saying "Who are they" or "Where are they", or something like that. I can't remember what the words were really, but it sounded like they were trying to get something out of the fellow and he wouldn't say. It was the voices of the two Krays that I heard because I recognised the voices.

By this time several men were standing outside the room, but I can't tell you who they were. There was people going in and coming out of the livingroom so I am not sure who was where at any one time. I know the Krays never came out of the livingroom because I could hear their voices in there all the time.

I don't know who it was because I don't think I even looked at the face of who it was, but I saw someone take a knife into the livingroom. I saw the knife. It was a long knife or it had a long blade about eight or nine inches long like a carving knife. I think whoever it was must have got it from the kitchen, but I'm not sure of this.

I seem to think somebody ran up the stairs after I saw the knife taken into that room because I heard the noise on the stairs as if this was happening. I didn't see who it was because like I said I kept looking down at the floor all the time.

I forgot to mention it before, but a little while before this after the men [?man] in the photo arrived but I think before the knife was taken into the room, I heard the breaking of glass as though a window had been broken.

Another thing I should have mentioned was that just before the glass was broken, I looked into the room and the man in the photograph was standing over the other side of the room to the left of the window as I looked towards it and Ronnie and

Reggie Kray had a hold of him. I think one on each side of him. They were holding him by the arms and the front of his shirt by his chest. When I first saw them, the man in the photo was standing side on to me. his left side towards me, but as I watched he jerked suddenly as if struggling to get free and he turned to face me as he did so. The next thing was that the door of the room was slammed shut from inside so I couldn't see any more. Within seconds of this I heard what sounded like the window breaking.

Very shortly after this I heard noises from the room like loud moans and although I couldn't see what was happening, I knew from the noises I heard, they were stabbing him with a knife. Then it all went quiet.

One of the Krays came out of the room after a short while, I can't remember which one and said, "Get the boys away". As soon as he said this, me and Terry got out of the house together as quick as we could without running, but as soon as we got outside onto the pavement we walked as fast as we could to the main road at the top of the turning the house was in and we saw a cab and took it. It dropped us at Bethnal Green Station. I don't know what time it was then, but I suppose it must have been 2 a.m., or something like that, but I don't really know.

About three days later I was with Terry in Pillens Betting Shop, now called the City Tote, in Bethnal Green Road. Somebody, I can't remember who, told me and Terry that Ronnie Kray wanted to see us. We were told to be at Bethnal Green Station at a certain time that evening. I think it was 8 o'clock. We went in there and I think it was Ronnie Hart picked us up in a motor and took us to a flat somewhere where we saw Ronnie Kray. He said, "The fellow's alright now. He's in hospital, but he's alright, and there is nothing to worry about. Don't worry." I said, "Alright", but I didn't really believe him. I thought the man must be dead, from what I had heard that night.

After you saw me when I made the statement to you that I knew nothing at all, Tony Lambrianou and Chrissie Lambrianou came into Tony's cafe in Bethnal Green Road, or it may be Peter's cafe – I'm not sure what it's called, while I was in there with a friend of mine. I think this was the day after you had seen me. They knew I had been seen by the Police and they asked me what I had told the Police and I said, I had made a statement to the Police denying that I knew anything about it. Tony told me to keep it that way.

The next time you saw me, Tony came to see me again. I think on the next day. He asked me what had happened and I told him I had said the same as before.

After I saw you the first time Terry said we should go up and see Sampsons the Solicitors and we went up there together. We didn't have an appointment. We just went up there and said it was about the Kray case and we were then seen by a man who looks like a Greek or Indian and who talks with a stutter.

We told him we had been seen by the Police and he took a written statement from us which we signed. This was to say we knew nothing about what had happened or any part of it. The man at Sampsons told us if we were seen by the Police again we should say we wished to say nothing and to ask for him. He gave me a card with his telephone number on it so that I could ring him.

I am sorry I had not told you the truth about all this before, but I am terrified for myself and my mother if it ever came out that I have told you this. I have no father and we live at Bethnal Green and we can be got by anyone at any time. I told you when I first saw you today, I will never go into Court and give this story as a witness. I am afraid to and I would die if necessary to avoid doing so. I don't want anybody except you and Mr. Hemmingway [Det Sgt A. Hemmingway, taking notes of the interview] to know that I have told you all this. I don't want to sign this, but it is the absolute truth.

INDEX

BIBLIOGRAPHY

Begg, Paul, and Keith Skinner, *The Scotland Yard Files,* Headline, London, 1992

Courtney, Dave, *Stop the Ride I Want to Get Off,* Virgin, London, 1999

Dickson, John, *Murder Without Conviction,* Sidgwick & Jackson, London, 1986

Donoghue, Albert, and Martin Short, *The Krays' Lieutenant,* BCA, London, 1995

Du Rose, John, *Murder was my Business,* W.H.Allen, London, 1971

Fido, Martin, *The Chronicle of Crime,* Carlton, London, 1993

 - and Keith Skinner, *The Official Encyclopedia of Scotland Yard,* Virgin, London, 1999

Fraser, Frankie, and James Morton, *Mad Frank,* Warner Books, London, 1995

Foreman, Freddie, and John Lisners, *Respect,* Arrow Books, London, 1997

Fry, Colin, *The Kray Files,* Mainstream Publishing, Edinburgh, 1998

 - and Charlie Kray, *Doing the Business,* Smith Gryphon, London, 1993

Gibb, Lee, *The Joneses How to Keep Up with Them,* Frederick Muller, London, 1959

 - *The Higher Jones,* Frederick Muller, London, 1961

Glatt, John, *Evil Twins,* St Martin's Press, New York, 1999

Hart, Edward T., *Britain's Godfather,* True Crime Library, London, 1997

Hebdige, Dick, *The Kray Twins A Study of Closure,* University Centre for Contemporary Cultural Studies, Birmingham, 1974

Hill, Billy, and Duncan Webb, *Boss of Britain's Underworld,* Naldrett Press, London, 1955

Hobbs, Dick, *Doing the Business Entrepreneurship, the Working Class, and Detectives in the East End of London,* Clarendon, Oxford, 1981

James, Trevor, *"There's One Away",* Orchard Books, Newton Abbott, 1999

Janson, Hank, *Jack Spot, Man of a Thousand Cuts,* Alexander Moring, London, 1959

Kelland, Gilbert, *Crime in London,* Grafton, London, 1987

Kelly, Patricia and James Morton, *The Barmaid's Tale,* Little, Brown, London, 1996

Kray, Charles and Robin McGibbon, *Me and My Brothers,* HarperCollins, London, 1997

Kray, Kate, *Lifers,* Blake, London, 1994

 - Ronnie Kray *Sorted,* Blake, London, 1998

 - and Ronnie, with Mandy Bruce, *Murder, Madness and Marriage,* Blake, London, 1993

Kray, Reg, *Slang,* Wheal and Deal Publications, Birmingham, 1984

 - *Born Fighter,* Arrow Books, London, 1991

 - *Thoughts, Philosophy and Poetry,* River First, London, 1991

 - and Ron with Fred Dinenage, *Our Story,* Pan Books, London, 1989

Kray, Ron, with Fred Dinenage, *My Story,* Sidgwick & Jackson, London, 1993

Lambrianou, Chris, and Robin McGibbon, *Escape from the Kray Madness,* Pan Books, London, 1996

Lambrianou, Tony, and Carol Clerk, *Inside the Firm*, Pan Books, London, 1992

McConnell, Brian, Norman Lucas, et al, *The Evil Firm*, Mayflower, London, 1969

McVicar, John, *McVicar by Himself*, Arrow, London, 1979

Mason, Eric, *The Inside Story*, Pan, London, 1994

Millen, Ernie, *Specialist in Crime*, Harrap, London, 1972

Morton, James, *Gangland London's Underworld*, Warner Books, London, 1993

- *The Who's Who of Unsolved Murders*, Kyle Cathie, London, 1995

- *Gangland Volume 2*, Warner Books, London, 1995

Munn, Michael, *The Hollywood Connection*, Robson, London, 1993

Payne, Leslie, *The Brotherhood*, Michael Joseph, London, 1973

Pearson, John, *Profession of Violence*, Grafton, London, 1985

Read, Leonard, and James Morton, *Nipper*, Warner Books, London, 1991

Reynolds, Bruce, *The Autobiography of a Thief*, Bantam, London, 1995

Richardson, Charlie, with Bob Long, *My Manor*, Sidgwick and Jackson, London, 1991

Samuel, Raphael, *East End Underworld Passages in the Life of Arthur Harding*, Routledge & Kegan Paul, London, 1981

Sharpe, Fred 'Nutty', *Sharpe of the Flying Squad*, John Long, London, 1938

Shaw, Roy 'Pretty Boy', with Kate Kray, *My Story*, Blake, London, 1999

Sifakis, Carl, *The Encyclopedia of American Crime*, Smithmark, New York, 1992

Simpson, Keith, *Forty Years of Murder*, Grafton, London, 1980

Thompson, Tony, *Gangland Britain*, Hodder and Stoughton, London, 1996

Tullett, Tom, *Murder Squad*, Granada, London, 1981

Webb, Billy, *Running with the Krays*, Mainstream Publishing, Edinburgh, 1995

Also, *passim*, *Daily Mirror*, *Hansard*, *News Chronicle*, *News of the World*, *Private Eye*, *Real Crime Digest*, *The Times*, and Home Office (HO) and Metropolitan Police (MEPO) files held at the Public Record Office or awaiting deposit there, and Lord Chancellor's Office papers kindly copied by Carlton TV.

CREDITS

The publishers would like to thank the following sources for their kind permission to reproduce the pictures in this book:

Hulton Getty

Topham Picturepoint

Every effort has been made to acknowledge correctly and contact the source and/copyright holder of each picture, and Carlton Books Limited apologises for any unintentional errors or omissions which will be corrected in future editions of this book.

ACKNOWLEDGEMENTS

Thanks, first, to Frank Simmonds and Andy Weir of Carlton Television, who discovered the major new information on the evil deeds of the Kray firm and made it available for publishing. Their cooperation and assistance since I came on board have been unstinting, generous and invaluable. Carlton Television Production Co kindly made office space available for me and provided facilities for me to work on Frank and Andy's collected material in Portman Square.

Thanks to those at Carlton Books who made a preliminary evaluation of the material and decided to take it up; and as ever to my agent Richard Jeffs for looking after the complicated rights dealings; also for giving me a relevant book on Dartmoor escapes as soon as he knew what the project was.

Research assistance from Karen has been as valuable as ever, and her enthusiasm as she becomes involved is always a real plus.

Alan Oakley, Andrew Brown, Richard Sharp, Maggie Bird and the Records Department at Scotland Yard have been helpful and obliging as ever. The staffs of the British Library, the Family Records Office, the Guildhall Library and the templeman Library at the University of Kent have assisted. And the librarians of Kent County Public Library Services, computer-catalogued and linked for readers' benefit and their extra work, have put themselves out repeatedly for me, Borough Green library being especially helpful. The staff at Canterbury have seen most of me; and thanks, too, to the County Library at Springfield, and to Dartford, Dashwood, Folkestone, Higham, Hythe, Maidstone, Sandwich, Sevenoaks, and Whitstable Libraries.

Without asking their permission, I have recounted anecdotes and observations gleaned from conversations at various times over the past fifteen year with police officers, criminals, East End residents, well-informed West enders, and one of the "boys" who attended Kray parties as part of Ronnie's retinue.

And, as usual, thanks to Paul Savory without whose Apple Mac and hospitality when London library research was indicated, this book could never have happened.